CULTURESHOCK!

A Survival Guide to Customs and Etiquette

MAURITIUS

Roseline NgCheong-Lum

Marshall Cavendish
Editions

This edition published in 2006 by:
Marshall Cavendish Corporation
99 White Plains Road
Tarrytown, NY 10591-9001
www.marshallcavendish.us

Other Marshall Cavendish Offices:
Marshall Cavendish International (Asia) Private Limited. 1 New Industrial Road,
Singapore 536196 ▪ Marshall Cavendish Ltd. 119 Wardour Street, London
W1F 0UW, UK ▪ Marshall Cavendish International (Thailand) Co Ltd. 253 Asoke,
12th Flr, Sukhumvit 21 Road, Klongtoey Nua, Wattana, Bangkok 10110, Thailand
▪ Marshall Cavendish (Malaysia) Sdn Bhd, Times Subang, Lot 46, Subang Hi-Tech
Industrial Park, Batu Tiga, 40000 Shah Alam, Selangor Darul Ehsan, Malaysia

Marshall Cavendish is a trademark of Times Publishing Limited

ISBN 10: 0-7614-2501-2
ISBN 13: 978-0-7614-2501-4

Please contact the publisher for the Library of Congress catalog number

Printed in Singapore by Times Graphics Pte Ltd

Photo Credits:
All photos from the author except page 93 (S Narayen); pages 41,
42 (Msiri). ▪ Cover photo: Photolibrary.com

All illustrations by TRIGG

ABOUT THE SERIES

Culture shock is a state of disorientation that can come over anyone who has been thrust into unknown surroundings, away from one's comfort zone. *CultureShock!* is a series of trusted and reputed guides which has, for decades, been helping expatriates and long-term visitors to cushion the impact of culture shock whenever they move to a new country.

Written by people who have lived in the country and experienced culture shock themselves, the authors share all the information necessary for anyone to cope with these feelings of disorientation more effectively. The guides are written in a style that is easy to read and covers a range of topics that will arm readers with enough advice, hints and tips to make their lives as normal as possible again.

Each book is structured in the same manner. It begins with the first impressions that visitors will have of that city or country. To understand a culture, one must first understand the people—where they came from, who they are, the values and traditions they live by, as well as their customs and etiquette. This is covered in the first half of the book.

Then on with the practical aspects—how to settle in with the greatest of ease. Authors walk readers through topics such as how to find accommodation, get the utilities and telecommunications up and running, enrol the children in school and keep in the pink of health. But that's not all. Once the essentials are out of the way, venture out and try the food, enjoy more of the culture and travel to other areas. Then be immersed in the language of the country before discovering more about the business side of things.

To round off, snippets of basic information are offered before readers are 'tested' on customs and etiquette of the country. Useful words and phrases, a comprehensive resource guide and list of books for further research are also included for easy reference.

CONTENTS

Acknowledgements vi

Dedication vii

Map of Mauritius viii

Chapter 1
First Impressions 1

Chapter 2
'Mauritius Welcome You' 7

The Nine Districts 8

Wildlife Conservation 24

When the Dodo
Roamed the Land 26

Rodrigues:
The Other Mauritius 37

Big Brother Mauritius 43

New Developments 44

Chapter 3
As One People,
As One Nation 47

Indians 48

Muslims 53

Chinese 56

The 'General' Population 60

Communalism 65

The Family 67

Religion 71

Superstition 73

Chapter 4
Socialising 75

Foreigners 76

Socialising with
Mauritians 78

Visiting 82

Conversation 87

Making Friends 88

Causes for Celebration 90

Divorce 99

Cohabiting 100

Children's Rites
of Passage 100

Chapter 5
Settling Down 105

Arriving In Mauritius 106

What to Bring 108

Accommodation 108

Around the House 113

Safeguarding
Your Valuables 120

Transport 121

Public Phones 125

Shopping 126

Public Toilets 130

Education 130

Personal Finances 134

Medical Care 136

Cyclones 139

Culture Shock 143

Chapter 6
A Taste of Mauritius 144

Ethnic Cuisines 145

The Melting Pot 149

Fast Foods 151

Drinks 153

Food Taboos 156

Food Shopping 157

Eating Out 162

Entertaining 172

Chapter 7
Enjoying Mauritius 177

Fun in the Sun 178

Beach Culture 178

Outdoor Fun 188

The Arts 193

Gambling 197

Clubs	200
The Night Life	201
Festivals	201

Chapter 8
Language and Communication 217

The Official Languages	218
The Real Mauritian Language	225
Mother Tongues	229
Language as a Status Symbol	230
Body Language	231
The Media	233

Chapter 9
Doing Business with Mauritians 236

Opportunites	237
Setting Up	246

Business Meetings	247
Women in Business	252
Business Ethic	253
The Work Ethic	255
Labour Unions	262

Chapter 10
Fast Facts 265

Writing Numbers	268
Famous People	268
Acronyms	269
Helpful Hints from A to Z	269

Culture Quiz	272
Do's and Don'ts	279
Glossary	281
Resource Guide	287
Further Reading	305
About the Author	309
Index	310

ACKNOWLEDGEMENTS

When my great-grandfather Ng Yin Cheong left his native village of Meixian in southern China for Mauritius at the end of 19th century, his only aim was to escape starvation. According to family folklore, he had only one pair of underpants which he washed every night and put out to dry before going to bed so that he would have clean clothes to wear the next morning. Furthest from his mind was the intention to establish one of the first Sino-Mauritian families whose members can now be found in Asia, Europe and North America.

This book would not have been possible without my great-grandfather and other pioneers like him, for the simple reason that it was they who laid the foundations of what Mauritius is today. I would also like to thank the other members of my family, in particular my father Raphael and brothers Ronald and Rodolphe. They have offered invaluable help in collecting research data and taking photographs. I am also grateful to Shova Loh of Times Editions for suggesting that I write this book. But above all I am most indebted to Mauritius itself for teaching me how to live among different peoples.

DEDICATION

To Hon Fye and the girls

MAP OF MAURITIUS

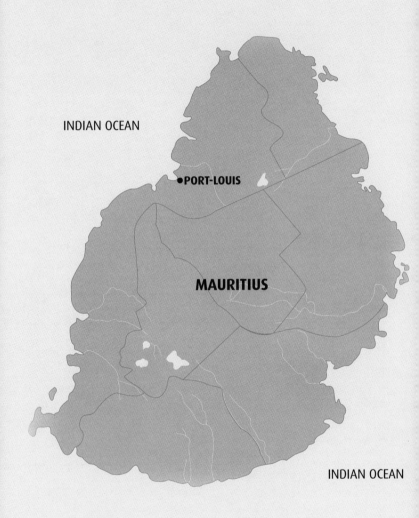

INDIAN OCEAN

●PORT-LOUIS

MAURITIUS

INDIAN OCEAN

The three dependencies (Cargados Agalega, Saint Brandon and Rodrigues Islands) are not shown.

FIRST IMPRESSIONS

'You gather the idea that Mauritius was made first and then heaven, and that heaven was copied after Mauritius.'
—Mark Twain

FOR THOSE VISITORS who arrive in Mauritius in the daytime, the first impression is that they have really reached paradise, of the type depicted in the tourist brochures. The view from the plane is simply breathtaking: jade green cane fields fringed by brilliant white beaches. And beyond the powdery sand, the turquoise blue sea. Those pictures did not lie. The island is indeed enchanting.

Go snorkelling and you will be treated to a display of beautiful coral formations off the coast of Mauritius.

Lush greenery and plantations dot the landscape of the island. Almost every square inch of arable land is under cultivation.

Moving away from the airport, they come upon quaint little villages and bustling small towns. And everywhere they go, the vegetation presents a riot of colours. The green of the palm trees and sugar canes merges with the purple of the bougainvillea flower or the red of the flame tree.

If you are coming from Africa or are familiar with African cities, you will be pleasantly surprised with the attitude of the country's officials. Dr Chris Du Preez, a university professor from South Africa, felt that 'the staff at customs was far more friendly than at other international airports, especially in some other African countries'. The Mauritians he came into contact with were efficient and displayed a high level of service. He was also impressed by the cleanliness and general state of the roads and buildings.

On the other hand, for this Malaysian lady married to a Mauritian, 'the reality of the big difference of standard of infrastructure, building, living amenities between Mauritius and Malaysia set in and it became quite scary to have to live in a foreign country, away from family and friends and with a much lower standard of living in terms of shopping, food and dwelling'. It took her about four years to feel utterly comfortable in the country and she can now appreciate the

It is the idyllic resorts such as Belle Mare Plage that attract
thousands of tourists to Mauritian beaches every year.

slower pace of life, after nearly ten years. The support of her in-laws and work colleagues was invaluable during her settling-in period.

The Mauritian population is an impressive lot. Coming from such diverse backgrounds, they have learnt about each other and built a harmonious society out of the injustices of slavery and colonisation. Everyone is friendly to each other and it is fascinating to watch people from different ethnic groups conversing happily in the Creole language.

'The whole island, with its sloping border and central
mountains, was adorned with an air of perfect elegance.'
—Charles Darwin

'MAURITIUS WELCOME YOU, Mauritius welcome you, welcome to our island paradise' goes the song. You are bound to hear this ditty at some point during your stay in Mauritius. The Mauritius Tourism Authority rides on the island paradise tag to generate millions of dollars of revenue each year. Surely, this is doing a disservice to a fascinating country whose people do believe they live in an island paradise, but not of the type described in the song. Mauritius is small, and it is an island, but this does not mean it can be contained in a few clichés.

An island of volcanic origin, Mauritius is ringed by a reef of coral and surrounded by a clear blue lagoon. Only 1,865 sq km (720.1 sq miles) in size, the island is home to a cosmopolitan population of more than 1.3 million. It lies slightly above the Tropic of Capricorn and enjoys a summery climate throughout the year.

THE NINE DISTRICTS

For administrative purposes, the island was divided into nine districts during the colonial period and it has remained so until today.

Port-Louis

Port-Louis, the capital of the country, is both a town and a district. Located on the north-western coast of the island, it is also the only town with the administrative status of city. The

The island of Mauritius and its nine districts.

city is composed of the town centre, bustling with commercial activity during the day and leisure activities at night, and is ringed by suburbs on all sides. The district is hemmed in by the Moka Range of mountains that stands directly opposite the harbour, leaving no room for expansion. The overriding impression one has of Port-Louis is of stuffiness and overcrowdedness. It is, after all, home to 15 per cent of the population. Here is the only place where one does realise that Mauritius is one of the most densely populated countries in the world.

In the town centre, tall ugly monsters of steel and concrete stand cheek by jowl with old wooden buildings with beautiful wrought-iron balconies and awnings. It is a perfect example of savage urbanisation and lack of planning. Streets are congested and traffic is a nightmare. Yet Mauritians go about

Silos in the distance (above) point to the origin of the Caudan and Port-Louis Waterfront. The harbour area has now been turned into the Caudan shopping complex and the Labourdonnais Hotel (below). A marina welcomes yachters from all over the world.

their daily activities with confidence, and you will too, after a short while. Away from the commercial centre are some fine examples of colonial architecture with their cool verandahs and sloping roofs, but these too are being overtaken by concrete structures making the maximum use of the land available. The suburbs are populated by the lower income groups and here, houses tend to be box-like and built quite close to the road.

Port-Louis is the seat of government and Government House stands at the end of a lovely palm-lined avenue that leads to the waterfront. Here, the Caudan Waterfront and the Port-Louis Waterfront—two shopping, dining and entertainment complexes—attract both tourists and locals. Le Labourdonnais and the more recent Suffren, the best business hotels in the country, are both located on the waterfront. Behind Government House is the National Assembly Chamber. The Treasury is also in the vicinity, with the Supreme Court a little further down the

> Like all capitals of developing countries, Port-Louis is the political, commercial, financial and religious centre of the country.

street. Port-Louis even saw the birth of industrialisation as the industrial area of Plaine Lauzun on the south-western end of the district was the first site of the EPZ (Export Processing Zone). All financial activity is conducted in Port-Louis and retailers from all over the island come here to replenish their stocks from wholesalers.

The main places of worship of the major religions are also in Port-Louis. The Catholic St Louis Cathedral has been on the same site in Pope Henessy Street since 1725 while the Jummah Mosque in Royal Road is one of the finest mosques in the Indian Ocean region. The Port-Louis Theatre, with its magnificent colonnaded front, is said to be the oldest and one of the finest structures in the southern hemisphere. Most cultural activity, however, has now moved away from Port-Louis to Curepipe and Rose-Hill, and the theatre is usually rented out for weddings.

The Champ de Mars is another outstanding feature of Port-Louis. The oldest race track in the southern hemisphere, it attracts joggers and families taking in the evening breeze on weekdays. At the Central Market, called *Bazar Central* in Creole, you can buy almost anything under the sun. The souk-like atmosphere, the colours, fragrances and aromas of food, and the cacophony of sounds make for a heady mixture. There are people everywhere, selling, buying, pushing and shoving. The Citadel, on the other hand, is deserted and still. An ugly fortress standing on a hill in the middle of Port-Louis, it was never used for military purposes. But you can get the best panoramic view of the city from here. Light and sound shows and rock concerts are sometimes staged in the fort.

Pamplemousses

To the north-east of Port-Louis is the district of Pamplemousses, so named by the Dutch for the *pampelmoes* (grapefruit) trees they planted there. The grapefruit are long gone and in their place is a mixture of rural settlements and cane fields. Pamplemousses occupies half of the Northern Plain, and much of the terrain is flat land ideal for agricultural cultivation. As you travel along the M1, the highway leading from Port-Louis to the northern part of the island, you will see large expanses of sugar cane fields punctuated by mounds of black rocks. Mauritians like to jest to foreigners that these were used for human sacrifice in the dark ages of slavery, but their origin is much more prosaic—they were just the rocks cleared from the fields and which were never taken away.

The 'jewel in the crown' of the district of Pamplemousses is the Botanic Gardens, about 11 km (6.8 miles) from Port-Louis. Better known as the Pamplemousses Garden, it is one the finest in the world. Dating back to 1729, the garden was made famous in the latter half of the 18th century by Pierre Poivre, who devoted himself to the cultivation of spices and gave his name to the pepper spice in French. Today, Pamplemousses Garden is home to over 500 species of plants, including the Talipot palm which flowers just once (when it is 40–60 years old, and not 100 according to popular folklore) and then dies. Other highlights are the water lily and lotus ponds as well as the tortoise and deer pens. In one corner of the garden lies the reproduction of an old sugar mill, a highly educational exhibit for both children and adults.

The largest settlement in the district of Pamplemousses is the village of Triolet, called the longest village in the country. It is also the largest village, but for political reasons, has never been elevated to the status of town. A mixture of residential settlement and industrial area, Triolet now boasts a large shopping centre and is likely to attain the same level of commercial development as a small town. Other big villages in the district are its namesake village adjoining the Botanic Gardens, Terre Rouge just outside Port-Louis, Piton and Baie du Tombeau. Alternately called Baie du Tombeau or Tombeau Bay, this coastal village grew significantly when citizens moved out of Port-Louis to build houses there. With its rural atmosphere, it offers the advantage of proximity with the city. The village of Pamplemousses itself has retained a certain colonial atmosphere.

To the north-east and north of Pamplemousses lies a series of beaches popular with both locals and tourists. Several high-class resort hotels dot the coastline, including Club Med at Pointe aux Cannoniers.

The First Sugar Estates

One of the first two sugar estates was built in 1745 at Villebague by Mahé de Labourdonnais. Sugar has, since then, played a predominant role in the prosperity of the district. The Château de Villebague, built at a later date, is a carbon copy of the headquarters of the French East India Company in Pondicherry, India. Set in beautiful grounds, it is private property and, unfortunately, not open to the public.

Rivière du Rempart

Sharing the Northern Plain with Pamplemousses is Rivière du Rempart. It takes its name from the Rempart River whose steep banks resembled ramparts. The northern coast has some of the best beaches and most expensive hotels in the country, but the district gets progressively poorer as you go further inland.

Grand Baie, which used to be a small seaside village, is now booming from the tourist trade. It was the first place in Mauritius to be given over to mass tourism. Souvenir shops, low budget accommodation and eateries abound, together with a boisterous low life and seedy activities. It is probably the prostitution capital of the country. Owners of former village shops had a windfall when low budget tourists started flocking in and they have now turned their premises into prosperous supermarkets. The activity of Grand Baie is spilling over towards Péreybère as the village develops. Cap Malheureux is the northernmost point in Mauritius and still relatively untouched. It was here that the British first landed in 1810 and captured the island from the French. The eastern coast of Rivière du Rempart is less welcoming and thus not so developed.

Inland, a few villages such as Goodlands and Rivière du Rempart are experiencing the benefits of industrialisation. However, overall, the district is still very close to its agricultural roots.

Sanctuary

A few islets dot the sea off the coast of Rivière du Rempart. Round Island is a nature reserve, home to some fascinating plant and animal species which have evolved in isolation from the mainland. Two snakes on the endangered list and the last representative of a species of lizard live here, sadly going the way of the dodo. Serpent Island, which paradoxically has no serpents or snakes, is a bird sanctuary. Here can be found a unique seagull with a long black tail, the paille en queue. A stylised reproduction features as the logo of the local airline. On the eastern coast lies Amber Island, so called for the ambergris that was found here. It is on the reefs of the island that the ill-fated *St Géran*, immortalised in Bernardin de St Pierre's novel *Paul and Virginie*, sank in 1744 with heavy loss of life.

Flacq

South of Rivière du Rempart is the district of Flacq, which also got its name from the Dutch. Originally called Groote Vlakte (Great Plain), it became Flacq under the French. The ebony forests that used to cover this region were felled, first by the Dutch to clear a road from the former south-eastern harbour to the north, then by the French for building houses and ships. Today, Flacq is largely agricultural, producing sugar, of course, but also tobacco for the local cigarette industry and anthurium flowers for export. Oyster and prawn farms have been established along the coast around Trou d'Eau Douce

The 18-hole championship golf course on Ile aux Cerfs was designed by world-renowned golfer Bernhard Langer from Germany.

with some measure of success. Lime, extracted by melting coral over wood fires, is another product of coastal Flacq.

In recent years, several new hotel developments have been added to the coast from Belle Mare to Trou d'Eau Douce. The first professional 18-hole golf course opened at Belle Mare in the early 1990s. A challenging course, it plays host to international tournaments and has boosted the profile of golf in Mauritius. The only major island off the coast of Flacq is Ile aux Cerfs. Despite its name, no deer will be found there. Preserved in its natural state, but with modern conveniences and restaurant facilities, it is easily reached by boat from Trou d'Eau Douce. In spite of vehement protests from environmentalists, a new golf course opened on the island in late 2003.

The heart of the district is the aptly-named Centre de Flacq. The village square is dominated by an imposing stone building which houses the courthouse and post office. It is a miniature reproduction of the Aberdeen family residence in Scotland. A huge banyan tree punctuates the scenery and the square comes to life every Sunday morning with the weekly market, called *foire* (fair). Villages with quaint names

The Grand River South East (GRSE), which runs across Flacq, is one of the few navigable rivers in Mauritius.

dot the coastline. Going to Quatre Cocos (four coconuts) is almost like saying going to the end of the world, this village being the easternmost point in Mauritius. And south from the village of Deux Frères (two brothers) lies that of Quatre Soeurs (four sisters).

Running eastwards across Flacq from the centre of the island is Grand River South East (GRSE), the longest river in the country at 27.67 km (17.19 miles). This is the only river that is usually crossed by boat, a barge serving as transport for traders going from one village to another and even for children going to school in a village on the other bank. The southern boundary of Flacq is the Grand Port Range of mountains which separates it from Grand Port District.

Grand Port

Grand Port is the historical district of Mauritius. It was here that the Dutch and the French started the colonisation of the island. Ruins (cannons, towers and fortifications) abound, but are in a sad state of disrepair, despite being gazetted national monuments. The oldest buildings are to be found here, some dating back to the 17th century. Several monuments and memorials have also been erected since the end of the last century to commemorate historical events, such as the landing of the Dutch and the abolition of slavery.

Pronounced 'Mayberg' by those with English pretensions, Mahebourg (Mai-boor) was the first town of Mauritius. The whole village exudes a historical feel that is not matched by any other place in the country. In a district with a predominantly Indian population, Mahebourg stands out with its Creole fishermen. The descendants of the French *colons* still keep weekend bungalows along the coast near Mahebourg

The Naval and Historical Museum

The Naval and Historical Museum is housed in the former Château Robillard at Mahebourg. Built in 1772 in the style of the French colonial period, it houses a motley collection of furniture and relics from the French East India Company as well as items salvaged from shipwrecks. Although most of the artefacts displayed pertain to the French period, the museum is well worth a visit.

and consider this area as theirs. In recent years, the town has undergone a revival with the opening of a few hotels and the growing affluence of its residents.

Grand Port is a varied district, with mountains, rivers and plains, and the natural phenomenon of Le Souffleur. This blowhole formed in the rocks of the coast used to spout water up to a height of 20 m (65.6 ft). Erosion, however, has greatly diminished its power, but it still roars a little at high tide. At Le Val Estate, watercress is cultivated and freshwater prawns called Rosenbergi are reared in ponds. The estate has encountered mitigated success. A more successful venture is that of Le Domaine du Chasseur, a commercial enterprise with an ecological vocation. Nestling in the Grand Bois forest, the Domaine rears deer for hunting in a protected environment and tries to preserve the forest and its species. Here can be seen the highly-endangered Mauritian kestrel and pink pigeon. Wardens offer guided walks and wooden accommodation makes for the perfect nature retreat.

In addition to having the first seaport of the country, Grand Port also boasts the only airport, the Sir Seewoosagur Ramgoolam International Airport, better known as Plaisance Airport. Despite calling itself the best airport in the Indian Ocean, it has no facilities for people dropping off and waiting for passengers. It was here that an English primary school teacher called Clark unearthed the bones of the dodo in 1854.

Savanne

Going clockwise from Grand Port is the district of Savanne. The name has now become a real misnomer for the coastal palm savanna has long been cleared to make way for sugar cane fields. The northern boundary is the mountainous forest region of Plaine Champagne, the largest nature reserve in Mauritius. Here the scenery is completely different from other parts of the island, with trees displaying tortuous trunks. Reforestation efforts are slowly bearing fruit as some of the threatened trees take centuries to grow to maturity. The view from Plaine Champagne takes in the Black River Gorge, the most breathtaking sight on the whole island. Grand Bassin, the lake held sacred by the Hindus of Mauritius, is in the vicinity, at 702 m (2,303.1 ft) above sea level. Also known as Ganga Talao, it is surrounded by Hindu shrines and temples. Devotees and hikers visit the lake year round, with the peak in March during the Maha Shivaratri festival. To the north, beyond Grand Bassin is the crater of Trou Kanaka. This extinct volcano is thought to have given birth to the island, it being at the centre of the volcanic explosion that produced Mauritius.

The deep south is plantation country with no less than five sugar estates. Income disparity is very obvious as the sugar barons lead an opulent lifestyle in their estate mansions while the rest of the population toil in the fields for a meagre salary. Commercial development is only slowly reaching Savanne and some factories have started to venture into the district, but keeping a respectable distance from the sugar estates. A 'nature' enterprise is La Vanille Crocodile Farm which stands in the midst of a superb tropical forest near Rivière des Anguilles. In addition to rearing crocodiles for their skin and monkeys for laboratory purposes, the farm also features a mini zoo with monkeys, deer, tortoises, lizards and reptiles as well as crocodiles, of course. More recent tourist developments include a golf course and a resort hotel at Telfair built around the beautiful colonial-style Château Bel de Ombre on a former sugar plantation.

Savanne's bleak coastline is not popular with Mauritians for the reef surrounding the island breaks in the south. This is the only place in Mauritius where one can feel the power of the waves crashing against the rocky cliffs. Bleak, windswept, with no land between here and Antarctica, the Savanne coast is evocative and poetic.

Black River

Taking up more than half the western coast, Black River is the longest district in Mauritius. Arid and mountainous, it is sparsely populated and the country's poorest region. Settlement has mostly concentrated along the coast with the economy centring on activities related to the sea. Fishing is the buzzword here; from sport fishing for big game like the black marlin to the more humble occupation that provides a living for hundreds of families. Most of the fishing is done on a small scale inside the lagoon. Boats are made of wood, 6–7 m (19.7–23 ft) long, with a small motor. Two to three men use hand-lines, basket traps, seines, gill nets and harpoons to catch the fish. Although this is the major source of fresh fish supply in the country and fresh fish commands a high price on the market, fishermen are poor because the fish is sold through an intermediary called a *banian* who sometimes also owns the boat. Since this

Some villagers in the poorer, rual regions still raise their own goats and chickens.

occupation is subject to the vagaries of the weather, the fishing communities are a poor exploited lot who do not have a stable income and no life insurance. Every now and then a boat does not come back and the families are left destitute. The dry climate of Black River is favourable for the making of salt, and salt ponds line both sides of the road from Tamarin to Riviere Noire.

Black River's landscape is dominated by mountains, with Piton de la Petite Rivière Noire standing at 828 m (2,716.5 ft), the highest mountain in the country. The most outstanding, however, is Le Morne, whose sheer cliff seems to rise out of the sea on the peninsula that sticks out of the south-westernmost coast of the island. Runaway slaves used to take refuge there and threw themselves down to their deaths when their masters' search parties got close.

In the south of the district lies Chamarel which is well known for its coffee and the 'seven coloured earths'. Due to a phenomenon of oxidisation, the different mounds of soil have taken bluish, reddish or greenish tinges. It is said that, if you mix the soil from one mound with another, the colours will re-separate overnight. Although the mounds do look distinct from each other, calling them seven coloured earths is something of an exaggeration. The little test tubes that are on sale containing distinct layers of earth in bright colours have been enhanced with coloured chalk.

In contrast to the rest of the country, the population of Black River is predominantly Creole. This is the home of the *séga*, the song and dance performed by the slaves of yore. It is here that the most authentic form can be heard, called *séga typique*.

Plaines Wilhems

One of the two inland districts, Plaines Wilhems is home to all the country's towns apart from Port-Louis. Settlement began in earnest in 1861 when a cholera epidemic pushed people away from Port-Louis towards the healthier climes of the Central Plateau. The malaria epidemic of 1866–1868 brought even more people. It is now home

Undulating fields extending towards infinity; such scenes are becoming rare as Mauritius continues to develop.

to 30 per cent of the population. The district is divided into the lower (at elevations around 200 m [656.2 ft]) and upper Plaines Wilhems (over 500 m [1,650 ft]). Although there are six towns, they form an almost continuous line from Beau Bassin to Curepipe. Still, the towns have distinct characteristics.

Beau Bassin and Rose-Hill are called sister towns and are managed by the same municipal council. Actually, since both towns are expanding at an alarming rate, they will eventually form just one big town. The climate is warmer here than in the upper towns but without the sultriness of Port-Louis. Originally populated by the coloured gentry, Beau Bassin/Rose-Hill is still home to a large Creole population. Those living in and around the town centres work in banks and offices in Port-Louis while those living in the suburbs of Trèfles, Plaisance and Mont Roches are engaged in manual work such as construction or as factory operators. Some beautiful Creole houses still exist, but many are being destroyed in the name of development. When Port-Louis and Curepipe ran out of room for commercial expansion, Rose-Hill became the target for shopping centres. It now has a bustling shopping area centred round the bus terminus. The town hall is called the Plaza and it includes the largest theatre in the Indian Ocean region. Both the theatre and the open space in front of the town hall are the venue for drama and musical performances. An art gallery is also housed in the town hall complex. Just oustide Rose-Hill, at Ebène, the new cybercity development aims to turn Mauritius into an international IT powerhouse.

The town of Quatre Bornes proclaims itself as the town of flowers, and most houses here have beautiful gardens. Of more recent settlement, it is smaller than the other towns. Quatre Bornes derived its name from the four milestones that used to stand at the entrance to the town. Its population is mixed, but with a slight predominance of upper income Indians. Being a more affluent town, it offers good shopping and restaurant facilities. The old nondescript buildings of the town centre are in the process of being razed to make way for modern shopping complexes of a somewhat dubious architectural taste. The side streets off the Royal Road lead to beautiful old villas and tasteful modern houses hinting at a more laid-back way of life. The town is overlooked by the Candos Hill, and the Princess Margaret Orthopaedic Hospital, commonly called Candos Hospital, is just outside Quatre Bornes.

Vacoas and Phoenix are also joined towns but, unlike Beau Bassin/Rose-Hill, they do not have much in common. Since the departure of the British forces which were stationed here, Vacoas (named after the pandanus trees that grew in profusion in the area) is slowly sliding into dereliction. However, it boasts the only country club in the country. Opened in 1844 as a polo club for British officers, the Gymkhana now has a golf course, swimming pool, snooker room, restaurant and tennis courts. Vacoas is mainly residential and agricultural, with a predominantly Indian population. Bonne Terre, between Quatre Bornes and Vacoas, carries its name well and its vegetable gardens produce the main supply of the town markets. Even a small patch in front of the house can produce considerable yields. Unlike Vacoas, the residents of Phoenix are overwhelmingly Muslim. With the Indira Gandhi Cultural Centre and the Phoenix Commercial Centre, the town gets quite lively during weekends and in the evenings.

Wet and depressing, Curepipe bills itself as the town of lights, perhaps to cheer up its residents. Inhabited from the outset by the moneyed white upper class, it is still home to a large portion of the white community. Shops abound in the town centre selling tourist knick-knacks and pseudo Chinese antiques, but its heyday as the foremost shopping area is definitely over. Curepipe seems to have been largely spared the trend of pulling down old colonial houses and replacing them with monstrous, soulless concrete apartment blocks. Beautiful white mansions with tiled roofs sit on well-tended grounds fenced by bamboo hedges. One of them has been turned into an expensive French restaurant, Le Gourmet. From the mouth of the Trou aux Cerfs crater that overlooks the town, one can see Reunion Island on a clear day.

Moka

Another plateau district, Moka is covered with sugar cane and tea in the Midlands area. The name points to the origin of the region as a coffee planting area. The Mauritian president's residence is at Le Réduit which started off as a small fort in 1748 on a 290-m (951.4-ft) high bluff between two rivers. It is now a beautiful mansion sitting in the middle of superb French gardens leading down to Le Bout du Monde (End of the World), the point between the two gorges.

The area around Réduit and Moka is the intellectual centre of the country (some call it the country's brain), with its many institutes of learning. Adjoining the Le Réduit gardens is the Mauritius Sugar Industry Research Institute, the foremost sugar cane research centre in the African region. Standing in front of the president's residence, the University of Mauritius, which started off as the College of Agriculture, is now a full-fledged university. Across the road is the Mauritius Institute of Education and Examinations Syndicate. A few kilometres away at Moka, the Mahatma Gandhi Institute houses a secondary school as well as an institute for Asian and African studies. Traffic used to be a nightmare around Réduit, but with the new by-pass roads, the area has regained the quietness and tranquility befitting a centre of learning.

The Moka Range
North of Moka is the Moka Range with its assortment of odd-shaped mountains. The most striking is the Pieter Both, a conical mountain topped by a huge boulder, like a head sitting on a human body. Folklore explains how a young goatherd was changed into this rock as a punishment for disturbing the fairies. Les Trois Mamelles mountain points to the humour of the Mauritian population. The three peaks of this mountain are indeed reminiscent of a woman's breasts. Pouce Mountain looks like an upturned thumb. Both Pouce and Pieter Both are fairly easy to climb, except for the topmost part which is steep and tricky. A few climbers have lost their lives there.

WILDLIFE CONSERVATION
It is said that Mauritius holds the record for the number of extinct animal species. Of those, the most well known is the dodo which disappeared almost as soon as the Dutch began settlement in the 17th century. It was first seen in 1681 and was extinct by 1692.

Less well known is the giant tortoise which was also killed off by the Dutch. It was so big that two grown men could sit comfortably atop its shell. The dugong, which lived in the mouths of rivers and gave rise to the legend of mermaids,

also went the way of the dodo. In addition to those animals killed for food, others such as insects and reptiles disappeared when their habitat was cleared for settlement. And, for a long time, this did not seem to bother anyone.

Today, however, the picture has changed. Of course, history cannot be reversed and the extinct animals are dead forever. But, with the help of the World Wildlife Fund for Nature (WWF), there is hope for those on the endangered list. It is among the birds that the highest success rate has been encountered. The Mauritius kestrel is one of the rarest birds in the world, with only four remaining in 1974 when the conservation programme began. They are hand-reared in an aviary in Black River close to their natural habitat. The kestrel is still a highly endangered bird although the conservation efforts were successful enough to release some into the wild. If you are lucky, you may see one hovering in the Black River Gorge area. The pink pigeon has also been rescued from the brink of extinction. But, although enough have been reared to be donated to bird parks overseas, it remains the rarest pigeon in the world.

Pollution

With the frenetic pace at which Mauritius has been growing in the past few decades or so, it is inevitable that pollution will exact its toll on the natural environment. The first culprit is, of course, the industrial sector. The textile industry was the driving force of the economic 'miracle', but the pollution the industry left behind is no miracle. Toxic waste resulting from the use of chemicals and dyes was dumped indiscriminately into rivers and waterways. There are now anti-pollution laws and great publicity was given to those caught flouting the law, but the rivers have irretrievably lost their crystalline quality and the life forms they supported.

One area where legislation is still required is the coastline. Hotel developments have caused erosion of the coast in some areas such as Le Morne and the related water sports industry has wreaked havoc with marine life. As the delicate balance of minerals in the sea is disturbed, the reef is slowly being demolished. This can lead to a potentially drastic situation where the coast is no longer protected by the reef and will ultimately lead to the destruction of the lagoon. The presence of motorboats, on the other hand, favours the growth of algae on the seabed. One tragic example is Mon Choisy, a favourite beach for family picnics. There are no boats at the Mon Choisy beach itself, but those berthed at the hotels next to it have resulted in the seabed being covered with an underwater 'lawn' that is creeping closer and closer to the beach, reaching within one metre in some places. The same lawn is now appearing at Péreybère a few kilometres away. The Mauritian government sets great store by what it calls eco-tourism, but ecology it seems is often furthest from the minds of those who operate the tourist industry.

WHEN THE DODO ROAMED THE LAND
Although short, the history of Mauritius makes exciting reading as imperial powers battle for its possession while its population fights for equality and an end to injustice. The island first appeared on medieval Arab maps as Dina Arobi. But it is the Portuguese Fernandez Pereira who is credited with 'discovering' the island in 1507. He called it Cerne, after

his ship. However, there was no attempt at colonisation until the Dutch moved into the Indian Ocean.

Mauritius

There were two phases to the Dutch colonisation of Mauritius. In 1598, a Dutch admiral called Wybrand van Warwyck sailed into Grand Port Bay and took possession of the island in the name of the Dutch king. He pompously named the bay after himself and called the island Mauritius after Prince Maurice of Nassau, the stadtholder of Holland. But it was not until 1638 that settlement began. A group of 26 men were assigned to prevent the French and the English from taking Mauritius and to provide food for Dutch ships calling there. Sugar cane was introduced from Java and slaves were brought in from Madagascar. However, the settlement was beset by problems with runaway slaves and the settlers themselves did not set their hearts to their task. In 1658, the Dutch left the island to devote themselves to the more prosperous Cape colony in South Africa.

The second attempt at settlement took place in 1664. The roads were improved and the fort repaired. A sawmill was

constructed and Javanese settlers began to produce a variety of vegetables, pineapples, bananas and some rice. However, the Dutch population was not hard-working and preferred to live off the land, hunting wild deer and cattle for food rather than growing crops. Dutch officials themselves did not have the drive to develop the colony, enduring their three-year stint as a tour of duty before returning to Holland. The same mentality prevailed among the settlers. Thus it is no surprise that colonisation of the island came to nought. In 1710, after destroying all their buildings and stores, the Dutch finally abandoned the island and went back to the Cape or Batavia (present-day Jakarta).

Ile de France

For a few years, Mauritius became the favourite base for the pirates who were skimming the Indian Ocean in increasing numbers. Gaining possession of the island for any of the colonial powers would therefore deprive the pirates of their base and offer a supply harbour for trading ships plying from Europe to the East.

In 1715, French Captain Dufresne d'Arsel called at Mauritius and promptly claimed it for France under the name Ile de France. Like the Dutch before them, the French also did not set up a colony immediately. It was not until late 1721 that a small reconnaissance group came from the French-occupied Bourbon Island (now Reunion) and landed at the north-west harbour. They were followed by a larger group of settlers from France. The north-west harbour was renamed Port-Louis and Warwyck Haven was now called Port Bourbon. The latter was still the main port and centre of government. It was more than ten years later that the French East India Company, which managed the French crown's overseas possessions, decided to shift all operations to Port-Louis. Due to personality conflicts and damage caused by cyclones and rats, the colony did not develop much in the early years.

In 1735, Bertrand François Mahé de Labourdonnais came to take charge of Ile de France as governor and started a flurry of activity that turned Port-Louis into the main port of the

Indian Ocean. Labourdonnais brought qualified architects and other artisans from Madras and dock workers and sailors from Pondicherry. With their help, he built Port-Louis into a well-constructed harbour and naval base, and turned it into the administrative capital of all French possessions in the Indian Ocean. A Government House was set up and the governor's official residence, Mon Plaisir, was at Pamplemousses in the grounds of today's Botanic Gardens.

A Man on a Mission

Labourdonnais was a Breton from Saint Malo and, like his countrymen, seafaring ran in his blood. A man of vision and boundless energy, he had a keen understanding of the island's strategic location and knew that whoever had control of Ile de France could effectively control the trading route between Europe and the Far East. Thus he saw his task as being twofold: to develop the resources of the colony and establish a permanent settlement; and to use these resources to help France in its struggle with the British in India and the Indian Ocean.

Labourdonnais brought in manioc (cassava) from Brazil and encouraged the cultivation of sugar cane, setting up the first sugar estate at Ferney near Grand Port.

The settlement flourished and slaves were brought in in great numbers to work on the sugar estates. In 1766, the island came under direct rule from France and in 1776, with the winding up of the French East India Company, trade was freed. The social life of the island blossomed, with high-society ladies vying with each other in fashion and entertaining. But, as France was continually at war with Britain, the island was used as a base for naval expeditions against British forces in India and the Far East. Soon the possession of Ile de France itself became a serious source of conflict and the British decided to capture all the islands in the Mascarenes.

One man, other than Labourdonnais, who marked the French period was Robert Surcouf. Nicknamed 'the king of the corsairs,' he led 47 successful raiding operations against British trading ships in the years preceding the British conquest of the island. From 1793 to 1802, the protection of the island depended on the

Corsairs had written permission from the authorities to attack and plunder enemy ships, and should not be confused with pirates. To be a corsair was an honourable profession and, even today, the word still carries a certain romanticism.

corsairs and commerce raiding activities were a major source of revenue.

The conquest of Ile de France was essential to the British in order to stop the corsairs from destroying their trade. In 1809, they captured Rodrigues and in 1810, Bourbon. In August 1810, Captain Willoughby captured Ile de la Passe at the entrance to Grand Port harbour. A few days later, he lured the French squadron led by Captain Duperré into the harbour by hoisting the French flag over the island. But the stratagem went wrong and Willoughby suffered a humiliating defeat after two days of fighting. Both captains having been wounded, they were treated in the same room in what is today's Naval Museum in Mahebourg. This was the only French victory in the Indian Ocean during the Napoleonic Wars.

Despite this victory, the French knew that their days on Ile de France were numbered, and when a British force of 10,000 landed in the north of the island in November 1810, they put up only a token resistance. On 3 December 1810, Governor Decaen capitulated on honourable and generous terms. The property, laws, customs and religions of the French inhabitants would all be respected. Those who wished to return to France could do so within two years and be allowed to take their property with them. Most of them stayed. Soldiers were treated as civilians and not as prisoners of war, and they were allowed to leave the island.

Mauritius Again

As the British captured Mauritius solely for strategic reasons, they let the French settlers be and did not try to colonise the island in the true sense of the word. They had no intention of sending large numbers of settlers and did not foresee any lucrative trade with the island. As long as the British were in political and military control, the French were allowed to remain in a dominant and influential position. Today, very few Mauritians have British ancestry and most people do not feel any affinity for the British language and culture.

The island was renamed Mauritius and Robert Farquhar, a dashing and energetic young man, became the first British governor. As he was anxious for the transition to take place as smoothly as possible, he tried to win over the French settlers by turning a blind eye to the slave trade, which had already been abolished by Britain. Life for the settlers and their slaves went on as before. Farquhar promoted the cultivation of sugar cane and opened up Port-Louis as a free port. He stimulated food production and road building.

Slaves continued to be brought into Mauritius until 1835 when the abolition of slavery was effected on the island and the planters received a generous compensation. Four years later, all slaves were freed and they left the sugar estates for the towns and lands that were so poor no one had claimed them before. The emancipated slaves and the emerging coloured population were subjected to deplorable prejudice and nothing was done to help them integrate into society. Two mission priests stood out in their treatment of former slaves: Father Jean Lebrun and Father Jacques Désiré Laval, the 'apostle of the poor'.

Very soon, Mauritius became a major exporter of sugar and the number of sugar factories increased to a high of 222 in 1853. The abolition of slavery left a huge gap in labour that was filled by indentured labourers from India. The lot of the labourers was not much better than that of the slaves.

Slaves and Coolies

Slavery had existed in Mauritius right from the beginning of colonisation. The Dutch brought slaves in from Madagascar and Java. The French initially also took slaves from Madagascar, but from the late 1720s their main source was West Africa, mainly from the French East India Company's base at Goree off Senegal. Smaller numbers also came from India and Malaya, mainly transported convicts. The slave population far exceeded that of whites and *affranchis* (freemen), to the ratio of five to one. The majority of the slaves worked in the sugar cane fields, clearing the land and cultivating the canes. A few, known as royal slaves, built roads and bridges for the government. Indian slaves were preferred as domestic servants for their cleanliness and mild manners.

The slaves were governed by the Code Noir which came into effect in 1723. The code, which in theory afforded a measure of protection to slaves, in fact labelled them as *meubles* (furniture) to be bought and sold at their owners' will. In 1767, the government laid down a decree that masters had to provide their slaves with two pounds of maize, or its equivalent, daily and with adequate clothing annually. They could complain to the Procureur Général (Attorney-General) if their masters failed to do so. In reality, however, the illiterate slaves did not even know their rights and ill-treatment of slaves was rife. Estate slaves were housed in small, one-roomed thatched huts in slave compounds. They were also allotted a small patch of land round their hut to cultivate and make some money. In this way, some of them managed to buy their freedom. Working hours were long, from sunrise to late afternoon with only one break for food around midday. If the camp commandant was not satisfied with them, they were whipped mercilessly. Runaway slaves, called *marrons*, were branded with the *fleur-de-lis* when captured. Those who were captured a second time had a limb amputated. However,

Le Morne, former refuge of runaway slaves, can be seen from any beach along the western coast.

many still risked their lives to escape the ill-treatment and took shelter on the slopes of Le Morne, diving off the cliff when they felt cornered.

The issue of slavery pitted the French settlers against the new administration right from the start of British rule. The slave trade had been abolished by Britain since 1807, but the authorities allowed it to continue in Mauritius. The planters were strongly against any attempt to end slavery and openly defied the government on the issue. Slavery itself was abolished by the British parliament in 1833 but it only took effect in Mauritius in 1835. Slave owners were generously compensated and still had the use of their slaves for another four years as apprentices to prepare them for free life. Seventy thousand slaves were emancipated in 1839 and almost every one of them left the sugar estates to try their luck elsewhere. The sugar estates were a humiliating symbol of their servitude and relations with their owners were so bad that none wanted to continue the same lifestyle.

The planters were prepared for this and, as early as 1829, were already sourcing for alternative labour from Madras and Singapore. The first batch of 75 hill coolies, as they were called, came from Calcutta and Bombay in November 1834 and, a year later, immigration of indentured Indian labourers began in earnest. Many peasants made landless by new property laws in India and out-of-work artisans saw emigration as the only way to make a living. They were offered five-year contracts to work on sugar plantations for 5 rupees a month plus free food and clothing. They were also guaranteed their return journey to India after the five years. However, most of them were deceived about the conditions of work and even the whereabouts of Mauritius, being told that it was only a few days' from India when in fact the voyage took more than a month.

In actual fact, the hill coolies were treated no better than the slaves. They were housed in the camps deserted by the slaves, often six men to a room. Working from dawn to dusk six days a week, they were fined for being sick and not being able to work. The 'double cut' system, which was in effect from 1847–1909, allowed the employer to retain two days' wages for every day off work. This meant that workers frequently found themselves in debt after having worked a whole month!

The inhuman conditions under which the coolies lived and worked were made known to the central government by officials and even by a planter, Adolphe de Plevitz, who organised a petition for better treatment. Unfortunately, few employers treated their coolies the way he did his. Despite a temporary stop to immigration and recommendations made by several commissions on the rights of the labourers, repressive labour laws were passed that almost institutionalised ill-treatment.

One decision by the authorities, though, had a favourable impact on the lives of the coolies: more women were encouraged to immigrate to Mauritius and coolies were encouraged to bring along their families. This resulted in a better social life for the workers who gained the support of their families. It also led to many deciding against going back to India at the end of their contracts. The frugal Indians saved up money during their indenture so that they could buy a small plot of land to farm when their contract was up.

The system of indenture was not abolished until 1916. When Mahatma Gandhi visited Mauritius briefly in 1901, he was shocked by the lot of the Indian labourers. In 1907, he delegated Manilall Maganlall Doctor, a young Indian lawyer, to come and champion the rights of the Indian immigrants in Mauritius. It was largely due to the efforts of Manilall Doctor that indentured labour was abolished. By then, more than 300,000 Indians had settled in the island.

Immigration

The Indian coolies ultimately became the largest group of immigrants the country has ever welcomed. With them came traders and artisans to cater to their needs. Their staple food was rice, which was not grown on the island, and they needed cotton cloth for clothing. The traders who came to deal in these two commodities were from the western Indian state of Gujarat and, unlike the Hindu coolies, practised Islam. Moreover, they were well off and thus constituted a distinct community from the labourers.

The last influx of immigrants came from China during and after World War II. Fleeing the Japanese invaders and later the Communist onslaught, they brought their meagre possessions with them and initially set up small shops to cater to the labourers on the sugar estates. Some came with their families, others came alone and later sent for their wives and children after they had settled down. Like all the others before them, the Chinese assimilated well into Mauritian society while preserving their culture and customs.

Since then very few people have migrated to Mauritius. In fact the reverse actually happened. Thousands of Mauritians, uncertain about what independence would bring, emigrated to Europe, Australia and Canada in the late 1960s. In the 1980s, however, many came back as there were more jobs for them in a developing Mauritius than in their countries of adoption.

Independence

For a long time, economic power equalled political power. The Council of Government was composed of British officials and the oligarchy of Franco-Mauritians who controlled most of the wealth of the country. In 1947, only 12,000 people out of a populatioin of 450,000 were eligible to vote, mostly Franco-Mauritians and a small number of urban, middle-class Creoles and Indians.

The first signs of unrest showed up in 1937 when the worldwide economic slump drove Mauritian wages down and prices up. Several strikes and demonstrations by sugar workers went off peacefully, but eventually violence broke out on the Union Flacq estate in the east and spread to other parts of the country. Labour unrest then reached the urban centres and the docks where most of the workers were Creoles. The movement for independence started with the call for more political rights for the Mauritian masses. Led by Dr Maurice Curé, who founded the Mauritius Labour Party in 1936, the movement called for better wages for the workers, the inclusion of non-white members in the governing body, and universal suffrage. In 1947, the right to vote was given to anyone who could read and write simple sentences in any of the languages used in Mauritius, not quite universal suffrage but good enough to elect several non-whites (11 Indians and eight Creoles) into the Legislative Council.

Subsequent elections saw the birth of several political parties and the emergence of Seewoosagur Ramgoolam as the leader of the Labour Party and the most outspoken advocate for independence. Ramgoolam spent 14 years in London, training as a medical doctor and serving a useful political apprenticeship as secretary of the London branch of the Indian National Congress. This was the time when India was fighting for independence and his meeting with Mahatma Gandhi and Rabindranath Tagore convinced him that the only way ahead for the Mauritian people was independence.

Self government was granted in August 1967, immediately after election results showed that there was strong popular support for independence. At the first meeting of the new Legislative Assembly, the motion to request for independence was passed, and 12 March 1968 was fixed by the British authorities as Independence Day. Mauritius thus became a sovereign country within the British Commonwealth with a parliamentary system based on the British model. Power rested with the prime minister who was at the head of a cabinet of ministers chosen from among members of the Legislative Assembly, all elected by direct voting. The representative of the British crown was the governor whose role was ceremonial.

The Republic

After several years of Labour government in coalition with the rightwing PMSD (Mauritian Social Democratic Party), dissatisfaction with the political and economic situation was running high. Thus the Mouvement Militant Mauricien (MMM), a left-wing party of students and young adults with revolutionary ideals, came into being and started to garner support from the labour unions and young people clamouring for change. The party quickly became a force to be reckoned with and won all of the 60 seats being contested at the 1982 general election. Despite its popularity being at an all-time high, the MMM itself split up soon after. However, it had always been on the agenda of the MMM and its splinter parties to throw off the final vestiges of colonialism by turning the country into a republic. In 1991, then Prime Minister Jugnauth proposed to amend the constitution to change Mauritius from a dominion to a republic. It was passed unanimously and on 12 March 1992, Mauritius acceded to republic state. Loosely modelled on India's presidential system, the new republic's head of state is a nominated president whose role is mainly ceremonial and with limited executive powers over Parliament or the cabinet. The Legislative Assembly was renamed the National Assembly.

The country's accession to republic state made no change to the daily lives of the Mauritian people. The system of government is more or less the same as before, and the vestiges of colonialism are still obvious in the street names, monuments, statues and even in some local attitudes.

RODRIGUES: THE OTHER MAURITIUS

The Republic of Mauritius consists of the islands of Mauritius and Rodrigues, Saint Brandon and Agalega, plus a few other islands whose sovereignty is in dispute, such as Diego Garcia and Tromelin. Rodrigues is the largest of these islands and politically, it counts as one of the regional constituencies of Mauritius. Rodriguans elect two representatives to the National Assembly in Port-Louis, one of whom is nominated as the Minister in Charge of Rodriguan Affairs. They have a certain amount of autonomy with their own 18-member elected regional assembly, based on the model of Trinidad and Tobago.

Another Tropical Island

Located about 650 km (403.9 miles) north-east of Mauritius, Rodrigues is shaped like a fish. Some 18 times smaller than Mauritius, it is also surrounded by coral reefs and has white-sand beaches in some places. Around 20 small islets dot its coast, mainly on the western side. The climate is hotter and drier than in Mauritius, and Rodrigues is, unfortunately, more prone to droughts and cyclones.

The Rodriguan relief is stark and mountainous, dominated by Mounts Limon and Malartic, the highest mountains at nearly 400 m (1,312.3 ft) above sea level. The landscape is made up of a series of hills and valleys, with sharp slopes descending abruptly from the mountains towards the sea, especially in the southern and eastern parts of the island. The succession of narrow, deep valleys and steep hills gives the impression that the country is much bigger than it actually is. The ravines cut the country from north to south.

Port Mathurin in the north is the major township and harbour. Since 1972, there has been an airport at Plaine Corail in the south-west. A few pockets of settlement dot the interior, but most of the activity is centred around Port Mathurin.

Rodrigues was discovered in 1528 by Don Diego Rodrigues, and has kept its Portuguese name throughout Dutch, French and British colonisation. Although it shares its history with Mauritius, it was always of lesser importance than its bigger neighbour. The first settlers were a group of French Protestants in 1691. In 1725, the French forces decided to colonise Rodrigues, but their attempts at settlement proved to be unsuccessful. The first settler who stayed permanently was a Frenchman who arrived in 1793 to engage in fishing and trading. A few more came later, but the island was never popular. When the British decided to capture Mauritius, they landed first in Rodrigues. That was in 1809 and the British made a greater effort at settlement, not least of all because they were using the island as a launching pad for their attack on Mauritius.

Throughout the 158 years of British rule, Rodrigues was administered as a dependency of Mauritius, very much like a poor relative, which was occasionally mentioned in official reports. When Mauritius was granted independence, the island became an integral part of the territory of Mauritius. In 1976, the setting-up of a Ministry of Rodriguan Affairs gave slightly more autonomy to the island and helped to make its voice heard in the corridors of power.

The population of Rodrigues has been stagnating as many young people leave their island to find work elsewhere. Mainly Creole, it is composed of three broad categories: the blacks, descendants of African slaves, make up about 85 per cent of the population and farm the mountainous interior; the 'Reds' are mulattos living in the coastal areas and are mostly fishermen; and the tiny Asian minority of traders hold much of the wealth of the country. Rodriguans speak the same Creole language as Mauritians and also learn English and French at school. The island is overwhelmingly Roman Catholic and Rodriguans are still very conservative in practising their faith. Here, a hat is obligatory for going to church. As for their cultural heritage, the *séga* has been preserved in its traditional form, away from the influences of pop music. *Séga tambour* with its rapid staccato rhythm is a particularly attractive version. Other olden dances with quaint names like *kotis* (Scottish), *mazok* (mazurka), polka, lancers, square dance and waltz are still performed regularly at weekend dancing parties.

A trip to Rodrigues is very much an off-the-beaten-track experience. Independent travellers do not fare very well for the lack of a proper system of public transport. Few areas are accessible by bus and the service stops quite early in the afternoon. The best way to see the country is to rent a moped and ride it along the roads until you come to the end. Some kind and friendly soul is always available to give you directions.

The Rodrigruan Lifestyle

For many years the local population has been living on the poverty line, without much concern from the administration in Mauritius. Basic facilities such as education, health care and public transport need much improvement. However, things are looking up for the island and it is slowly benefiting from the economic success of Mauritius.

The Rodriguan lifestyle revolves around the traditional occupations of farming, fishing and animal husbandry. Houses are perched on steep slopes, at the mercy of cyclones and landslides resulting from serious soil erosion.

The landscape of Rodrigues is rugged, with sharp cliffs and deep ravines.

Most of them are built of wood and/or corrugated iron. In the more affluent region around Port Mathurin, concrete houses are more common and on the coast, coral is used as a building material.

Socialising is limited to house visits and the occasional Saturday night dancing party. Drinking is a serious problem, probably the result of a lack of meaningful entertainment. Boredom is also driving hordes of young people away from the island to look for a more exciting lifestyle in Mauritius.

Farming

Agriculture is still the major sector of the economy. However, the large plantations that characterise Mauritian agriculture are not to be found here. The government owns 95 per cent of all land and farmers lease small plots for cultivation of produce, mainly at subsistence level. Most Rodriguan households own a pig, a cow and a few chickens for their own consumption.

Onions and garlic are grown for export to Mauritius. Corn, which is the staple of the Rodriguan diet, is produced on a large scale for local consumption. The production of local fruits is encouraged with grants from the government. Rodriguan limes, in particular, are greatly appreciated

Rodrigues' economy still depends mainly on agriculture.

by Mauritians. Full of flavour, they are best squeezed for lime juice drinks. Local chilli is another favourite. They are reputed to be one of the hottest chillies and are usually preserved in vinegar or oil, to be eaten as a condiment with local dishes.

Funded by the European Union, the production of honey has taken off successfully. Half of the harvest is exported to Mauritius. One of the best in the region, it is reputed to cure common colds and protect regular consumers from disease.

Although it is a major economic activity of the country, livestock breeding is still conducted through traditional methods. Cows, pigs, sheep and chickens are reared on a small scale by farmers gathered into co-operatives. The only market is Mauritius. Rodriguan chickens have become a delicacy for the price they fetch and the difficulty of obtaining them. Free-range and fed with corn, they have less fat and a better texture.

Farming is a difficult occupation in Rodrigues. Apart from the ruggedness of the terrain, farmers have to contend with droughts and devastating cyclones that can wipe out the whole harvest in a few hours.

Not too long ago, farmers still helped each other out with harvesting their corn and beans. However, people have become more materialistic now and such solidarity is rarely shown. The old barter system has also died out.

Fishing

The island's 12,000 fishermen are grouped in co-operatives. Although they receive much aid in terms of training and technical assistance, Rodriguan fishermen still use small scale traditional methods. Most of them restrict themselves to the waters within the lagoon and go out only when the weather permits. Using a rod and line, they fish to feed their families rather than to make a living. Professional fishermen bring their catch to the area co-operative for distribution throughout the area or cold storage at the plant in Port Mathurin. Most of the fish are small, such as parrot fish or snapper. Not much fresh fish is exported towards Mauritius because production is irregular. Instead, the fish is salted and then exported.

In addition to fish, octopus is also caught and dried before being exported. Octopus fishing is practised mainly by women who use a kind of spear to catch them. Prawns are exported to Mauritius, but in very small quantities. Since there are no farms, prawn fishing is done in the sea with nets.

BIG BROTHER MAURITIUS

With the creation of the Rodrigues Regional Assembly, Rodriguans now enjoy more autonomy and greater responsibility. Independence is not on their minds, but they do want the means to better their lot. Two political parties look after the interests of the Rodriguan people: the Organisation du Peuple Rodriguais (OPR) founded in 1976 and the Rassemblement du Peuple Rodriguais (RPR) founded in 1986. Whichever party gets elected to represent the island depends on the political alliance they make with the major Mauritian parties. The Ministry of Rodrigues oversees the administration of the island and formulates policies.

Rodriguan Local Government

Local government is administered by the Regional Assembly made up of 12 elected members and six others who are nominated to represent the various components of the Rodriguan population. Their leader is the Chief Commissioner, who is in effect the prime minister of Rodrigues. Only certain aspects of life, such as law and order or national security, are managed by the central government in Mauritius. The Island Chief Executive is nominated by the government and represents Mauritius in Rodrigues.

The Rodriguan stereotype is of a simple-minded, naïve rather than stupid, person whose artlessness gets them into funny situations. Much like Irish jokes in Britain, Rodriguan jokes abound in Mauritius. And you will hear well-meaning friends and colleagues advising you to make allowances for a certain person because they are from Rodrigues. The truth, of course, is that Rodriguans are not more stupid than anyone else in the world. They are simply less streetsmart because of their sheltered lifestyle. Do not make the mistake of treating people from Rodrigues like dim-witted morons. Rodriguans living and working in Mauritius are just as worldly-wise as the next person.

The Rodriguans do not have much affinity for the people of Mauritius who are ethnically different and whom they believe treat them with condescension. They feel closer to the Creole population of the Seychelles. In fact, Radio Seychelles is much more popular than the special programmes tailored for Rodrigues by the Mauritius Broadcasting Authority. For one thing, it is in Creole and the reception is better.

NEW DEVELOPMENTS

Modernisation is slowly reaching Rodrigues since the central government realised that it was in their best interests to have a prosperous neighbour. Although the road network is still limited, most of the island has access to electricity and running water. The telephone network covers most of the island, but subscribers tend to be commercial businesses and government bodies. International Direct Dialing (IDD) as well as facsimile and Internet services are also available. The island now has a total of three post offices, with postmen doing their rounds on foot. Several banks, including international ones, operate in Rodrigues, and they are slowly opening more branches all over the island.

In the domain of social development, the government built a sporting complex in Port Mathurin to stage annual national games. Television broadcasts to Rodrigues have now been extended to almost the whole evening. Sea and air links have also been extended.

The Tourist Industry

Tourism in Rodrigues is a new development. It is encouraged, but not aggressively promoted as it is in Mauritius. The aim is to create a type of tourism that is compatible with the 'untouched' nature of the island.

Tourism began in earnest with the building of a resort hotel at Pointe Coton by Air Mauritius, the local carrier. Small and unsophisticated, it caters to Mauritian tourists looking for a quiet, 'away from it all' holiday but who are not willing to give up their creature comforts. They come for the beach and maybe a tour of Port Mathurin, to experience the backwardness of the country. Very few venture far beyond the hotel and almost none are interested in the daily life of the Rodriguans. There are now more tourist facilities and the tourism industry is developing at a steady pace.

Visitors from Reunion and other neighbouring islands tend to have more respect for the local population and take more interest in their lifestyle. They come for the isolated beaches, hill walking and to have a relaxed time.

If you want to make a trip to Rodrigues, there are several flights a week on Air Mauritius by Twin Otter or ATR-42. It takes about an hour. Although not expensive, the ticket for a foreigner is almost double the cost of that for a Mauritian. You need to bring your passport and fill in an embarkation form, even though it is a domestic flight. Going by sea is slightly cheaper, and takes much longer. The Mauritius Pride is the only passenger ferry.

Rodrigues presents many attractions for the 'green' tourist. The landscape of ravines and hills is almost untouched by modern development and white sandy beaches are not easily accessible, but deserted. The hills and bracing air of the interior are very conducive for long walks, and you can explore the whole island without much contact with 'civilisation'. You will only meet friendly Rodriguans going about their traditional activities. Of special interest is Caverne Patate which are caves near the southern coast. About 600 m (1,968.5 ft) long, it offers a fascinating 20-minute walk among dripping stalactites and stalagmites. A permit is necessary, but it is free and there are daily guided visits at 10:00 am. Nature observers can watch a variety of birds, but the most interesting animal is the unique Golden Bat, which is highly endangered. As for flora, the rarest plant in the world can be found here. Only one Café Marron (a member of the coffee family) plant exists at Eau Claire and efforts to save it have encountered some measure of success. If you are interested in treasure hunting, local folklore has it that treasures are buried on the islet of Hermitage and at Anse aux Anglais.

Industrialisation

The first industrial park was built by the Development Bank of Mauritius and the building rented to entrepreneurs who are interested in investing in the country. Several Mauritian business people have taken advantage of the low labour rates to start simple factories. However, problems of transportation make investment on a large scale not viable.

Rodriguan entrepreneurs, on the other hand, are not affected by these problems. With financial help from the bank, several small scale industries have been set up, mainly in furniture making and garment manufacturing for the local market.

Possibilities definitely exist for making money in Rodrigues, but on a small scale. If you are interested in investing in Rodrigues, the same procedures for setting up in Mauritius apply. (*Please see* Chapter Nine: Doing Business with Mauritians *for more details.*)

AS ONE PEOPLE, AS ONE NATION

CHAPTER 3

'The various races of men walking in the streets
afford the most interesting spectacle in Port-Louis.'
—Charles Darwin

THE PEOPLE OF MAURITIUS are a nation of immigrants. However, today's Creoles, Indians and Chinese consider themselves 100 per cent Mauritian and would not be anywhere else in the world. The size of the population has grown to over a million and it is unlikely to grow much further. As it is, Mauritius is one of the most densely populated countries in the world. Indians make up more than half of the population, followed by what is euphemistically termed the 'general population', then the Muslims and Chinese.

INDIANS

In Mauritius, the word 'Indian' is used to refer to Hindus only. Muslims, whose ancestors also came from India, are called 'Muslims', a distinct ethnic group in the Mauritian context.

You will surely hear the term *Malbar* used in reference to Indians. You can use it as well, but do so only in circles where you are sure it will not cause offence. The word, though not an insult in itself (since it refers to the Malabar coast from where the first Indians sailed to Mauritius), used to carry pejorative and racist connotations. It is not widely used today, the younger generation preferring to use the word 'Indian'.

The traditional Indian attire is the *dhoti* for men (called *lunghi* or *langouti* in Mauritius) and the *sari* for women. These days, you will see very few men in a *dhoti*—perhaps only among the older generation in rural areas—but Indian women still favour the elegant *sari*. Not for everyday wear, though, because Western-style dress is more practical for going to work or doing the housework at home. (However, some older women are not used to wearing short dresses and still put on a *sari* everyday.) On formal occasions, such as weddings or cocktail parties, almost every Indian woman wears a *sari*. Adorned in intricate gold jewellery, these ladies make a resplendent sight. Married women also wear a red *tika* on the forehead. Children wear Western clothes, except that little boys may get to wear a *kurta* (round-necked, long-sleeved shirt) on festivals. Young girls look forward to the day when they can don a *sari* as it is a sign that they have grown up.

Although Hindi is the official language of the Indian community and is taught to Indian children at school, each ethnic group has its own language. Ethnic dialects are used mostly on religious occasions. Bhojpuri, the dialect of the predominant Bihari group, is the dialect that cuts across ethnic groups. It is not a 'refined' language like Hindi, but almost every Indian knows it and can converse in it. Hindi is not becoming more common in daily conversation.

You can easily spot an Indian home by the two red or yellow flags fluttering on bamboo poles in the garden. These flags are planted behind the shrine of the deity which helps to protect the house.

The Various Ethnic Groups

Tamils are called 'Madras', in reference to the town in Tamil Nadu from which the early immigrants sailed for Mauritius. Madras and Malbar are two distinct entities: a person cannot be both. However, while Indians might resent the term Malbar when applied to them, Tamils willingly call themselves Madras.

Over the years, many Tamils converted to the Christian religion and are now known as *Madras baptisés* (Christian Madras). They have retained their Tamil surnames, but have Christian first names. Some have, however, changed their surnames to Westernised forms. During colonial times, Asians could hardly get a job in the civil service and uniformed services, let alone reach the top posts. To circumvent this prejudice, those Indians eyeing a government job changed their surnames to French-sounding ones so that they could pass off as Creoles. Several went on to become leading policemen, doctors or administrators. Today, their descendants have kept the Western names, but some have reverted to their traditional religion and way of life. They openly acknowledge that they are Madras and follow Tamil customs and traditions.

Tamils are physically different from other Indians in that they have a darker complexion and favour the colour yellow. They are noted for their fiery curries and awe-inspiring religious rites. The Thai Poosam Kavadee is their most important religious festival.

Telegus, who number about 50,000 in Mauritius, originate from the north-western state of Andhra Pradesh in India. Because of the proximity of Andhra Pradesh to Tamil Nadu, Telegus look slightly like Tamils and are also partial to hot spicy food. (This assertion will doubtless draw criticism from the Telegus because of historical differences with Tamil Nadu.) Their favourite colour is orange.

Some Telegus have converted to Christianity (for much the same reasons as the Tamils) or married Creoles, and they have now been absorbed into the Creole community. Creoles with Telegu ancestry are easily recognisable by their surnames. Somebody called Appadoo, for example, is likely to be a Creole of Telegu ancestry, whereas Appadu is still an Indian. Most of the Telegus of Mauritius have lost their original surnames. As the Telegus of India keep their surnames as an initial in front of their first names, many families now carry the first name of their ancestor as their surname. The same holds true for the Tamils.

The next group of Indians are the Marathis from the eastern state of Maharashtra. In Mauritius, they are concentrated in the urban area around Vacoas and Henrietta, and the villages of Grand Bois and Plaine Magnien in the south-east. They have a special reverence for Ganesh, the elephant-headed deity, and the festival of Ganesh Chaturti is celebrated with extreme enthusiasm in the Marathi-populated regions.

The majority of the Indian population descend from immigrants from the northern state of Bihar. According to other ethnic groups, Biharis are lazy and that is why they

Years of toiling in the sugar cane fields have left their mark on the weather-beaten face of this Indian villager.

are not doing as well as the rest of the community. But, of course, this generalisation is totally unfounded.

The Caste System

The caste system, being rooted in the Hindu religion, is still a strong factor in the Indian community. According to the Hindu world view, all humans on earth sprang from the body of Brahma, the supreme lord of the Hindu pantheon. Brahmins, the highest caste, issued forth from his head, Kesatria, the warrior caste, from his arms and chest, Vaisyas, the merchants, from his thighs, and Sudras, the lowest caste, from his feet.

In Mauritius, Brahmins are called Maraze, the Hindi word for priest. They are strict vegetarians and enjoy the respect of the whole community. Kesatria are called Baboujee. Maraze and Baboujee are referred to as 'Grand Nation,' the high-class people, and are lumped together for all intents and purposes. Each caste being quite small, intermarriage is the norm. Vaisyas are called Vaish and make up the bulk of the Indian community. There are three sub-castes within this group: *koyris*, *kurmis* and *ahirs*. Formerly, people married only within the same sub-caste, but this is no longer the rule. Sudras are also called 'Ti Nation,' the little people, a term laced with contempt.

Although all Indians are born into a certain caste, there are no restrictions in terms of occupations. Enterprising Sudras can start their own business and they will mingle freely with other business people, some of whom may be Baboujee. Although a Maraze would not take 'dirty' jobs, they would certainly not refuse to work as a clerk under a Sudra manager.

Having said that, the caste system is still a strong political tool. Even though the Grand Nation are small in numbers, their support really counts in an election. And in rural areas, political parties would make sure they field candidates who belong to the same caste as the majority of the village people.

People from the various castes socialise freely. It is when it comes to marriage that the caste system shows itself in its most cruel form. A Ti Nation woman who marries into a Grand Nation family is sometimes taunted and ill treated by the in-laws. This holds true for men too: a Ti Nation man would be looked down upon by his Grand Nation brothers-in-law. It seems that one can have lower caste friends but not relatives.

Indian Values

Like their coolie ancestors, today's Indians recognise the value of hard work. An honest and diligent group, they will put their best efforts into whatever task they are called upon to perform. White-collar workers are not afraid to use their hands and a group of friends would band together to help each other build their houses, especially among the village communities. This pooling of resources also points to their deep sense of thrift. Of course they would take a mortgage to buy a house or a loan for a car, but it will never cross their mind to borrow money for more 'frivolous' pursuits like going on holiday or throwing a big wedding party. For these, they will live frugally for a while and save up the money.

Rich Indians do not flaunt their wealth with big cars and a flashy lifestyle. They treat everyone with deference. Deeply religious, they are however not fanatical about it, preferring to follow their faith through their daily lives rather than showing off their religious fervour. A sense of community pervades the whole Indian population. The fact that they are Indians automatically qualifies needy Indians for help from other members of the community.

MUSLIMS

Muslims arrived in Mauritius at about the same time as the French colonisers. Mostly artisans and seamen, they came from India, just like all other Muslims who subsequently settled in Mauritius. Many of these early settlers immersed themselves in the local culture, mainly in terms of dress and language, and became known as Creoles Lascars. The majority of Muslim immigrants were indentured labourers who were brought in to work on the sugar estates after the abolition of slavery. With them came a small group of merchants trading mainly in textiles and rice. Unlike the labourers who hailed mostly from the state of Bihar, the latter came from Gujarat in western India. They soon became very successful and used their economic influence to uplift the social lives of the other members of the community. Several Muslim families are still very active in the textile trade and some have gone on to diversify into other commercial enterprises.

The word Lascar is sometimes used to refer to a Muslim. Just like Malbar, it carries derogatory and racist undertones and should ideally not be used. The word is actually derived from the Persian word referring to Muslim sailors and seamen working in the harbour during colonial times, but Muslims strongly resent it being applied to them.

Muslim men have long abandoned their traditional attire for the practicality of shirt and trousers. Only a handful still wear the *fez* (called *toque* in Creole), most men preferring the lightweight skull cap which can be neatly tucked into the pocket after prayers. Muslim women, too, have adopted Western dress, but the Indian combination of *salwar* (knee-length tunic) and *kameez* (straight-cut trousers) is also very popular. To distinguish themselves from Indian women,

Muslim women enhance the outfit with a *horni* around their neck (a long scarf made of a very light material).

Because they cherish their privacy, Muslim houses tend to be surrounded by a tall, rather fortress-like wall. They are painted white, pink or green and have rather small windows with heavy curtains.

Urdu is the language by which the Muslim community identifies itself. Children learn it in the *madrassas* and most sermons in the main mosques are conducted in Urdu. It is not widely used any more though, being replaced by Creole even in the home. Being a small group, the Gujarati section of the community has retained their dialect and they speak it at home and among themselves. Muslim children have the option to learn Arabic at school, but they treat it as a foreign language since Arabic is not an ancestral language for the Muslims of Mauritius.

An Axe to Grind

One sore point among the Muslims of Mauritius is the failure of successive governments to adopt the Muslim Personal Law. As they are a distinct religious entity, they feel that they have the right to be governed by the Islamic law of Shariat which is established in countries with a strong Muslim population. The Muslim Personal Law would cover aspects of personal and social behaviour as well as marriage, divorce and inheritance. Starting from 1932, there have been representations by the Muslim community for the administration to put the Shariat code into practice. However, such a law would be in contradiction with the overall laws of the country and every time there has been a push for it in recent years, the women's group Muvman Liberasyon Fam (Women's Liberation Movement) has come out strongly against it, condemning the Muslim Personal Law as being a tool to subjugate women. The rest of the Mauritian population is certainly resentful of the Muslims' claim for a separate code of law, but has kept quiet in order not to revive destructive communal feelings. The Muslim community, on the other hand, claims to be a victim of communal politics.

Rooted in Religious Tradition

As a group distinct from the rest of the population because of its religion, the Muslims believe it is their duty to preserve their faith and culture for the future generations. There are mosques in every locality with a sizable Muslim population and the call to prayers can be heard five times a day. All Muslim men who can make the necessary arrangements at work take part in Friday prayers. Among the small Ahmadiyya sect, women also go to the mosque to worship, though separate from the men. (The majority of Mauritian Muslims are of the Sunni faith.) Almost every household has a copy of the Holy Qu'ran, the Muslims' sacred book. Children (both boys and girls) attend the *madrassa* (religious school located in the mosque) after school hours to learn to read the Qu'ran in Arabic and also some rudiments of Islam and the Urdu language.

The number of Haj pilgrims to Mecca keeps on growing every year as the Muslim community becomes more affluent and logistical help becomes available. Those who have performed the Haj are called Haji (for men) and Haja (for women). However, these titles are not used in daily life.

All adult Muslims faithfully pay the *zakaat* (a 2.5 per cent annual levy on personal wealth which goes towards the well-being of the whole community) and many donate money and labour to build mosques and schools. Some rich people also leave all their property to the community, even though they have children. Such property is termed *waqf* and is used for mosques or to house *jamaats* (welfare associations). Revenues from property under lease contribute to the finances of the community.

Mauritian Muslims are rather pragmatic when it comes to food. Preferably they should consume only halal food, that is meat from animals slaughtered according to Islamic precepts and prepared in accordance with Islamic custom. Of course, home cooking is halal. But when it comes to eating out, not all Muslims insist on the establishment being halal and would just order those dishes that do not contain pork. However, it must still be said that the Muslim community is more reluctant than the others to eat food other than its own.

Plaine Verte and Phoenix
Two urban areas that are closely associated with Muslims are Plaine Verte, a western suburb of Port-Louis, and Phoenix in the Plaines Wilhems district. Both of them have

a predominantly Muslim population and members of other communities who used to serve the area as shopkeepers, for example, are selling off their businesses to Muslims and moving out of the area. There is a feeling among young Muslim residents, though, that these enclaves are not prestigious addresses and they move to other middle-class urban areas once they are successful in their careers.

Plaine Verte and Phoenix teem with 'teahouses,' a kind of non-alcoholic pub that serves tea instead of spirits and cafeteria-style Muslim food. Here you come for the best *briani* or *catless* (a spicy meat patty coated in bread crumbs and deep fried). They are also the rare places where *nan* bread is sold, not the type that you find in North Indian restaurants worldwide, but a round and flat loaf of unleavened bread redolent with *ghee* (clarified butter).

Houses tend to be built quite close to each other and there is a general feeling of 'shutteredness' that keeps outsiders at bay. Plaine Verte was the scene of much communal violence in the late 1960s and it takes very little to fan hostile feelings and incite mob-like behaviour. It must be said, though, that such opportunism is declining and most people are peaceful and mind their own business.

CHINESE

The first attempt to bring Chinese coolies to Mauritius in the 18th century proved unsuccessful as Chinese women refused to accompany their husbands. The first Chinese settlers in the 19th century were traders and artisans from the southern provinces of Guangdong and Fujian, Cantonese and Hokkiens. Most of the latter married local women and the tiny Hokkien clan has almost completely lost touch with its roots and traditions, having more or less been absorbed into the Creole population. The Cantonese also form a minority group now, but they have maintained their language and culture, greatly helped by the trading links between Mauritius and Hong Kong.

The majority of the Chinese population today is made up of Hakkas, also from the province of Guangdong. At first, only the men came over and they later sent for their wives

Although not the largest ethnic group in Mauritius, the Chinese have become an integral part of the multicultural population.

and children after they had made some money. Or, if they were bachelors, they went back to China to find a wife. Meanwhile they lived with local women with whom they had children. When the Chinese wife came along, the latter was relegated to the status of concubine and lived apart. The children, if male, would still inherit part of the father's fortune. The bulk of Chinese immigration took place around World War II. However, they account for a very small percentage of the total population.

The overwhelming majority of the Chinese community is Christian, mostly Roman Catholic. As the immigrants did not have any religion and the Confucianist and Taoist doctrines they practised were more a way of life than a religion, they were easy subjects for the proselytising Christian religions. Many converted because some of the best schools were run by the churches and conversion was the only way their children could gain access to those schools. Others found that asking their bankers or suppliers (who were mostly Christian Whites) to become their children's godparents was a good way to strike up a relationship with someone who was so essential to their business.

Nowhere is the erosion of traditional culture sharper than among the Chinese. It is estimated that in one or two generations' time, the ancestral language will have passed into oblivion and one of the pillars of Chinese society, ancestral worship, will have disappeared completely. Probably what will be left is the cuisine. The Chinese are rightfully proud of their cuisine and most restaurants in Mauritius are operated by Chinese and serve Chinese food. The other communities appreciate Chinese food and many have learned how to cook it.

Shopkeepers and Tycoons

Since the beginning of Chinese settlement in Mauritius, they have always been prominent in the retail business. During the 19th century, Chinese shopkeepers on the sugar estates catering to the Indian labourers devised a credit system called *roulement* which enabled the customers to buy provisions on credit during the low season and pay for them at harvest time when they had money. This system, while relieving the financial plight of the labourers, was sometimes abused by unscrupulous shopkeepers who would inflate the bill at payment time, a form of interest on the credit. As the sugar industry developed and experienced several booms, so did the shopkeepers. Having made a small fortune, they sold their estate shops and moved to Port-Louis to set up wholesale businesses or to other towns to open shops selling general merchandise, which was much less taxing.

From these humble beginnings, the Chinese entrepreneur has moved into property development, manufacturing and other 'big' businesses. In this they have been helped by the fact that they have always placed a strong emphasis on education and the Chinese community has a high number of university graduates and professionals. Shopkeepers whose children are now accountants or doctors have cashed in their shops and given the capital to their offspring to start their businesses. Today, several big firms are controlled by Chinese families and the economic contributions of the community are totally out of proportion with its small size. Wealthy Chinese are particularly conspicuous by their lavish lifestyle, driving luxury cars and sporting the latest fashions, sometimes arousing the envy of the other communities. The Chinese themselves would say that there is no worse show-off than a Chinese who has made some money. The majority, though, are middle class, with jobs in the banks or other big firms. And many corner groceries are still managed by Chinese shopkeepers.

Chinese Names

If you are familiar with Chinese names, you might well be taken aback to be introduced to someone with a name like Charmaine Lee Ka Tong. The Western first name is definitely a woman's name while the Chinese name is most certainly male. No, Charmaine is not having an identity crisis, nor did her parents have a sick sense of humour. In all probability, Charmaine is the daughter or granddaughter of Mr Lee Ka Tong, who migrated to Mauritius from China.

When children were born to the mostly illiterate Chinese migrants, they took along their passports to the registry of births. The non-Chinese clerk, seeing three Chinese names on the passport, assumed it was all the surname and recorded the father's full name as the child's surname. Thus, most Mauritian Chinese have a three-name surname, their progenitor's full name. They know that only the first name is actually the surname but use the whole name as their surname in the Western style, usually with a Christian first name. Charmaine might call herself simply Charmaine Lee, but in the eyes of the law, she is Charmaine Lee Ka Tong.

Clan Associations

Like Chinese all over the world, Mauritian Chinese also grouped themselves into clan associations. The focal point of community life in the old days, these associations are now dying a slow but inevitable death. Only old people, mostly men, frequent the association premises, for a chat or a game of cards or mahjong.

There have been some half-hearted attempts to revive the association by some clans, giving them more of a community club-like flavour in order to attract the younger generations.

Modern activities like dancing parties and sports and games were introduced in addition to the traditional mahjong, and membership was even open to people belonging to other clans, but these attempts have encountered mixed success.

More successful are clubs like Hua Lien which bring together young and old Chinese of the same social background and with common interests. These are social clubs offering a range of activities from sports to cooking demonstrations, with a special emphasis on Chinese history and culture. Some of your Chinese friends may bring you to one of their parties or talks and, if you are a Chinese, the club will welcome you to join in their activities.

THE 'GENERAL' POPULATION

It can be argued that everyone is a member of the general population, but in the Mauritian government lingo, only Creoles and Whites and anyone who does not fit into any of the other categories, are called 'general population'. They account for 30 per cent of the population. The Whites would like to be classified separately, but their numbers (2–3 per cent of the total population) are too small to warrant another category. And, when considered objectively, you will find that the only thing that differentiates them from the Creoles, apart from skin colour, is economic status.

Almost all Mauritian Whites are descended from the French *colons* who settled on the island in the 18th and 19th centuries. Although the country was also governed by the British for one and a half centuries, very few actually settled here. When Mauritius was granted independence, many Whites fled the country as they were afraid the majority Indian population would dominate the political sector and would make them pay for their ill-treatment of Indian labourers on the sugar estates. (As it turned out, these fears were largely unfounded.) This community is overwhelmingly Catholic and has raised quite a number of nuns and priests. A very small number are Jewish.

Despite the rise of many new players on the economic front, the Whites are still a force to be reckoned with, controlling the sugar industry, the hotel business and quite a large part of the banking sector as well. They have been successful in diversifying their interests, converting capital from the declining agricultural sector to the manufacturing industry.

Who is a Creole?

The word 'creole' actually refers to people of French descent born in the colonies but in Mauritius, this term definitely does not refer to the Whites. Creoles are Negroid and come in all shades of brown. They are descended from African slaves and have had a fair amount of mixing through the generations. Although dark-skinned and dark-eyed, Creoles have lost the wide nose and thick lips of their ancestors. Very few have kinky hair, with most of them sporting curly locks or even straight hair. Those who have retained African features are sometimes referred to as *mazambic*. Or they may be called *gros Creole* (big Creole), probably because they display 'bigger' (more pronounced) Negroid features.

Lighter-skinned Creoles are called *milat* (mulattos). As in other former French colonial societies, Mauritian mulattos enjoy a higher social standing since they are fairer than Creoles. Because of this, they have traditionally been better

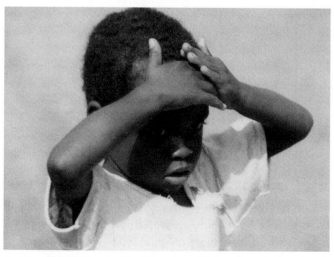

A young Creole boy—part of the 'general population'.

educated and work in the middle management of well-established firms and banks. Mulattos (and Whites) are remarkable by their absence from the civil service. Less fair mulattos are called 'two-coloured' mulattos, the two colours presumably referring to white and brown. All of them live in towns, mainly Rose-Hill, Beau Bassin and Quatre Bornes. Some Mauritians might refer to Whites as mulattos. This is just a way of putting down the Whites since they have long been the dominant community in the island.

Some people of mixed descent also call themselves Creoles even though they may not have any African ancestry. This is more practical than calling themselves Chinese-Indian or Muslim-Tamil for example. The Creole-Madras are Christian Tamils while Creoles Lascars are Muslims who have adopted a Creole lifestyle.

Almost all Creoles are Catholic and they make up the bulk of the congregation in every Roman Catholic church in the country. Many Creole women are very active in church-related activities, running sewing classes for young girls or managing the church's library.

The 'Nas' Way of Life

People of the same community would call themselves 'nation' referring to the fact that they belong to the same race (nation). The term has now come to mean exclusively a Creole. Its short form is *nas* and a *gros nas* or *gros nation* is more or less equivalent to *mazambic*.

Creoles come from all income groups, even though the majority are working class. They have acquired a reputation for living hand to mouth, spending their money as soon as they earn it (or even before) and living on credit. It is a fact that they do like to enjoy themselves to the utmost and would even put enjoyment before work. Contract workers especially would rather take the day off to have a drink with friends than complete the work and get paid for it.

The *nas* way of life then is to spend the minimum on basic necessities, making do with frugal meals every day of the week so as to splurge on good food and drinks (mainly drinks) during the weekend. Most of them live in rented

accommodation because they never save enough for a deposit on a house. If they can afford it, they would own a car (even if it is a bone shaker) so as to be able to move about freely and enjoy themselves. Some young people even buy a car in common, pooling their financial resources together and taking turns to use the car or using it during weekends only when all of them squeeze in to go to the disco or the beach.

It must be pointed out that the *nas* way of life is not exclusive to the Creole community. The older generations of Asians are bemoaning that their youth no longer appreciate the value of thrift and are now living just like the Creoles. But, after all, what is wrong with enjoying yourself while you can?

Séga

Mauritians make it a point to tell visitors about the *séga*. It is both song and dance. Accompanied by distinct instruments

Séga—the national song and dance of Mauritius.

such as the *ravane* (a thin, wide drum covered with a goat's skin), the *maravane* (a pebble filled box that makes a rattling sound when shaken) and the triangle, the singer sings about the tribulations of love or the humorous side of life. The instruments provide a rhythm only, no melody. The dance is a series of shuffling steps with no set pattern, with hips swinging and arms outstretched. The dancers shuffle around each other before facing each other and sitting down on the floor, bending their torsos forwards and backwards, much like a courtship dance. Commercial performances in hotels and nightclubs accentuate this suggestiveness and try to lend an air of eroticism to the dance.

Eroticism was certainly present in the original *séga* of the slaves, but today's watered-down versions fail to bring out the emotions that loaded the songs of the slaves. During the days of slavery, the *séga* was a link with the distant ancestral land and the only form of relief from their back-breaking labour. The slaves of old sang about their suffering and their yearning for the land they were cruelly snatched from. In the predominantly Creole region of Black River, one can still hear some of these emotions in the *séga typique* (traditional *séga*) performed on a non-commercial basis.

The *séga* is extremely versatile. It can be played with a full set of guitar, drums and trumpet or with no instruments at all. Anything that can make noise will do—an old jerrycan, two sticks, or a bottle and a coin, and that's the way a *séga* party gets under way at the beach. And, despite the sensuality of swaying hips and torsos, the *séga* is a family dance as well. Young children dance the *séga* with their grandparents at weddings, friends dance it when they meet in the village square.

In colonial times, the *séga* was banned by the slave masters because it could lead to unrest on the plantation and for a long time, it was considered crude and almost taboo. Today, however, it is no longer a Creole song and dance, but the national song and dance, enjoyed by all communities. It is performed on all occasions and no party is complete without the *séga*. Your friends will surely teach you how to dance it and you will have great fun doing the *séga*.

Integration

As the different communities get to know each other better, there is a certain movement towards greater uniformity throughout the Mauritian society. What the Mauritian population is going through at the moment is a gradual (and almost imperceptible) dilution of traditional lifestyle and values, so that Asian communities are brought closer to the 'general population.' Certainly in a few generations' time, everybody will be living a more or less Creole lifestyle. However, traditional religions and the Asian values of thrift, hard work, respect for elders still prevail. Integration means each community absorbing a bit of the others. The proto-Mauritian of the future will probably be a fun-loving person (like the Creoles) but also hardworking and thrifty (like the Asians).

COMMUNALISM

Racism does not exist in Mauritius—or so the political leaders would like the population to believe. Instead they prefer to use the word 'communalism', a euphemism certainly, but more acceptable because of its etymological association with the word 'community'. The word 'communal' is something

Walk along the street and you will see Mauritians from different racial backgrounds.

of a dirty word in Mauritius and praising a group of people for their communal lifestyle would more likely be taken as an offence than a compliment.

One People, One Nation?

The national anthem claims that Mauritians 'gather around' their country 'as one people, as one nation'. This is all very fine and it does seem so in times of prosperity. When the economy is doing well, everyone is happy with each other. However, it takes very little for communalism to rear its ugly head. Many Mauritians still remember the communal riots of 1969 when Muslims and Creoles fought it out in the suburban areas. And until the 1980s, football clubs were organised on a communal basis, with names like the Hindu Cadets or Muslim Scouts, and matches degenerating into fights between members of different communities. Such overt communal policies are now outlawed, and sports and social clubs are open to all segments of the population.

The slogan 'unity in diversity' is bandied about at every general election, but it is a fact that people vote for those whom they believe best represent their views, that is people of their own community. Political parties know this and candidates for the national assembly are selected on the basis of their community when standing in particular areas. The parliamentary system of 'best losers' which ensures that all communities are adequately represented in government is itself a pillar of communalism. When it comes to communal feelings, the solution then is to tread carefully. The apparent harmony of different races working and having fun together hides undercurrents which would be best left alone. And certainly most Mauritians are conscious of this and try their best to avoid rocking the boat.

THE FAMILY

The pillar of Mauritian society is the family. Married children either live with their parents or visit them frequently, sometimes taking their evening meals together even when they have their own house. The extended family of uncles, aunts and cousins also meet on a regular basis, and even distant relatives feel quite close to each other. Very often, one's best friend is a brother, sister or cousin. And many businesses are family ventures, with cousins or brothers and sisters in partnership. A family member is thought to be a more loyal and trustworthy employee than a stranger, even if the latter is better qualified.

A Typical Household

The three-generation family is still the norm. Children feel duty-bound to look after their parents and sending them to an old folks' home is tantamount to committing a crime. The home is seen as a place for only the destitute who have no one to look after them. In general, when sons get married, they continue to live with the parents while saving up for a house of their own. However, only one son's family lives with the grandparents. The extended family of several married children living together is no longer desirable. The grandparents help to look after the children and the grandmother cooks the meals, with the help of the daughter-in-law if the latter does not work.

In the nuclear family, if the mother goes out to work, then the children are sent to the grandparents for baby-sitting or after-school care. Today's families tend to be small in size, with one or two children. Some families still prefer boys, but girls are loved just as much and given the same educational opportunities as boys. Parents tend to shelter their children, doing everything for them so that they can concentrate on their studies, and this in a way inhibits independence and creativity.

Women

Various factors affect the degree of 'liberation' a woman feels. Through her upbringing, the Mauritian woman is still rather conservative in dress and moral attitude. Girls live with their parents until they get married (in fact, most men also do). Living on her own or sharing a place with friends would imply that a woman either has loose morals (she lives alone in order to entertain men) or is bad-tempered (she is too fierce to get along with her family), neither of which is desirable. A woman leaves her parents' home to be someone's wife or mistress, never to be by herself. Once a woman gets married or sets up home with a man, she is defined by her relationship with the man. This is changing though, as more women succeed in the professional world. And this is where a certain dichotomy lies. The Mauritian society expects women to be rather prudish and yet women receive as much education as men and many jobs are available to them. Daughters are treated no differently from sons. Girls fulfil their educational potential and go out to work after completing school. And they go on working even after marriage and childbirth. Some do eventually stop work, when the family's financial situation is secure or the elderly parents can no longer look after the children.

Despite equal opportunities, the 'glass ceiling' is very much present, and is set quite low by developed countries' standards. Women who have made it to middle management are considered successful, and promotion is slow, although women get paid the same salary as men for the same job. Even in the professions, women still play second fiddle. Certain types of jobs are considered more appropriate for women, such as teaching or jobs related to computers. However Mauritian women do not see themselves as being dominated by men. Very few feel the need to be liberated. They take their lot with serenity and know that liberation is a slow process. In the villages, women come together once a month for all-night women's parties, sing, dance and enjoy themselves in a ritual of female bonding. They are thankful for the opportunities they get for being themselves.

There are several women's associations ranging from the genteel Mauritius Alliance of Women to the more militant Muvman Liberasyon Fam and others based on religious affiliation. All of them aim to uplift the status of women in Mauritius but use different means to achieve it. They offer a range of activities but still do not really reach out to the majority of women. Most women are confident of themselves and do not see the need to belong to any feminine or feminist organisation.

Two young girls display the broad smile and zest for life that Mauritians are famous for.

Children

As the family is the pillar of society, children are highly prized. A childless couple feels lacking, and well-meaning friends and relatives would commiserate with them and offer advice even if they do not have children by choice. Of course, saying frankly that you do not want children is something of a faux pas. Everybody likes children in Mauritius and those who do not are like monsters.

Nowadays, most families have only one or two children and the latter tend to be spoilt by the parents, grandparents and uncles and aunties. Telling your friends that their children are spoilt or chiding them would not go down well at all. Adults marvel at the antics of children and sometimes misbehaviour is mistaken as a sign of intelligence. Your own children will be the object of much praise and attention and if you try to discipline them in front of your Mauritian friends, the latter will certainly speak up on their behalf. They do not see it as interference because children are defenceless and need protection. However, despite the indulgence of their parents and those around them, Mauritian children are generally well behaved and are, in fact, quite shy in front of strangers. Many are very self-conscious about talking in English or French, but they will soon play with your children without any reserve. Then you will realise that they are actually very fluent in both English and French.

Once a couple has children, they are considered a family, almost like a package. The parents of young children do not go anywhere without them. Adults-only functions are very rare. Parents leave their children with their own parents or siblings only on formal occasions. If you invite your Mauritian friends to your house, you should be prepared to see them arrive with their children in tow. Sometimes even teenagers accompany their parents. And, of course, when you are invited to a friend's house, they expect you to bring your children. And you might just have to do that because there are no baby-sitters in Mauritius.

RELIGION

The three main religions are Hinduism, Christianity and Islam. With complete freedom of religion interred in the Mauritian Constitution, there has also been a proliferation of sects and nearly 100 religious denominations have been counted. Mauritians are a pious people and the number of churches, mosques and temples bears witness to it. However, as the main religions have been established for centuries, some people only pay lip service to it. The newly arrived cults and sects, on the other hand, take proselytising to the

extreme, to the extent of harassment. Persevering converts go door-to-door trying to disseminate 'enlightenment' through pamphlets and brochures. Such tactics rarely succeed. Much more successful are those sects which, using modern management techniques, target specific groups.

Religious Tension

Like communalism, religious tension lurks beneath the harmony and understanding that characterises Mauritian society. (The two are actually closely related.) In general, the main religious groups leave each other alone, making no effort to convert members of other religions. There is no need for them to advocate tolerance because the people know each other so well. In fact, there is a movement to bring together the various religions while respecting each other and without any proselytising. Ecumenical services are organised to mark such occasions as the new year, national day or different religious festivals. Visits of religious figures, like the Pope or an eminent cleric, are attended by members of all religious clergies.

One indefatigable supporter of ecumeny is a Roman Catholic priest, Father Souchon. To mark festivals of the other religions, he chooses from an extensive wardrobe of chasubles with appropriate colours and motifs, such as bright red for Chinese New Year or green for the Muslim Eid-ul-Fitr.

Houses of Worship

Christian churches and Hindu temples can be found in almost every town and village. There are fewer mosques, but you can usually find one in the next village or the nearest town (which, in such a small country, is never far away). Buddhist and Taoist temples, on the other hand, are only located in Port-Louis. As for the minor religions, there might be only one house of worship throughout the whole island.

The main houses of worship are open whole day long and anyone is welcome to visit. However, remember that the people there are engaged in a deeply personal activity and any form of disturbance should be avoided. Mauritian churches do not contain any artistic treasures and have never attracted the kind of attention that tourists heap on those in Catholic countries such as Spain and Italy. Thus snapping pictures would really startle the devotees praying in the pews. Photography is much more common in temples and mosques, though. Shoes have to be taken off before entering and the inner sanctuary is forbidden to all but the priest.

Services are held weekly in the smaller churches and several times on Saturday and Sunday for the bigger ones. All mosques are open for Friday prayers and *pujas* are held daily in Hindu temples. Taoist and Buddhist temples do not have regular services, but you can offer incense any time of the day when they are open.

SUPERSTITION

Mauritians are not a particularly superstitious people. The older generation might still hold on to some folk beliefs, but most young people raised on a rational Western education do not indulge in superstitious practices. But this does not mean you should make fun of irrational beliefs because, while not really believing in superstitions, many Mauritians will still avoid certain things, just in case. The usual Western superstitions prevail: do not walk under a ladder; a black cat brings bad luck; touch wood to prevent misfortune. Others have a more local flavour, such as spitting out a piece of food if someone stares at you when you are eating. And yet others only subsist in folk sayings, such as roll your tongue seven times in your mouth before making any statement.

With the arrival of the Hong Kongers, some Chinese have adopted the Cantonese superstitions concerning numbers, favouring the number eight and giving a wide berth to unlucky numbers such as four. However, the belief is not very strong—but they reckon that there is no harm in putting all the chances on their side.

Witchcraft

You might come across a slaughtered black chicken with candles and other paraphernalia at a road junction. This means that some sort of witchcraft has been performed at that spot. The spot itself poses no danger, but most motorists would swerve to avoid running over the offerings. If your house is at a street corner and you do find some items of witchcraft in front of your door, just call the municipal cleaners and they will get rid of it. Such a scenario is, of course, highly improbable because belief in witchcraft, just as in superstitions, has almost died out. Most people live according to their religion, which forbids such practices. However, if you are interested, it is said that the witchcraft of Madagascar is the most potent and that some Creole women still practise it.

White Magic

What is more popular is white magic, that is using prayers and incantations for healing purposes. Faith healers use candles, heads of onion and needles to get rid of warts, cure a sprained ankle or get rid of pains. Prayers to 'legitimate' deities accompany the rites. Even though people still believe in the powers of the *guérisseurs* (as faith healers are known in Creole), they go to them only as a last resort, after visits to the doctor have proved unsuccessful. A few of them are known almost throughout the island, but they also are a dying breed.

SOCIALISING

CHAPTER 4

'You can make more friends in two months by
becoming interested in other people than you can in
two years by trying to get other people interested in you.'
—Dale Carnegie

FOREIGNERS

Foreigners have always been welcomed by Mauritius, more so now that the tourist industry is an important sector of the economy. And, inevitably, stereotypes have formed. The colonial past does not help, either, because the belief that 'white man is better' still prevails in certain circles. Many gullible young women have been taken for a ride by unscrupulous Caucasians promising marriage and a rosy future in Europe. Thus, having a foreign spouse or friends is still something of a status symbol, although Mauritians are now becoming more confident of themselves and treat foreigners on an equal footing. Still, Mauritian families tend to welcome foreign guests with more exuberance than local ones.

The Indian 'Expert'

When Mauritius was granted independence in 1968, the country needed administrators and technicians with the necessary expertise to put the infrastructure into place. Thus in the 1970s and early 1980s, a number of 'experts' were recruited from India. Many did a great job training doctors or planning the road network, but some were certainly not up to standard.

This was a time when the Mauritian people were exhorted to tighten their belts and work hard to make the country succeed. It was therefore not surprising that the very favourable conditions under which these experts were employed drew criticism from the locals. Moreover, the Indians did not speak French and did not make much effort to learn Creole, giving the impression that they were arrogant. Thus, much hostility was directed at them, though not openly. Today, there are fewer Indian experts and their contribution is better understood.

Chinese Entrepreneurs

At about the same time came the Chinese entrepreneurs from Hong Kong and Taiwan who took advantage of the very attractive incentives offered by the government to those who invested in the Export Processing Zone (EPZ). As the textile factories they set up were highly labour intensive, a large number of people found jobs as machine operators, mainly women. However, the Chinese were not welcomed as saviours bearing jobs and prosperity. Hardly. The problem here is again that of communication. The mid-level managers and technical staff running the factories were barely conversant in English and were deemed arrogant and uncouth. And, as people started to compare the wages paid to factory operators in Mauritius with those in Hong Kong, there was a general feeling that workers were being shamelessly exploited.

Many Hong Kongers and Taiwanese have become permanent residents because they truly appreciate living in Mauritius and they have adapted to the lifestyle. One undeniably positive aspect of the presence of Chinese expatriates is the blooming of good Chinese restaurants set up to cater to their tastes.

Whites

Because most tourists come from Europe, it is generally assumed that a Caucasian is a tourist. Thus it would come as a pleasant surprise if a Caucasian shows knowledge of the country. Mauritians are always flattered when a Caucasian chooses to work and live in the country. As old habits die hard, Caucasians are treated with respect, even deference.

Caucasians are physically different from most Mauritians and so tend to attract more attention when they move about.

White children, especially blonde and blue-eyed, are the focus of attention wherever they go. People smile at them, vendors offer them fruits at the market and some even try to touch their hair. No harm is meant, just curiosity. In general, Caucasians are viewed as charming, glamorous and fashionable, and good to make friends with.

Africans

Africans are called Zulus in Creole, with just a touch of condescension, even from those with African ancestry. Zulus are perceived to be naïve and unwittingly funny. This is the general perception. But when it comes to business, African business people are treated with as much respect and care as anyone else. And when Africans deal with Mauritians on an individual basis, their qualities are appreciated and a friendship is established as quickly as with other races.

SOCIALISING WITH MAURITIANS

The most wonderful part of your stay in Mauritius will be the many sincere and lasting relationships you will form with Mauritian friends. In a country blessed with good weather and where the pace of life is refreshingly leisurely, keeping in touch and enjoying convivial visits are that much more easy and frequent.

Etiquette

Mauritians are easy-going and open-minded about people having different manners and ways of doing things. Through their own multiracial heritage and the media, they have been exposed to many different practices and customs. Being a tolerant people, they will never be offended if you do certain things differently—unless offence is intended—and will understand that this is your custom. However, it is always more pleasurable if you show that you do know Mauritian rules and proceed to explain in which way they are different from yours. Because they live on an island, Mauritians are always curious about other people and cultures. Their interest in your customs is genuine and they will make a point to remember them.

Forms of Address

Mauritians tend to be quite formal and would address each other as Mr, Mrs or Miss So-and-so. Even the person performing the introduction will use the titles in addition to the full name.

In the office, all superiors and people from other departments are addressed as Mr or Mrs. Unmarried women are usually called by their first names preceded by Miss (in Creole, *Mamzelle*). Bosses are never called by their first names, except out of their hearing. If your surname is more difficult to pronounce than your first name, then most people will use the latter, but still preceded by the title.

In social situations, always use the title and surname unless people ask to be called by their first names. No Mauritian will address a foreigner by the first name upon introduction. If you want to be called by your first name, say so. Your friend will not get the hint if you just use their first name, expecting them to do the same. If you want to be known by your nickname, explain the nickname to them and ask them to use it. You might hear some people calling colleagues by a shortened name (Renga for Rengasamy or Venkat for Venkatasamy, for example); do not use this short form until you are very familiar with the person. Although it denotes intimacy between friends, it is a sign of condescension when used by a casual acquaintance or a superior at work.

Married women are always called Mrs, followed by their husband's surname or first name, whichever is easier to pronounce. The term Ms is never used because there is no equivalent in French and Creole. People would be very puzzled if a married woman asked them to use Miss and her own surname. Using a double-barrel surname also leads to confusion because most people would not know which name to call her.

Older people expect to be addressed as Mr and Mrs. As you get more familiar, you can call them Uncle and Auntie (Ton and Tantine in Creole) followed by their first names, but never use their first names alone. It is a sign of great disrespect.

Professional titles are not used in the social context, except for medical doctors and dentists (who are both called Doctor). Lawyers (both male and female) are addressed as Maître in the course of their work, but not socially.

Introductions

Mauritians do not stand on ceremony when performing introductions. There is no hard and fast rule, although in polite society, a man is introduced to a woman and younger people are introduced to their elders. When a man and a woman are introduced, they shake hands and the man says 'Enchanté' while the woman accepts the compliment with a smile and perhaps a 'How do you do?'. With older people, 'Pleased to meet you' is an adequate greeting.

As you are the foreign guest, the tendency will be to introduce others to you—men, women or older people. This is just a sign of respect.

Dress

Mauritian men and women like to look smart when going out. Even if you specify that your little party is a casual one, your male guests will still come in long trousers and a smart shirt or polo-neck T-shirt and the women in pretty dresses and high heels. Wearing shorts and T-shirts is sloppy and would be a mark of disrespect to you. Such attire is good only for the home or the beach. To go shopping, even if it is to the market, a change of clothes is still required.

Mauritians dress smartly, but not formally. Men wear mostly short-sleeved shirts, except in the cooler months when they would put a jacket or woollen sweater over it. Jeans and cotton trousers are appropriate when visiting as well as sports shoes. Dress shoes are worn only with the suit and for formal occasions.

As for women, trousers can be worn anywhere, although they tend to be the tailored type when worn for weddings and cocktail parties, not jeans or cargo pants. Ankle-length skirts are not popular, knee-length or mid-calf being more favoured, even for formal wear. There is no rule about sleeves; it all depends on the season. Long, short or no sleeves are appropriate for any occasion. Court shoes with one- to two-inch heels are the most popular footwear. In the summer, sandals can replace the shoes.

Beachwear is not appropriate for going about town. You will not get kicked out of restaurants or shops, but the locals will not like it. Such attire only reinforces their belief that foreigners do not care about their sensitivities. Places of worship have a strict dress code. Even if it is not advertised, you should follow it. The guideline is to dress modestly: sleeves and knee-length skirt or trousers for women, and shirt and trousers for men. Headgear is not required.

Children Welcome

Children are welcome anywhere. When visiting Mauritian friends, do not worry about bringing your children along. Friendships are formed between families, not just individuals. When receiving an invitation, you will be reminded to bring the children. It is a sincere desire to get to know your whole family and Mauritians just love children. They would be horrified to hear that you have left them alone at home while you are having fun. Likewise, when you extend invitations to your house, you should expect your friends to arrive with children in tow. And, really, the thing to do is to tell them not to forget to bring the little ones.

All restaurants welcome children, even if some of them are not equipped for it. If you have young children who cannot sit on adult chairs yet, it is wise to bring along their stroller since high chairs might not be available. At least you will not have to keep them on your knee for the whole meal. If your children get restless, just send them to play outside the restaurant. The management does not mind, and your kids will make friends with the children of the other restaurant patrons. But, despite being family-oriented, very few restaurants have a children's menu. They are expected to share what you order. So, when trying out a new restaurant, bring along their favourite snacks so that they will have something to eat even if the menu does not cater to them.

VISITING

Mauritians are a hospitable lot and like to receive guests at home. Now that most houses have a phone, unannounced visits are less common, but some friends might still drop by if they happen to be in your area.

Hospitality

Visiting usually takes place in mid-morning or mid-afternoon, rarely at meal times to avoid embarrassment to the host. After dinner is also not a good time to visit because most families settle down to watch television in their most comfortable house clothes or pyjamas. This is family time when the children do their homework or everyone gathers around the television to talk about the day's events and enjoy each other's company. (Mauritians generally do not go out in the evening.)

You do not have to take your shoes off when entering a house since Mauritian houses are not always spotlessly clean. Making guests walk barefoot is also a sign of disrespect. However, if you see that your host is barefoot, do bend down to remove your shoes; they will certainly tell you not to bother. In that case, just walk in.

A drink is always offered to the visitor, tea or some fizzy soft drink. You should always accept it, even if you take only a few sips. If you really cannot stand cola or tea, it is all right to ask for plain water. Sometimes biscuits are also offered, but nothing really fancy. Your host might prepare some local snacks only if this is your first visit and it has been scheduled well in advance. For a casual visit, you do not have to bring a present. However, if your hosts have children, some sweets will always be appreciated.

Most visitors are entertained in the living room, or the garden if the weather is nice and your host has some nice garden furniture. If this is your first visit, you may ask about the house, the number of rooms, when it was built, etc, but do not ask for a tour of the house; wait for your host to suggest it.

When you arrive, the children will come out to greet you, but they will not stay in the living room. After welcoming you, they go back to their rooms or outside. Your children can go with them, but if they are shy, they can remain with you. Sweets and chocolates will be offered to your children. It is no use telling your host that your children are not fond of them because they will coax them to take at least one. Even if you are very strict about this at home, here you should urge your child to accept the sweet.

A social visit rarely lasts more than one hour. If it is near dinner time, your host might ask you to stay back and be quite persistent about it. But do not accept the offer unless they tell you that they have actually prepared your share because they expected you to stay longer.

Greetings

The most common form of greeting is the handshake. Both men and women shake hands, except for some conservative Muslim women who will not touch a man's hand. The same applies to conservative Muslim men; they might not want to shake hands with a woman. To avoid embarrassment, it is safest to wait for the Muslim person to proffer their hand before extending yours. Most men have a firm grip but some women offer a limp hand and just touch yours before removing it. Do not be offended: they just believe it is more ladylike. If you have just been introduced, the handshake is de rigueur.

Becoming more common, even among Asian communities, is the kiss. Women kiss each other upon meeting and women kiss men. Men do not kiss other men (at least, not in public). Kissing is performed among friends, or perhaps when you meet a friend's friend at the friend's house, but never with casual acquaintances or colleagues. Mauritians kiss both cheeks, while a few add a third kiss, after the French fashion. These are usually the younger and more trendy lot. Most people do actually kiss the other person's cheeks, except when women are heavily made-up. In that case, they just touch their cheeks to the other person's. Children always kiss adults (of both sexes) although some boys might think that shaking hands is more 'manly.' If a little hand is proudly extended towards you, shake it in all seriousness. You can follow the handshake by a little pat on the head.

Hugging is not that common, except when friends who have not seen each other for a long time meet again. But back-slapping and draping one's arm around another person's shoulders (for a few seconds) are considered friendly gestures. Leaving your arm there for too long denotes sexual intimacy. Holding hands too. But touching another person, like a casual brush of an arm or tapping a shoulder with a finger, is socially acceptable.

When leaving a party, you do not have to shake hands with or kiss everyone. A general wave in their direction is enough. However, you should shake your host's hand and kiss your hostess goodbye if they walk you to the door.

If you come from a society where physical contact is limited, you might be taken aback and embarrassed by all the kissing. But do not shy away from it. Treat it as going native. Kiss your friends, slap their backs, hold their shoulders. You will be surprised at how fast kissing will become second nature to you.

Being a House Guest

When staying with Mauritian friends, you will be asked to make yourself at home and treat the house as being yours. They do mean it—to a certain extent. The saying 'Make yourself at home—but don't forget that you are visiting' sums up the attitude.

As most Mauritian houses are quite small, a child would have had to move in with a sibling to make room for you. So leave the room exactly as it is. If you need to move some things on the writing table, ask your host to help. The child would probably need to come in from time to time to get books and other school materials or clothes. As far as possible, do not use the stuff in the room. Get your own pens and paper if you need to write. You can certainly read the books on the shelves, but remember to put them back. Make your own bed everyday and tidy up the room in the morning. Even if your hosts have a maid, her duties would not include making the beds. However, you do not have to sweep the floor or dust the furniture.

Most Mauritian households are early risers, so make it a point to wake up before 8:00 am. However, families do not sit down to have breakfast together in the morning, so you can eat at any time. As most houses have only one toilet and one bathroom, do not take your own sweet time. Reading in the loo is definitely out of the question. Others might be waiting outside. In general, people are in a rush to go to work or school in the morning. So it is a good idea to wait for them to have finished before you emerge from your room. You can leave your pyjamas on when you go to the bathroom, but as soon as you have brushed your teeth, you should change. When taking a shower, bring your clean clothes in with you. Do not come out of the bathroom with a towel draped round you. Your host might find such behaviour brazen.

Do not shut yourself in your room when there are other people in the house. It would be regarded as antisocial behaviour. In general, the bedrooms are meant for sleeping only. During the day, everybody is in the living room or kitchen. Your hosts will certainly tell you to eat and drink whatever you want from the fridge and larder. But you should wait for them to offer food and drink. If you do want to have something, then you should always ask for permission. When you are alone in the house, of course, you help yourself but remember to tell your hosts what you have taken when they come back. You do not have to replace it, but it would be a nice gesture to bring some snacks or pastries back the next time you go out. Never consume liquor if it is not offered, or anything expensive.

Neighbours

Being on good terms with your neighbours will make your stay that much more pleasurable. As soon as you move in, introduce yourself to the immediate neighbours and tell them something about yourself. There is no need for you to go knocking on their door and effecting a formal introduction. You will surely see them in the garden within a few days of moving in; take the opportunity to have a small chat over the fence. Always greet your neighbours when you see them and ask how they are doing. If you have children, encourage them to make friends.

Usually neighbours do not interact that much on the social level. They do not visit each other, but do invite each other for important events, like their children's weddings. You do not have to entertain your neighbours, but it is nice to offer some of your country's specialities when you prepare them. Just go to the fence and call out your neighbour's name. When they come out, pass the dish over. If you have seasonal fruit trees in your garden you should always distribute some to your neighbours when they are in season.

Being a good neighbour means being considerate. Do not allow your parties to drag into the wee hours of the morning, and never play music in the garden. Ask your guests not to park their cars in front of your neighbours' gate. If your pet makes too much noise at night, go out and discipline it. Your neighbours should hear you doing that so that they will know that the noise is really out of your control.

CONVERSATION

What do you talk about when you meet Mauritian friends? It all depends on your gender and your relationship with them and whether you are colleagues or new acquaintances. In general, women tend to gather together and talk about their children, fashion or the latest television programmes.

Do not dismiss these conversations as being frivolous because they give you an idea about Mauritian society and you will be able to make judgements on how to integrate better. In addition, you can garner a lot of practical information from the other women present.

Politics

One sure topic of conversation when men get together is politics (women in general shy away from such talk, even in mixed company). It pays to learn a thing or two about the local political scene the moment you arrive; you will be able to appreciate the subtleties of the conversation much better. However, remember that politics in Mauritius is very much community based, so avoid launching into any harsh criticism of politicians, especially in front of people of the same community. Even if the others are shredding the politician's reputation to bits, limit your comments to some witty remarks about the person's flaws.

When it comes to politics, Mauritians are like the proverbial frog in the well. They may make passing remarks about the tension between China and Taiwan or ask you who you think will win the presidential elections in the United States, but these are quite superficial and they do not expect you to embark onto a detailed analysis of the situation. Above all, do not try to engage them in an earnest discussion of international politics. You might find such arguments stimulating, but your Mauritian friends will be taken aback at what they perceive to be your aggressive attitude.

Gossip and Rumours

In a small country like Mauritius, it is inevitable that gossip and rumours rule daily conversations. Gossip about public figures and their families abound, some really malicious and bordering on slander. Even respectable newspapers pepper their reporting with innuendoes and carry articles about 'a certain political figure' without revealing the person's identity but insinuating wrongdoing.

Rumours also tend to focus on public figures and some are so persistent that they are taken for fact in some quarters. Sometimes nationwide rumours lead to attacks of panic, like the occasional talk about werewolves roaming about at night. One such rumour after a cyclone (when there was no electricity) led to the formation of vigilante groups patrolling the streets at night and the beating-up of unlucky people who happened to arouse the suspicions of the group. Actually the word 'rumour' is so popular that most people would say, "There is a rumour..." rather than "I heard that..." If someone mentions that there is a rumour about you, do not get on your high horses; it only means that they heard the information from a third party.

MAKING FRIENDS

In the Mauritian version of French, there are two words for friend—*ami* and *camarade*. You use one or the other depending on the degree of intimacy of the friendship. The distinction is important because Mauritians are so hospitable that they will make friends with anyone, but to be an *ami* takes time and interaction, plus the X-factor that makes two persons click. It is interesting to note that in Creole, only the word *camarade* is used; to give the sense of *ami*, the adjective *bon* (good) is prefixed to it.

The first thing that strikes you as you arrive is the friendliness of the people. Everyone is helpful and eager to please you. You will receive invitations to people's home and will probably be overwhelmed by the amount of attention you will receive. Don't worry; all this will die down after a month or two and you will just blend in with the rest.

Friendliness

Everyone you meet is friendly—from your greengrocer to the tax collector—because Mauritians are friendly to all foreigners. There is still this subtle perception that foreigners are superior and thus good to make friends with. However, some of this friendliness might be more self-interested. If you hold a managerial post in your company, colleagues might see friendship with you as a means to advance their careers, or they intend to visit your country and are hoping for free accommodation from you. Do not be too bothered about it: you will soon be able to distinguish true friends from those who only want to make use of you.

Friendliness does not extend to greeting everyone on the street in the morning, and strangers will not approach you to wish you a good day just because you are a foreigner. But if you look lost, a kind soul will certainly come forward and offer you their help, to the extent of walking or driving you to your destination.

Friendship

Even if you are here for only a short stay, you will still be able to forge enduring friendships. Being a friend means that you try to spend as much time with each other as possible, perhaps every weekend and some evenings during the week as well. Friends visit each other to have a drink and chat about everything under the sun or go to the beach together. All this is very informal; you do not have to invite your friend over or wait to be asked to their house. You just drop in on a Saturday afternoon and stay on until after dinner, sharing the family meal.

If you have a family, you all participate in the friendship. Spouses and children become friends with each other. If you are going to spend your weekends with your friend, your family will not feel neglected because they too will be sharing in your activities. If your spouse does not click with your friend's spouse, you will find that it is not as easy to cultivate the friendship. In general, friendships develop between people of the same sex only. Mauritius is still a rather conservative society and you will find that people of the opposite sex will be more reticent to make friends with you for fear of rumours.

Friends are there for each other in times of need, or whenever you need help. If you can do with an extra pair of hands to move some furniture about, ask your friend, or just wait for the day they come to visit. But, because you are friends, your friend will never let you know they are in difficulties, especially financial ones. You do not borrow money from your friends; you ask your boss for an advance or go to the bank, but never bother your friends. And if you detect that your friend might need some help, never for one minute suggest lending them some money. Don't even ask them about it; just offer your help in subtle ways, like giving the children some clothes that you 'found at a bargain price.'

Other problems can be shared among friends, especially work-related ones. If you are considering a career switch, discuss it with your friends. They can offer advice and can even use their connections to put you in touch with relevant people.

CAUSES FOR CELEBRATION

Mauritians are fond of having fun and occasions for merrymaking are exploited to the fullest. Being less inhibited, the Creoles have traditionally been viewed as a fun-loving people, even as wastrels. But younger Asians are now following suit.

Weddings

In all communities, a wedding is eagerly awaited by both the couple and their families and friends. Preparations start months in advance, sometimes even more than a year, as an auspicious date is chosen according to the almanac and the more popular reception halls have a very long waiting list. Everyone chips in to help, relatives serve the guests on the wedding day itself and friends decorate the hall and wedding car.

Previously, a couple had to go through a civil marriage ceremony before the religious one. To give more protection and full legal rights to women who have only gone through a religious ceremony and the offspring of such marriages, the government has now introduced legislation to make religious marriages legally binding as well. However, most people still hold both ceremonies and foreigners who go through a religious marriage in Mauritius might have problems getting their marriage recognised in their home country. The legal wedding is more of a formality, with the couple taking half a day off from work or turning it into an engagement party. The real wedding is the religious ceremony.

The Indian Gamat

Indian families hold a wedding party called a *gamat* on the eve of the wedding day, one for the groom's family and another for the bride's. If you are invited to an Indian wedding, you also go to the *gamat*. The invitation card will state the address and the time. You do not have to make it a point to be punctual; guests arrive in a steady stream and food is served continuously. And, as the *gamat* is not the official part of the wedding, you do not have to dress formally. But remember that Indian men and women are still rather conservative, and scanty clothing would be considered offensive.

The *gamat* is basically a dinner held in the garden, under what is called a 'green hall' which is a marquee made of green tarpaulin sheets and decorated with palm fronds and other ferns. The bride or groom is seated in the house, not in the green hall, and relatives come in to rub some turmeric on their hands or face in a symbolic gesture. For this reason, the *gamat* is also called the 'saffron'. At the bride's house, the dowry can be inspected and the groom's gifts of *saris* and gold jewellery are laid out for everyone to see. At the groom's house, you can visit the newlyweds' room. In Mauritius, the dowry is not very big and some ethnic groups do not even have it. But if the parents are rich landowners, they usually give a plot of land or a house to their daughter.

As soon as you arrive, you will be led to the 'green hall' by relatives. Guests are seated at long tables covered with a basic plastic sheet. A banana leaf is laid in front of you and dollops of curry are dropped onto the leaf. This is a vegetarian meal consisting of curried potatoes, curried beans, pumpkin curry, jack fruit curry, chilli curry, a thick aubergine and dholl soup and various fruit and vegetable *achards*. It is all accompanied by *puris*, small round pancakes deep-fried until fluffy, and some tamarind sauce. The food is cooked in the backyard by members of the family or hired caterers. You are expected to eat with your fingers. Indians use only their right hand, but you can use both to tear the *puris* and pick up the curries. For drink, you will be given cool tap water served in a steel goblet. You can eat as much as you want to and you will see many of the other guests calling to the servers for more food. As the servers are relatives of the couple, they are certain to offer more food to you and taking a second helping will really make them happy.

After the dinner or before, you can ask the helpers to lead you to the bride or groom to offer your congratulations. This visit should not last very long as many relatives will be coming in. Leave the chit-chat for another day. The *gamat* sometimes ends with a dancing party and you are very welcome to join. But it is perfectly all right to leave immediately after eating; it will not be considered rude.

The next day, the wedding ceremony takes place in a temple hall or reception hall. Guests are seated in rows facing a raised dais where the couple sits together with the priest. The bride wears the red wedding *sari* trimmed with gold threads and gold jewellery given by the groom. He is either dressed in a traditional costume complete with turban or a

The bride and groom in front of the sacred fire, solemnising a Tamil wedding.

suit. Prayers are said and the groom puts the *thali* round the bride's neck. This is a piece of yellow cord with a pendant and it embodies the married status of the wearer. After that, one end of the sari is tied to the man's clothes and the couple walks three times round the sacred fire, with the groom leading the way. After the ceremony, everybody goes home, with the guests receiving a cake at the door. (Even though the wedding takes place in mid-afternoon, no food or drink is served.) You will not get to talk to the newlyweds, but the immediate family (parents, brothers and sisters) will be there to greet you.

The Muslim Nikah

The Muslim wedding is also preceded by a meal, but on the same day. As it is for the Indians, Muslim weddings are usually held on a Sunday. The ceremony itself takes place in the afternoon, and guests are treated to a lunch of *briani*, a wonderfully fragrant dish of rice, meat, potatoes and spices, at the bride's or groom's house. If the family has invited a large number of guests, then a 'green hall' is erected in the garden. Otherwise, lunch is served in the house. The invitation card will probably only mention the ceremony, but it is understood that a meal is included.

As you arrive, the relatives will lead you to the bride or groom so that you can offer your congratulations. Afterwards, you are taken to a long table for lunch. Men and women eat separately, so you should be prepared to be away from your spouse, at least during the meal or even longer. In general, men tend to congregate in the garden while the women stay in the house. Children, if they are in their teens, have to go to the section of their own sex. The *briani* is served on a plate, together with a fork and spoon. You can either have plain water or rose syrup for a drink. As *briani* is a very rich dish, you will generally not want a second helping, but if you do, just ask the servers. Many guests even ask for just meat or potatoes.

The wedding ceremony, or Nikah, is also separate for men and women. Usually, the men go to the mosque where the priest says prayers for the groom. After this, the priest and groom go over to the wedding hall where the bride and women guests are waiting. Many brides wear a white Western-style wedding dress and grooms don a suit. The marriage rites are performed on a stage with the guests watching from their seats. While waiting for the men to arrive, sweets are served. You can decline if you do not have a sweet tooth. After the ceremony, guests receive a delicious pastry called *soutal fine* to take home. This is a fluffy disc of white hair-like threads soaked in sugar and rose syrup. Sometimes a second cake is also distributed.

The Creole Bash

You have to attend a Creole wedding to understand the intensity with which this community devotes itself to merrymaking. The evening before the wedding, the groom and his friends get together to 'bury his bachelor's life'. Much like a stag party, the evening consists of a good dinner with lots of drinks. Women, however, do not usually have a hen party or wedding shower. A Creole wedding is held on a Saturday so that the guests have the Sunday to recuperate. And after you have attended one, you will understand why.

When a Creole family goes to a wedding, they do so in style. Women buy new party dresses and men wear a suit. If they do not own a car, they hire a taxi for the whole duration of the wedding, about five to six hours. And the whole family turns up, not just the parents. If the grown-up son or daughter has a girlfriend or boyfriend, they also go along.

The church is beautifully decorated with flowers, and white ribbons and flowers are tied to the pews. Guests wait in the church for the wedding party to arrive. The groom walks in first, on his mother's arm. If he does not have a mother, his godmother or an elder sister or aunt takes her place. He then stands at the altar to wait for the bride, who walks in on her father's arm, preceded by the flower girls, ring bearer and bridesmaids. Everybody has to stand up to welcome the wedding couple. The service itself lasts only half an hour, although some couples might opt for a full-scale mass. The ceremony is characterised by beautiful singing and expressions of love from the couple to each other and from the families to the couple. After the wedding, the newly-weds walk out of the church, arm-in-arm, with the bridesmaids and all the guests following them. As the bells peal, pictures are taken on the church steps. The couple then gets into the wedding car and everybody proceeds to the reception hall for a cocktail party.

The newly-weds enter the reception first and stand at the door to shake hands and greet every body. The bride is kissed by both men and women whereas the groom is kissed only by the women. As they enter, guests are offered a glass of champagne or *ponch* (an anise-flavoured sherbet). After all the guests have walked in, the newly-weds stand at the bridal table and somebody, usually an uncle, makes a speech and proposes a toast to the couple. Then snacks and drinks are served, with the bride's family serving their guests and the groom's family theirs. The costs of the reception are split with each side providing their own food and drinks for their guests. However, it is becoming more common for both families to get one single caterer and foot half of the bill each. Wine, whisky and beer flow freely, but the stocks frequently run out before the end of the party.

After the cake has been cut and everybody has been served a slice, the bride and groom open the ball with a Viennese waltz. Afterwards all kinds of music is played, with *séga* being the most popular. Everyone joins in the fun, children dance with their grandparents and every man tries to have a dance with the bride. Unfortunately, with the ingestion of so much liquor and the desire to have as much fun as possible, wedding parties frequently end in a brawl.

Even though the whole affair lasts from mid-afternoon to late evening, only finger foods are served. So you might have to get some form of sustenance waiting for you when you get home or leave the party midway to go to a restaurant for dinner and then come back to resume the fun, which is what many guests, in fact, do. And, of course, you can always leave early to go home for dinner. Or skip the early part altogether and turn up when the party is in full swing, after an early dinner at home. Just say that you were held up by work.

The Chinese Feast

As most Chinese are Catholics, the wedding celebrations are quite similar to those of the Creoles. Traditionally, the bride's parents throw a dinner party about a week before the wedding for her close relatives and friends, in a kind of farewell to her. On the day of the wedding, offerings are made to the ancestors and the groom eats two hard-boiled eggs, egg being the symbol of fertility. The bridal bed is made by two women who are considered fortunate or successful in marriage and who have a son and a daughter. Then a young boy performs a somersault on the bed. It is an honour for both the women and the boy, and if either you or your son receives such a request, you should accede with thanks. It is a unique opportunity to see tradition at work.

A Chinese wedding fuses together the best of Western and Chinese customs. The bride wears a long white gown and her father puts on the headdress and veil for her. When the groom's party goes to pick up the bride, his mother gives her new daughter-in-law a set of gold jewellery. Her mother then hands her the bouquet and they proceed to the church in separate cars. The church set-up and service are the same as for a Creole wedding, but not all Chinese guests attend it. Many, especially the older folks who are not Christian, make their way straight to the reception hall to wait for the couple. As the newly-weds walk into the hall, a long string of firecrackers explodes, ending with a loud bang. The couple, with bridesmaids in tow, walk round the hall to the strains of the wedding march and then food and more food is served. Speeches and toasts are not very common because the emphasis here is on eating well. You can safely come with an empty stomach because the amount of food catered is just incredible. Quite a lot of wastage occurs but Chinese hospitality dictates that you should provide more than enough food and drink to satisfy the guests. Otherwise, the hosts lose face. Whisky, the liquor of choice, flows freely, but you can also have beer and soft drinks.

Alternatively, many couples choose to throw a traditional dinner party in a restaurant after the church ceremony. Seating is quite flexible and you will usually be placed at a table with people you know. Each course is placed in the middle of the table and you help yourself with the serving spoon.

After the cake-cutting, the guests start to disperse and you can safely leave the reception. Most Chinese weddings also end with a dance and the *séga* is becoming more and more popular. Food and drinks are still available, but now you help yourself at the bar counter.

The Mauritian Chinese also practise the tea ceremony, one of the traditional rites of a Chinese wedding. Now this is where Chinese weddings can get a little bit tricky. Some couples consult the almanac for the appropriate time and the tea ceremony can very well take place between the church service and the reception, meaning that the couple and bridal party would make a detour to their house before moving on to the reception hall. Depending on the distances to be covered and the degree of formality involved, this can take anything between one and two hours. Meanwhile, the guests wait and wait in the reception hall, presumably getting more and more hungry and thirsty because food and drinks are not served until the newly-weds arrive. Fortunately, most people leave the tea ceremony until after the reception.

Wedding Gifts

Traditionally, the Chinese give money to the newly wedded couple as a way to help set them up for married life. The older generation puts the money together so as to have a larger sum to present to the couple. You can do the same, but try to get a *foong pao* (red envelope) to put the money in. Ask around to find out what is an appropriate amount. If the couple throws a wedding dinner instead of a cocktail reception, your gift should be equivalent to your share of the meal. Again, ask around.

Among the other communities, money is not usually given and more and more Chinese are also buying gifts now. The presents of choice are functional or semi-functional items that look 'presentable' when wrapped up. This means things that come in a box. Glassware and chrome or steel platters are favourite choices. Small electrical appliances (iron, toaster or kettle) are also very popular. Unless you know the couple really well, don't attempt to buy decorative pieces. As a guideline, the closer you are to the couple, the more expensive the gift should be. Your present should be wrapped up with a card carrying your name and best wishes attached to it.

The custom of wedding lists is not practised in Mauritius and most couples end up with several sets of the same item. If you do not want your present to go to waste, you can ask the couple what they would like. However, do not tell them what your budget is as Mauritians are rather embarrassed to talk about the monetary value of gifts. Make a few suggestions of things that are within your budget and they will get the message.

If you are attending the Indian *gamat* or Muslim *briani* session, you should bring your wedding present then. For Creole and Chinese weddings, give your present to the couple at the reception. If it is something bulky, then of course you can always drop it off at the house a few days earlier.

DIVORCE

The divorce rate is still low in Mauritius, mainly because the family-based Asian communities are still rather conservative and the other sections of the population are Catholics who consider divorce a sin.

However, more young and not so young people now consider divorce as a viable alternative to a life of misery with someone they cannot agree with. If children are involved, they may wait until the latter are in or near their teens in the hope that the divorce will affect them less.

The stigma surrounding a divorcee, especially the woman, is decreasing. Usually, it is the parents who feel more embarrassed by their children's divorce, in particular if a third party is involved. They think that, as parents, they have failed to inculcate the right moral values in their children. A woman who divorces her husband for another man is labelled promiscuous. However, the same does not always hold true for the man; perhaps his wife was not a good wife to him or the other woman possesses more qualities.

In Mauritius, an uncontested divorce is granted if the couple has lived apart for a minimum of five years. Most people do this rather than go to court to avoid the 'shame' of a hearing. Before a divorce is pronounced, the court puts a notice in the daily newspapers advertising the hearing and calling upon anyone who has any objection to come forward.

COHABITING

Even though marriage is an entrenched institution in Mauritian society, cohabitation exists, mainly among the lower income group. A couple live together without getting married because they do not have the money to throw a wedding party or because this is what their ancestors used to do.

Before the legislation making religious marriages legal, many couples lived in 'concubinage' in the eyes of the law. The spouses are known as concubines, but they call each other husband and wife because they do not consider their union to be any different from those who are legally married. If you are not legally married to your partner, there is no need to publicise it. Most of your acquaintances would assume that you are married and referring to each other as husband and wife would make things much simpler.

CHILDREN'S RITES OF PASSAGE

As Mauritian society places a high value on children, the life events of children are accorded much importance. Most parents try their utmost to celebrate birthdays and events of religious significance on a grand scale so that their children will have a 'good life'.

Baptism

Children are baptised when they are very young, usually before they turn one. Baptism sessions are conducted once a month, usually after the Sunday morning service. If you are asked to be a godparent, you may have to attend some preparatory sessions in the weeks preceding the ceremony. A white outfit for the child, with or without cap, is essential.

Creole parents and godparents tend to dress very smartly, in suits and hats. However, sober trousers and shirt will usually do for men and a modest dress or pant suit for women.

In the life of a Christian, baptism is one of the most important events and the family celebrates it on a grand scale. It is usually a lunch party with ham, roasts, curries and cake with white icing to symbolise the purity of the child. Appropriate gifts for a newly baptised child are clothes, religious images and small items of jewellery. As most Mauritian Christians are Catholics, the image of the Virgin Mary is very popular for both boys and girls. These are sold at the Montmartre Church in Rose-Hill.

When a child is baptised, the parents give out *dragées* to friends and relatives. These are small sweets with an anise centre contained in a *bonbonnière*. Some are very creative and make pretty souvenirs for the receiver. When you receive a box of *dragées*, congratulate the parents but you do not need to give any present in return.

First Communion

The second most important event in the life of a Catholic Christian is the First Communion. This takes place when the child is about 7 or 8 years old. Girls dress in white, like little brides or in a nun's outfit, while boys either wear a suit or a monk's robe. Most parents opt for the bride's outfit or suit because they can be altered for other occasions.

Early in the morning, the children are taken to the church. As this is organised by the Roman Catholic School Authority, hundreds of children are involved. The service is a normal mass with the priest stressing the importance of the communion in his address to the children and their parents. Again, the parents are smartly turned-out. After the mass, the parents and children go home for some refreshment and then it's off to distribute the *brioches*, round sweet loaves with a cross on top, much like hot-cross buns. The family stops at the house of every relative and friend, even those who live quite a distance away. For those parents without a car, this can be quite an expensive exercise as they need to hire a taxi for at least half a day. Some, of course, do take the bus.

In return for the *brioche*, the children are given gifts of money, preferably in an envelope or a *foong pao* for the Chinese. They also receive a religious image, a book, a crucifix or a rosary.

Creoles and some Chinese throw a small First Communion party for the child's godparents and close relatives and friends. Depending on the time they get home from the distribution of *brioches*, it can be either lunch or dinner. The food served is very much the same as for a baptism party.

Two years after the First Communion, the children are confirmed. This is a less celebrated event for the Catholics, as opposed to Christians of other denominations. The children put on a smart outfit and attend mass in church.

Name-Giving Ceremony

The equivalent of baptism for the Indian community is the name-giving ceremony. This takes place at the maternal grandparents' place because Indian mothers stay with their parents after giving birth. Mother and child do not return home until the baby is 27 days old. The naming of the child takes place on the ninth day. A priest is invited to the house and prayers are said wishing the child well. The parents choose a name with the qualities they would like their child to have, usually something formal and dignified. In daily life, however, the child is called by either a short form of the name or a totally different name which is more casual and affectionate. After the name-giving ceremony, the grandparents host a small lunch or dinner for close relatives. All other expenses are also borne by the mother's family. Generally outsiders are not invited to the name-giving ceremony but, if you are, bring along a present for the child, a baby's outfit or toiletries. The child's head is shaved after two months, but there is no form of celebration.

First Month 'Birthday'

When a Chinese baby is one month old, the parents and grandparents make offerings to the god of heaven and to Kuan Yin, the mother figure of Chinese mythology. Relatives and friends are invited to a dinner celebrating the occasion, either at home or in a restaurant. The scale of the dinner depends on the financial means of the parents and also on whether the child is a first-born. The first dish served is chicken cooked in rice wine and ginger. It is delicious but can be quite potent for those who are not used to alcohol. The rest of the meal is the usual banquet fare. The traditional food associated with the first month birthday is hard-boiled eggs stained red, but they are no longer offered to guests because of the cheapness of eggs. Many parents have a cake instead.

Grandparents and close relatives traditionally give a gold ornament to the baby. As for the other guests, a *foong pao* or any other baby gift is appropriate.

Birthdays

With growing affluence, children's birthdays are now celebrated on a grand scale. For adults and older children, a lunch or dinner party takes place. An 18th birthday is special and parents sometimes rent a beach bungalow for a barbecue party followed by dancing. This is when a young person is considered an adult and is given the right to vote. It is also usually at 18 that teenagers leave school and start work, so

the 18th birthday is an important rite of passage. In Creole, they are now called *majeur*, as opposed to being a minor. The birthday boy or girl receives rather more expensive gifts than usual, some branded apparel or jewellery.

Children's birthdays take place at lunch time or in mid-afternoon. Little friends and cousins are invited together with their parents, and sometimes the parents also invite their own friends. Children (and adults too) take part in party games and everyone ends up with a prize. Party favours are not common but home-made hats are sometimes given out. Cake, sandwiches, fried snacks, pies and fizzy drinks are served to the children. Fried noodles are a tradition among the Chinese. Adults have no qualms quaffing down whisky or rum. Some organisations and fast-food restaurants like Pizza Hut or McDonald's now offer theme parties for children's birthdays. Books, toys and clothes are popular gifts.

SETTLING DOWN

CHAPTER 5

'Nothing great was ever achieved without enthusiasm.'
—Ralph Waldo Emerson

HOWEVER OFTEN YOU HAVE MOVED HOUSE, arriving in a foreign country can still be a rather unsettling experience. The logistics involved can be overwhelming, more so in a country where people are not that physically mobile. Most Mauritians are born, live and die in the same town or village. For an immigrant people, the notion of continuity, of having roots in a certain area, is important.

ARRIVING IN MAURITIUS

If you are coming to Mauritius from a yellow fever area, you need a certificate of vaccination. It is also wise to be inoculated against tetanus; beyond that, you do not need any other inoculation, although your home doctor will recommend that you be vaccinated against cholera and typhoid, and that you protect yourself from malaria. These diseases have been almost eradicated in Mauritius, with only an odd case or two surfacing once in a while. Unless you have documents proving that you have received employment in the country, you must have a return ticket and show proof of your financial means.

Visa Regulations

All visitors to Mauritius need a valid passport. The passports of some countries, such as Taiwan, are not recognised by the Mauritian government. So check that your country's papers are all right; otherwise you will have to apply to the Mauritian Immigration Authority for an entry permit.

Citizens of the Commonwealth, the European Union and several other countries are not required to apply for a visa. If you do need one, you should make your application at the nearest diplomatic representative of Mauritius or through a British consulate. All visitors are usually issued a visa of one month upon arrival. If you wish to extend your stay, you can apply for a visa extension from the Immigration Office at the Police Headquarters in Port-Louis, commonly called Line Barracks, or *casernes* in Creole. There is no fee.

Permanent Residence

To apply for permanent residence, you need to write to the Prime Minister's Office. If you are investing in the country, then you should provide information on the nature of your investment. In general, permanent residence is granted to those people whose investment is substantial and who will help in the development of the country.

If you are already residing in the country and are a work permit holder, your application will still be thoroughly investigated to make sure that your employment is secure and that you have integrated into the local lifestyle.

If you fulfil neither of the above conditions, you can still apply for permanent residence, but have to prove that you have sufficient funds overseas to support you. The Mauritian government does not actively encourage foreign retirees to buy a house in Mauritius and live out their retirement here. The spouse of a citizen is usually granted permanent residence without too much trouble, although it is easier for spouses and children of Mauritian men than the other way round.

Citizenship

To become a citizen of Mauritius, you have to satisfy certain residence requirements. Application should be made to the Prime Minister's Office. Mauritius allows dual citizenship, so you can still keep your present passport.

WHAT TO BRING

You can actually find almost everything that you need in Mauritius, except perhaps for some prescription medicines and high-end branded goods. You should certainly not bother shipping bulky items such as furniture and electrical appliances.

Bring cool clothes, preferably in cotton, ranging from what is termed 'smart casual' to beachwear. The latter, you will certainly find all over the island and in a greater variety and at lower prices than back home. Do not load yourself with formal wear and dressy clothes, but you certainly should bring a few outfits because the local shops are not very well stocked in such items. A light jacket or sweater is necessary for evenings out during the cooler months. And bring all your favourite shoes; local shops offer very little variety and imported shoes tend to be very expensive.

You do not need to bring Mauritian rupees with you. There are money changers at the airport and if you need to tip a porter upon arrival, they will not mind foreign currency. If you are here to do business, it is wise to bring a substantial amount of cash (in traveller's cheques) because you will need to grease a few palms in order to open some doors.

ACCOMMODATION

The first thing to look for is accommodation, especially when you are here with your family. Living in hotels is not an option for they are prohibitively expensive, and very few have the sort of service accommodation that would see you through several months.

You can start by scanning through the newspapers. *L'express* has a comprehensive classified section and you might just find your dream home advertised there. Get a good French/English dictionary before you embark on this exercise because most of the advertisements are in French. You could also put in your own advertisement. The best person to help you, though, is a real estate agent. A few agencies specialise in finding accommodation for foreigners and they are quite good. They usually advertise their services in foreign publications.

The attitude of Mauritian landlords to foreign tenants is rather ambivalent. On the one hand, they believe (and quite rightly too) that foreigners can afford to pay higher rents; but on the other hand, if the foreign tenant leaves some major damages behind, there will be no avenue of redress whatsoever. So you should not take it personally if a prospective landlord seems reluctant to sign a lease with you.

If you have a job already lined up for you then, of course, the office will make all your accommodation arrangements. But it might still be a good idea to make a short 'recce' trip so that you can survey what is available. For example, a house in town might be closer to the office, but then you might prefer a slightly longer commute and savour the peacefulness of a beach front bungalow.

Finally, there are a number of consultancy firms that, in addition to offering business advice, will also assist in the search for appropriate housing. The Mauritius Export Development and Investment Authority (MEDIA) has a list of such firms.

Short-term Accommodation

If you are in Mauritius for just a business meeting or a short preliminary trip, then there are a variety of hotels to suit your purpose and budget. Beachside resorts—many operated by well-known international chains—offer well-appointed rooms, water sports, restaurants and nightly entertainment, all at a price. Of a lower standard (and price) are the smaller hotels that are not quite resorts, but still have a stretch of beach in front and provide clean rooms and friendly service. Whatever type you choose, though, you should be aware that residing on the coast requires your own transportation. Exclusive resorts are so exclusive that public buses do not stop there. Taxis are an option, but they might not always be available.

A few hotels offer self-catering chalets in addition to normal rooms. These are probably best for families who would like some form of independence but with the reassuring presence of hotel facilities, such as swimming pool, tennis courts and restaurants. Cooking facilities are really basic, but you can always have a few meals at the hotel restaurant. Also a grocery might not be within easy reach, so having your own means of transport would be a great help.

Compared to beachside hotels, business hotels are few and some are not quite up to the mark. They number less than ten and can be found only in Port-Louis, Quatre Bornes and Curepipe. Rates in town are lower than in resorts, but not that much lower considering they do not provide water sports and entertainment. However, you do get photocopying and secretarial assistance as well as meeting rooms. (Some resorts also offer the same business facilities.) The main advantage of a business hotel is that it is near government and private sector offices and that public transport does not pose a problem.

If you are combining business with pleasure, you can rent an apartment in Grand Baie, Péreybère or Flic-en-Flac on a short-term lease (by the week or day). These are usually rather basic, with one or two rooms, kitchenette and bathroom. Furnishing is durable plastic or Formica top while decoration is kept to a minimum. In general, apartments do not sit right on the beach, but you might still get a sea view from your balcony. Restaurants are plentiful in these resort villages and the beach is just a few minutes' walk away. However, there is no guarantee that you will get peace and quiet during your stay. Your neighbours might be a group of teenagers on holiday, having the time of their life partying into the wee hours of the night or several families packing into the apartment to save costs.

Living in Town

The most popular towns for expatriates are Floréal, Curepipe and Quatre Bornes. Port-Louis is definitely not an alternative, even though your house might be within walking distance from the office. It is always hot and humid in the capital, even in the winter months. And most houses are built too close together for comfort and you have to contend with pollution and traffic. Actually, you can live in any town and work elsewhere because public transport is quite good and commuting time is about an hour at most.

The upper plateau towns have the advantage of a balmy climate year round, even though it can get really wet and dank in Floréal and Curepipe during the rainy season. Most

Beautiful colonial houses with well-laid out gardens can still be seen in the plateau towns.

embassies and consulates are located in Floréal. Quatre Bornes has probably the best weather of all the towns. It combines a mixture of modern high-rise apartments and elegant houses with pretty gardens. (High-rise buildings are still the exception rather than the norm, though.) Good shopping, restaurants and other amenities are all within easy reach. Rents here are lower than in Floréal and Curepipe, but you will probably not be able to secure the type of high-end luxurious accommodation that is available in the other two towns. If you are looking for an expensive house, then you should live in Floréal, but if you want a nice house at an affordable price, then Quatre Bornes is for you.

If you and your family want to interact with as many layers of society as possible and experience the Mauritian lifestyle, then you should definitely elect to live in town. Neighbours are at closer range, you can go to the market every day and your children will get to meet more people when taking the bus to school.

A Beach Bungalow

Nothing is more symbolic of the good life than sitting on the verandah of your seafront bungalow, sipping a drink and watching the sun sink slowly into the ocean. And you can have it—if you have a big budget. Beautiful bungalows sitting directly on the beach are available, for rent and for sale. The best are those that were built by wealthy White families because they sit on extensive grounds with well-tended lawns and gardens. The house itself may not be very big—three to four bedrooms, one common bathroom, sitting/dining room and verandah. But they usually come with an annex and a sort of servants' quarters that can be easily converted into guests' quarters. Airy and tropical in design, they are whitewashed and furnished in rattan and other natural materials. Despite being located in popular areas like Grand Baie or Blue Bay, they retain an air of exclusivity thanks to the stone walls that surround them. The beach, although being state land, does not attract members of the public because it is not directly accessible from the road. If you can afford it, it is definitely a piece of paradise on earth.

There are other houses nearby, not quite as big and secluded, but at a much cheaper price. Those that are rented out by the day should be avoided because they tend to be in rather bad condition. They usually attract groups of students (more than ten) pooling their resources for a few rowdy days at the beach and who do not have much respect for the owners' furniture. Appliances and furnishings are quite basic because the owners know how their day-tenants treat them. The same applies to apartments. Look only at those where the whole block is leased on a long term.

In areas around Grand Baie and Péreybère, there are now condominium-style houses that might not be within walking distance of the beach. These are quite small (three bedrooms at most), but are a nice option if you cannot afford the bigger stand alone houses. They are quiet because many owners use them as weekend homes and the security staff patrol the grounds regularly. These condominiums may be advertised as 'bungalows' because, in Mauritius, any house, or even apartment, near the beach is called a bungalow.

If you do not have children, or you do not mind driving your children to school every day, a beach bungalow is really the most enjoyable option. Of course you need to own a car, but commuting times may not be longer than living in town. The best area is in the north. Despite being highly commercialised, it is the only region with good road links to Port-Louis and the plateau towns.

Rent

Rent usually includes the water bill, sometimes electricity also, but never telephone charges.

AROUND THE HOUSE

If you come from a society where everything moves like clockwork, then you might find Mauritius utterly inefficient. Red tape pervades all official business and getting things done requires a good dose of patience and diplomacy. It helps also to have the right connections. So it is of utmost importance that you know exactly which doors to knock on when you are trying to settle into your house. Queuing in the wrong line could make you waste one whole day, not to mention your effort and patience.

Furnishing Your House

Most houses that are rented out to foreigners on a regular basis come already furnished. In general, new houses are bare except perhaps for some basic furniture like beds, dining table and chairs. Houses that are rented to locals are not furnished for the simple reason that the tenants already have their own furniture.

It is actually a blessing in disguise to move into an empty house for it gives you the opportunity to get better acquainted with the superb local furniture industry. There are not many furniture shops around because Mauritians still order their furniture and have it made according to their own specifications. Mauritian artisans are highly skilled and artistic. A few companies specialise in reproduction period pieces and these will probably be your best buys. Beds, tables, armchairs and cupboards are hand crafted from the finest wood for a fraction of the price elsewhere. The furniture is made to last and it will adapt to most types of weather, so you can safely take it back with you when you leave. If you have a certain design in mind, the cabinet maker will make a faithful copy for you. Alternatively, if you wish to adapt an existing model, this will also be done according to your specifications. Of course, ordering your own furniture will take some time and Mauritian craftsmen are not known for punctuality. However, if you go to a reputable company, you should get your items more or less on time. If you do not want to wait, there are always a few ready-made pieces on sale in the showroom next to the factory or in the factory shops. You should probably start your furniture hunting by paying a visit to the shops first. The best ones are in Curepipe and Quatre Bornes.

You might have admired the beautiful colonial furniture displayed at Eureka or in the Mahebourg museum. Unfortunately Mauritius does not have much of an antique market, especially in furniture. Most antique shops are rather rundown and the only items you would find there are lights, glassware and trinkets, all not much more than 50 years old. Your best bet is actually to make a reproduction of the pieces you have taken a liking to.

Water, Electricity and Telephone

Water is supplied by the Central Water Authority (CWA) which has its head office in Curepipe. To apply for water, you should go to the nearest CWA office (there is one in almost every town). This is also where you pay your monthly bills. If water is not included in the rent, then your landlord will present the bill to you every month and you remit the correct amount at the same time as the rent. Most of the island now has access to running water but the supply tends to be erratic, especially during the dry months. Water stoppage is a regular feature in some areas. In any case, even if your area is not subjected to regular water rationing, it is wise to fill a container in the morning. When the CWA carries out repair works on the pipes that supply your house, they do so without warning, and sometimes supply may not resume until the next day. And there is always the danger of a burst pipe since the piping system is quite old and badly maintained. Water is safe to drink in most areas and at most times, except when there are filter problems after prolonged heavy rains. At such times, you only need to boil the water to make it drinkable.

Electricity might not be included in your rent because of varying consumption. If your house is not wired up, you

Most houses have running water but some poorer housewives have to do the dishes at a communal tap located outside.

should go to the nearest Central Electricity Board office (CEB) to apply for electricity. The head office is in Curepipe, but there are regional offices in the towns and villages. The bill will be in your landlord's name but you will be required to pay it yourself. The distribution voltage is 230v single phase and 400v three phase. Incoming high voltage is 6,600v or 22,000v or 66,000v with 50Hz frequency. You will find both two-pin as well as three-pin wall sockets, all depending on the fancy of the electrician who did the wiring for the house. In general, sockets for heavy-duty appliances, such as cookers or refrigerators, tend to be the international standard square three-pin type. Power outages are not frequent, but they can happen. All electrical cables are above ground and disruption of supply occurs during cyclones or heavy winds. It takes a while for the CEB technicians to repair any fallen cables, so it is wise to keep some candles in the house. Electricity meters are usually located near the front door, and every month the meter reader drops by, notes the reading and hands you the electricity bill for the previous month.

If water and electricity supply are taken for granted, it is a different matter when it comes to the telephone. Not every house in the country has a phone and sometimes, it might take a while for you to get a line. Calls within the same exchange are charged a flat fee while calls between exchanges are timed. IDD services are provided by the Overseas Telecommunication Service (OTS) and are available to every phone subscriber who applies for them. If you do not have a telephone line, overseas calls can be made from the OTS office in Port-Louis during office hours or from the OTS headquarters in Cassis just outside Port-Louis round the clock. OTS also offers telex, telegram and fax services.

Cellular Phones

Cellular phone services are provided by two companies: government-owned Cellplus and Emtel. Both offer the usual range of services. Since the island is so small, mobile coverage is quite good everywhere.

Pets

Most households keep a dog, not as a pet but to guard the house. Once it has outgrown its purpose, for example if it has an accident and cannot run after intruders, it is put down without a second thought. Thus Mauritians view foreigners' attachment to their pets with indulgent amusement, much like adults treat a child's fondness for the family dog. When you are faced with an emergency concerning your pet, you can appeal to local friends for help, but do not expect them to go all out and drop everything on the spot.

Guard dogs are usually let loose in the evening and they roam the streets, fouling pavements and grass verges. If your neighbour's dog has dirtied the pavement in front of your house, you should just clean it up and keep quiet, even if it is on a regular basis. Confronting your neighbour over the matter will not achieve much because they cannot control what their dog does since the animal is free to roam. Also, Mauritians believe that it is a natural thing and though it is a nuisance, they just put up with it. However, if you are walking your pet and the latter does its business in front of your neighbour's house (or anybody's house, for that matter), then they might get annoyed. However, Mauritian laws do not require you to clean up after your pet. You should also not let your dog stand at your gate and bark at passers-by—they may just get angry and hurl something at the animal.

Since pets are not such a big thing here, there are very few pet shops, with a limited range of products and services. Dog and cat food is sold in the supermarkets and some of the high-end grocery stores. But don't expect your corner boutique to stock it, unless you live in an area with a large concentration of expatriates. And there is no need to look for grooming services because there are none.

Rubbish

Since the municipal authorities have subcontracted refuse collection out to private cleaning companies, rubbish disposal is much less of a headache. You will see rubbish trucks visiting homes every day, but they will stop at your house only once a week. You should line your bin with the black plastic bags provided, but the cleaners will still empty it if you have not used bags. You are not required to bring your bin outside, but if there will be no one in the house during the day then, of course, you should leave it outside your gate. Most people keep their bins in the backyard and the cleaners will pick up the rubbish from there.

Waste disposal fees are included in your municipal taxes, but if you are asking the cleaners to remove some bulky items or you have an unusually large amount of rubbish on a certain day, then it would be nice to give them a small tip. However, do not make a habit of tipping them because they might just refuse to remove your garbage when you do not 'pay' them.

If you have just moved in, the cleaners may not be aware that your house is occupied and may pass by without stopping. Ask your neighbours when the collection day is and wait for the truck for the first week or two. You will need to call them and explain that you have just moved in so that they will collect your refuse every week.

Household Help

It is still quite easy (and affordable) to get someone to come in every day and do your housework. Married women with school-going children are more willing to work as maids since they cannot work the long hours required by the factories. They come to the house after they have dropped the children off at school, clean the house and do the laundry before going to pick up the children. Live-in maids who also act as baby-sitters are not easy to hire.

Wages vary depending on the size of the house and the number of people in the family. Be sure you spell out exactly what you want to be done every day and the level of cleanliness you expect. If you want your maid to bathe the dog once in a while or trim the plants in the garden, point it out right from the beginning. Otherwise, she would ask for more money. Of course your maid will agree to do some extra chores from time to time, but you do have to remunerate her. Your agreement with her is verbal only and, as most maids do not understand much English, you are strongly advised to ask a Mauritian friend to act as translator when negotiating the terms and conditions.

The key is to be flexible; your aim is to treat your maid fairly without her taking advantage of your generosity. You should also offer some form of refreshment every day, usually a cup of tea and a loaf of bread with some cheese or jam. Most maids have their own way of doing the housework, so it is best not to meddle with their work, even if you feel that your way is more efficient. It is perfectly all right to call your domestic helper a maid. Mauritians use the term 'servant' or *nénenne* in Creole.

Your maid's domain is strictly within the house. If you want someone to tend to your garden, it is quite easy to employ a part-time gardener who comes in once or twice weekly to remove weeds and prune the plants. Gardeners also bring new plants according to how you would like your garden to look. You pay them every time they come and separately for the plants. However, gardeners do not mow the lawn unless you own a lawn mower. There are a number of young men who bring their lawn mowers along on a bicycle about once a month and they will cut the grass for you. But you have to clean up the cut grass yourself.

SAFEGUARDING YOUR VALUABLES

This section is not meant to alarm you, but as the saying goes, better safe than sorry. Mauritius is a gentle society with a low crime rate, but criminals exist everywhere and housebreaking is one of the more serious crimes in the country. There are stories of home owners coming back to an empty house after a holiday or even a day at the beach! Cash and valuables are best kept at the bank. (Incidentally, not many banks offer safes for hire.)

Burglars are mostly attracted to electrical equipment such as hi-fi systems, computers and microwave ovens. The only solution here is to secure your house. The most popular (and cheapest) method is to keep a guard dog that would go after intruders or bark and create such a racket that neighbours would be alerted. Alarm systems and home safes are not popular because they tend to be quite costly and are not

readily available. Finally, there is nothing safer than having watchful neighbours. Make friends with your neighbours and let them know when you will be gone. Ask them to keep a watch for suspicious happenings.

If you are unfortunate enough to have your house broken into, make a police report, but do not expect much success. The police are chronically overworked and are unlikely to be able to trace a burglar unless enough fingerprints and incriminating evidence are left on the scene. And even when the burglar is caught, there is very little chance of retrieving all your belongings. So, to avoid being left with nothing at all, it is best to take out home insurance. If you live in rented accommodation, check that the landlord has insured the house and its contents so that stolen items can be replaced quickly.

TRANSPORT

The road network is extensive and in generally good condition, although many are quite narrow. Potholes appear after heavy rains but are patched up quite fast. Sometimes you may spot 'trenches' along a stretch of road. This is due mainly to a lack of co-ordination between different public departments. It is a real waste of resources to see telephone workers digging up the road to lay cables barely a month after the roads have been tarred, but Mauritians take it all in their stride.

The good news is that public transport is cheap and adequate. There is always some form of public transport wherever you live and you do not have to walk far to reach a bus stop.

Driving in Mauritius

Driving is on the left, but it only takes a short while to get used to. You might hit the wipers every time you want to signal a turn, but just remember to do everything the other way round. What is not so easy to get used to is the attitude of Mauritian drivers. Inching forward at a red light, overtaking on a slope, honking at pedestrians and other drivers are not really the norm, but they do happen often enough to require the utmost vigilance when on the road. Most roads are single carriage ways and the person behind you might get impatient if they feel you are driving too slowly. The solution in this case is to slow down to almost a crawl and allow them to overtake you. Do not road hog: a volley of insults might be hurled at you when the car behind does manage to overtake. However, violence is not common on the roads. Rarely do any traffic incidents degenerate into physical fighting. There is certainly a long way to go before road courtesy becomes second nature. Do not expect other drivers to give way to you, unless it is your right of way. But that should not stop you from being courteous. Other road users will be grateful for it.

You do not need an international driver's licence to drive in Mauritius. Just bring your home licence to the traffic branch of the police to have it endorsed. The headquarters are in the line barracks in Port-Louis. The minimum legal age for driving is 18. If you have children below 18 who hold a driver's licence, then it is best to check with the police if they are allowed to drive.

If you want to import your car into Mauritius, duty is payable on its whole value. It is probably best to buy one when you get here. Cars are by no means cheap, but there is always the option of getting a second-hand one or a 'retrofitted' one (two to three year old cars imported from countries like Japan or France). If you are employed as a consultant by the Mauritian government, you may be exempted from paying duty on a brand new car. The price is much more attractive in this case. About 20 makes of motor vehicles are available, with Japanese brands predominating.

A few car hire companies operate in Mauritius, including Hertz, Avis and Europcar. It is extremely expensive to rent a car and there are no packages for long-term rental. Rental cars are referred to as 'contract' cars. A high tax is imposed on petrol, but it is still affordable. Petrol stations are plentiful in towns, but not so in rural areas, so it makes sense to keep a full tank when touring the country and for distance driving at night. You do not serve yourself at the pump, but wait for the attendant to fill your tank. Stations take turns to remain open on Sunday afternoons, so it is wise to top up on Saturday or Sunday morning.

Public Transport

Buses operate between all the towns and between the towns and major villages. Different companies ply different routes, but if you live in a midway town like Rose-Hill, you will have a wider choice of services. Curepipe, Quatre Bornes, Port-Louis and Rose-Hill act as hubs for buses from the south, west, north and east respectively. So you might find yourself travelling a much longer distance to go to a village that is in a different zone. In general, bus travel is comfortable, except at peak hours when the vehicles tend to carry more passengers than they are allowed. Aside from the driver, a conductor collects fares and hands out tickets. The conductor waits for you to be seated before coming over and collecting your money. They also give change. Sometimes an inspector boards the bus to check tickets, so do not throw away your ticket until you have alighted. Services are quite regular although arrival times are not posted at the bus stops. Express buses between Port-Louis and the plateau towns operate at peak hours. These are not non-stop, but take a shorter route and run along the motorways. Above all, bus travel is cheap and the only means of transport for the majority of the population. Some (gentle)men still give up their seats to women passengers when the bus is full, but this custom is fast disappearing. Other passengers would squeeze a bit to allow young children to sit down. Travellers are a well-disciplined lot and form queues whenever there are more than a couple of persons at a bus stop. Queue-jumpers are politely told off. Buses run from 6:00 am to 9:00 pm, later on special occasions like the festival of Père Laval in September.

'Tip-tops'

Linking the town centres to the suburbs is a system of 'tip-tops', full-size or minibuses that depart from a separate terminus a few minutes away from the main one. This works along the same lines as commuter buses, with definite routes and well-marked bus stops. 'Tip-tops' are operated by the main bus companies which usually retire their vehicles to these routes. So the fleet may not be as new and the ride less comfortable, especially since the roads leading to the suburbs are not always in very good condition. As 'tip-top' services cater mainly to school children and working people, the last bus leaves at around 7:00 pm but starting times are the same.

Taxis are a real blight on the standard of public transport in Mauritius. In the first place, there are very few taxis and they do not cruise the streets. So if you want to take a taxi, you have to walk to the taxi stand near the bus station. They are all operated by individuals and some of the vehicles tend to be old and not quite roadworthy. Taxis are not metered and drivers do not adhere to the charges recommended by the National Transport Authority. It is always best to negotiate the fare before entering. In any case, taxis are expensive and drivers tend to quote even higher fares when they realise that you are not a local. Always ask friends or hotel staff for a guideline so that you can beat the price down.

Aside from the word 'Taxi' written on the doors, taxis are recognisable by their number plates: the numbers are black on white while private cars have white numbers on black.

Mauritians take a taxi only on special occasions, like when going to a wedding in their best finery, or when buses are not running.

The equivalent of the 'tip-top' in the car category is the 'taxi-train'. This is a licensed taxi, but it is usually quite old, about 20–30 years, since older cars are bigger and more boxy. Passengers are picked up near the 'tip-top' terminus and dropped off at specific points along the same route, not at their doorstep. Fares are fixed and the driver tries to cram as many passengers as possible, sometimes six or even eight. 'Taxi-trains' are actually breaking the law as they carry more passengers than allowed, but the authorities close an eye since they are providing a service to the population. Enter at your own risk: passengers are not covered by insurance.

PUBLIC PHONES

The situation concerning public telephones has improved tremendously over the last few years. Today, the cute little orange coloured booths can be seen in all town centres, at the beach and in village halls.

Most of the new phones are card-operated and it is wise to always have one on hand. You can buy them at some bookshops, the post office, or the Telecom office. As for the coin-operated machines, you need a Rs 5 coin to make a call. If you are really in a fix and cannot find a public phone, then you can try asking a shop owner to let you use theirs. This used to be the public telephone system, with shops charging Rs 3 for a three-minute call. However, most of them are very reluctant to do so now since overseas calls can also be made from the same telephone.

The Currency

The currency of Mauritius is the Mauritian rupee (Rs). One rupee is divided into 100 cents.

Emergency numbers are free, even from a public booth. For fire, police and ambulance services, dial '999'. Calls are picked up promptly and acted upon immediately. There is also a weather information service on '96'.

SHOPPING

Tourists complain that Mauritius has nothing to offer in terms of shopping and they are right. If you are looking for branded goods at bargain prices, you will be sorely disappointed. What you will find, if you live here for a while, is good quality, locally produced merchandise at affordable prices.

Markets

In addition to meats and fresh produce, you can find a variety of dried foodstuffs as well as spices in the markets. Most markets have a corner selling basketware and clothing. Rose-Hill's Arabtown across the road from the market has a souk-like atmosphere and you can find any cheap-looking household item as well as beads and bangles. Beware the prices though: the stalls have a reputation for bargain prices, but they are no cheaper than regular shops. Some, in fact, charge more, knowing that customers believe they are getting good bargains. It is the same with roadside peddlers selling their T-shirts or plastic toys right in front of the shops. If you make the effort to walk into the shop, you will find a greater variety at the same prices.

Shops

Sundry shops, called *magasins*, are only found in town centres or along the main road in villages. Most of them stock the same goods and charge the same prices. But it is still worthwhile to shop around when buying expensive items. There are a few luxury stores that carry more upmarket and expensive goods, and these are usually found in Curepipe.

The goods are displayed in glass cases and the shop assistants (mostly female) will help you find what you are looking for. When you request an item, the assistant will take it out and put it on the counter for you to check. Retail law requires that every item put up for sale be tagged with a price, but stickers are not that visible because some shop owners prefer to put them at the bottom of the objects. If you agree on the price, the assistant will put it in a plastic bag and you proceed to the cashier to pay. No receipt is given, unless you ask for it specifically. If you find out that you have bought a

Even though the owner calls it a 'store', this shop sells only snacks and confectionery.

defective article, you should take it back to the shop and ask for an exchange, even if you do not have a receipt. But do not delay. The shop assistant or cashier will remember you, but not after a long period of time. Gift-wrapping is available, but only during the festive period at the end of the year. At other times, you have to pay for the paper and ribbon.

Fashion shops sell mainly women's apparel, but there are several chains of shirt shops for men. The clothes are displayed on racks, with one or two mannequins in the window. The standard ranges from low-end shops selling clothes with poor finishing to designer boutiques complete with shoes and handbags. Imported dresses are very expensive with styles that cater mainly to middle-aged women. Shoe shops also put more emphasis on women's fashion. Most shoes are locally made and imported ones are expensive.

Best Buys

Aside from quality reproduction furniture which might be rather cumbersome to cart back, there are a number of more portable items that you should not miss. One of the best buys is duty-free cut diamonds. Mauritian master cutters turn out exquisite pieces that can be viewed at the cutting works in Floréal. A smaller selection is available at the Poncini shop in Port-Louis and in the duty-free shop in the airport departure lounge. You have to bring your passport along to prove that you are a foreigner. The catch is that the stones can only be collected at the airport, on your way out of the country.

Slightly cheaper (but not much) are model ships. Mauritius has developed a first-class industry in the production of scale models of old sailing ships. Assembling the ships takes much precision and everything is done by hand, from the cutting of the sail cloth to the turning of the tiny wooden barrels on deck. There are several workshops in the area around Curepipe and a visit is well worth it. The ships themselves can be bought from hotel shops and luxury stores in Curepipe and Port-Louis. After having displayed them in your house during your stay in the country, you can take the ships back to the workshop to be wrapped for taking home with you. You have to pay a small fee, of course.

The cheapest souvenir is the ubiquitous T-shirt. Quality is generally quite good, except for the really cheap ones with corny messages which might bleed or tear in the washing machine. What makes local T-shirts stand out are the colourful and creative designs. You can get some really beautiful T-shirts (and other clothes, as well as table cloths, aprons, etc.) for a very reasonable price at factory outlets. Tailored clothes are also a bargain. Many seamstresses work from home and they can copy any design you bring them. You have to buy your own material, but then dress material is cheap since it is tax exempted. Tailors can sew a suit in 24 hours, but you have to give them some more time to produce good workmanship.

Local crafts are cute but poor in finishing. Basketware makes pretty decorative pieces and showcases genuine local tradition and talent. But check all shell and mother-of-pearl objects: many are imported from the Philippines.

Trading Hours

Shops are required by law to close half a day on Sunday and one other day of the week. This applies to both *boutiques* (groceries; *see page 157*) and *magasins*. Shops in the plateau towns close on Thursday afternoon whereas village shops might choose another day, Tuesday or Wednesday. In Port-Louis, shops close on Saturday afternoon and all day on Sunday.

Boutiques generally open quite early, around 7:00 am or 8:00 am because many sell bread that their customers buy before going to work. Closing time is 7:00 pm. Some owners take some time off in the middle of the day when business is less busy. Supermarket opening hours are generally from 9:00–7:00 pm, with extended hours on one day of the week for late-night shopping.

Magasins work shorter hours: 9:00 am to 5:00 pm in Port-Louis and 9:00 am (sometimes 10:00 am) to 6:00 pm elsewhere. Many remain closed on Sunday, except in the month of December when business is better. Markets, on the other hand, are open from 6:00 am to 6:00 pm daily, except on Sunday when they close at around 1:00 pm.

The Customer Is Never Right

In general, shop assistants are not unfriendly. However, they do feel that you are imposing upon them if you ask to look at several items before making your mind up. Or (heaven forbid!) if you do not buy anything after having checked the goods and their prices. Shop assistants are not downright rude and they do not mean to offend, but their job is just to sell goods to you, and not to make you feel good. They will not go the extra mile to entice you to buy from them because, whether they make a sale or not, they still get paid the same salary at the end of the month. Few shop assistants are service-oriented, and when you meet one who is, it really restores your faith in human nature. You will certainly get better service when you deal with the shop owner, but even here some have a 'take it or leave it' attitude. The fault probably lies in the fact that the Mauritian consumer has very little clout. Traders have traditionally been the richer segment of the population and they can get away with bad service. Grocery owners tend to be much more friendly, because they get to know you better and also because they depend on regular customers for their livelihood.

If you receive only perfunctory answers to your queries in a shop, this does not mean that Mauritians do not like foreigners. Shop assistants behave the same way with everybody. Just treat a shopping trip as a business transaction, where you go and exchange your money for some goods.

PUBLIC TOILETS

One good thing about public conveniences in Mauritius is that you do not have to pay for their use. The downside is that there are very few of them and they are not always properly maintained. Most public toilets are located near bus stations or the post office, and at some of the more popular beaches. Newly-built shopping centres boast somewhat cleaner facilities, but they still smell a bit. If the urge to go to the loo grips you while shopping, it is perfectly all right to ask the shop owner to let you use their private toilets. Walking into a restaurant just to visit the toilet is definitely not recommended. The proper course of action is to explain your predicament to the staff and ask them in your politest manner to allow you to use their facilities. It would also be a nice gesture to purchase something on your way out, a can of drink or some snacks. Do not use the terms 'washroom,' 'restroom' or 'bathroom' or even 'loo' when asking for the use of the toilet. Most Mauritians would take these words literally and would answer that there is none on the premises. The local terms are 'toilet' or 'WC' (for 'water closet,' but only the acronym is a recognised term). The safest solution, though, is not to drink too much if you know you will be out for a length of time.

EDUCATION

Education is free for everyone, including children of expatriates, up to secondary level. The literacy rate is one of the highest in Africa, but the level of education is very inconsistent from one school to another. Primary school takes up six years, culminating in an island-wide examination (referred to by the acronym CPE, meaning Certificate of Primary Education) that determines which secondary school the child is entitled to go to. The syllabus and examinations are set locally. Secondary education is based on the British GCSE model. The first five years lead to the School Certificate and it takes another two years to reach the Higher School Certificate. Both examinations are set by the Cambridge Examination Syndicate in England. The form five and form six syllabi are recommended by the examination authority, but those of the lower levels are worked out by the local Ministry of Education.

Classes are conducted in English for all levels, in theory. In practice, many teachers have to resort to French or Creole to explain scientific principles or to paraphrase Shakespeare! The Mauritian system of education favours bookishness over critical enquiry. Because students take exams in what is basically a language foreign to them, they tend to learn by rote. The subjects offered at school leave very little scope for creativity and critical thinking. For a long time the Lycée Polytechnique in Centre de Flacq was the only proper school for technical education, but the government has now set up a more structured programme for job training.

Government Schools

Most primary schools are run by the government. Classes contain on average 30–40 pupils and the better students are grouped together in the same class under a 'good' teacher. All lessons are conducted by the same teacher, except for religious classes and oriental languages. A few schools are very popular, mainly because of the presence of one or two very good sixth standard teachers. ('Good' teachers refer to those whose students rank highly in the CPE exams, no matter what method they use.) Also very popular are the RCA (Roman Catholic Aided) schools because they offer some form of religious instruction and they are all located in towns. Having been around longer than the secular government schools, they enjoy a reputation for giving a good education as well as teaching good manners and morals. RCA schools admit pupils of all religious denominations.

Every town and village has at least one primary school, sometimes more. You should enrol your children into the school of your area. If there are several schools in the vicinity, then you do not have to go to the one nearest your house, you can choose any one. Schools admit children from other areas only when they have vacancies. RCA school heads have slightly more leeway over whom they can admit, but they cannot block the transfer of their teachers to government schools. Likewise, children can transfer from one to the other if there are vacancies.

There are government secondary schools almost everywhere, certainly a bus ride away from your house, wherever you may live. Secondary schools are called 'colleges' in Mauritius. Application is made through the Ministry of Education. You can state your preference for a certain school and they will enrol your child if there is a vacancy. Otherwise, your child will have to go to the neighbourhood junior secondary school. All secondary schools offer classes up to form five. After secondary school, Mauritian students continue their higher education at a sixth-form college. These are located mainly in the towns. The less academically-inclined go on to a vocational school.

Private Schools

Secondary education used to be dominated by colleges set up by religious authorities, mainly the Catholic Church. These fee-paying schools are now free and have to compete with government colleges for the best students. However, they are still managed by the religious authorities and are referred to as 'private' or 'confessional' schools. Principals are appointed by the religious authorities and each principal recruits their own teachers. If you want your child to attend a particular confessional school, you apply directly at the school, and the principal and teachers will assess whether your child is suitable for admission. Bring the child's latest report cards and any teachers' testimonials because these will be useful. The school might also require your child to sit for a test or go through an interview, so try to find out about the contents of school subjects from friends' children. If you live in town, or not too far from a town, it might be more expedient to look for a private college because principals can decide on their own whether to take in your child or not.

A few Catholic colleges also run a fee-paying primary section, some from standard one onwards or only standards five and six. Apply directly at the school, but your child will have to go through an admission test because the number of applications always far exceeds the number of seats available.

Despite the cost, private primary schools are popular because the children get automatic admission to the college to which they are affiliated.

A few local private secondary schools cater mainly to slow learners or those who have dropped out of mainstream colleges. Le Bocage High School near Moka, Northfields at Mapou and Saint Nicholas Grammar School at Phoenix, on the other hand, are based on the international model. (Saint Nicholas also has a primary division at Sodnac near Quatre-Bornes while Northfields is the high school equivalent of the International Prep School.) The medium of instruction is in English and students are exhorted to speak English to each other outside of the class, even though their first language may not be English. The schools are popular with foreigners because their courses lead to the International Baccalaureate and they offer foreign languages such as Spanish, which is not available in other schools. International schools are considered expensive by Mauritian standards, especially since all the other secondary schools are free. So, if your children attend any one of these schools, they might have little opportunity to mix with Mauritian youngsters of their own age.

Private Tuition

A parallel system of education is the phenomenon of private tuition. In primary schools especially, almost all students take tuition from their own school teacher, sometimes in their own classroom, after school hours. The good students take tuition to perform even better and the bad students do so in order to catch up. In some cases, children are coerced into attending (and paying for) the tuition classes by their teachers. The root of the problem lies in the fact that primary school teachers are badly paid and giving tuition enables them to make some money on the side. This has now become institutionalised and even mediocre teachers force their students to pay them for tuition. Methods of harassment of non-tuition students are: putting the child in the back row, nit-picking the work of the pupil or ignoring them completely. For an impressionable young child, such treatment can be quite traumatic and many actually beg their parents to pay for tuition. If this does happen to your child, report the teacher to the ministry and ask the principal to transfer the child to another class. However, you should be aware that not much will be done against the teacher.

Foreign Schools

The only foreign schools in the country are the two French lycées, one in Curepipe and the other in Goodlands in the north. They both take students from primary level through to the French baccalaureate. However, your child needs to be very fluent in French, especially if they are joining the school at a higher level.

PERSONAL FINANCES

Managing your personal finances in Mauritius should be quite straightforward. The banking sector is experienced and the banking network extends to almost every corner of the island. Apart from income tax, you need to pay property and municipal taxes if you are a house owner. The rest of your money, you are free to spend as you please.

Income Tax

Filling your income tax form is really simple. But if you have difficulty understanding some of the terms or are not quite sure under which section to declare what, there are a number of private individuals and bookkeeping firms that specialise in doing tax returns. One advantage of going to such professionals is that they would advise you on how to pay the minimum amount of taxes if you have different sources of income. But if your only source of income is your salary, then just ask a local friend or your company's accountant for some guidance.

Personal income tax ranges from 10 per cent on the first Rs 25,000 to 30 per cent on incomes of more than Rs 450,000. If you are a resident, you have to declare all your income from worldwide sources, but will only be taxed on the money remitted to Mauritius. Non-residents are only taxed on income earned in Mauritius. There are no withholding taxes on interests and dividends, and there is also no capital gains tax.

Income is taxed on a pay-as-you-earn basis, which means that you pay an estimated amount out of your salary every month and not one huge sum once a year. If you have made more or less money at the end of the financial year, your taxes are adjusted accordingly.

Banks

Banks work very short hours in Mauritius, from 10:00 am to 2:00 pm on weekdays and 9:30 am to 11:30 am on Saturday. But, of course, banking staff work the usual office hours, even longer at certain times of the month. The Bank of Mauritius oversees the business of all 12 commercial banks operating in the country, eight of which are international enterprises such as the Hong Kong and Shanghai Bank or Citibank. Of the local banks, the oldest and most experienced is the Mauritius Commercial Bank. The State Bank was incorporated only after Independence and has established itself as one of the leaders in the banking industry. It has the highest number of branches throughout the country and offers the same state-of-the-art services as the more well established Commercial Bank and international banks.

Outside of banking hours, you can withdraw cash and deposit cash and cheques at one of the many ATMs that dot the landscape. Most banks offer this facility and you can find ATMs in all town centres and at shopping centres. Most banks also offer Giro payment of bills and taxes. Internet banking is also available, but most Mauritians still prefer to physically go to the bank and have their transactions done in front of them.

Banks offer the usual savings and checking accounts. It must be pointed out that personal cheques are not widely accepted. Restaurants and shops will take them only if they know you well, but you can use them to pay your utilities bills and when buying expensive items. Banks also issue credit cards (Visa and MasterCard) but they will not be readily accepted for buying groceries and at the small restaurants.

You can also change foreign currencies at the main branches of most banks.

Tea Money

In the past, when a motorist was stopped by a traffic policeman, the driver would slip a Rs 50 note into the driver's licence when handing it over for checking. This was not considered corruption—although it is—it was merely a little 'tea money' to turn a blind eye to a minor traffic infraction. Elsewhere in the world, the driver would probably get off with a verbal warning, but the Mauritian driver just wanted to make sure that they were not going to get a summons.

Such practice is definitely disappearing, but a little cash is still needed to oil some deals. We are not talking of big amounts here, just a little something in an envelope for a middle person to devote more attention to your case or to put your file at the top of the pile.

MEDICAL CARE

The standard of medical care in Mauritius is generally quite good compared with other developing countries, but it certainly still needs to be improved. Most diseases have been eradicated through preventive measures and health education, and the occasional outbreaks of conjunctivitis or gastroenteritis are the result of specific events, like cyclones.

Mauritian doctors and dentists are well trained and offer sound medical advice. Most of them are in private practice and they operate out of medical or dental 'cabinets'. You will certainly find a general practitioner in even a small village, but not always a dentist. You do not have to register your family with any doctor in particular, just go to the nearest GP and if you are satisfied, you can consider them your family doctor. Mauritians tend to believe that specialists are better doctors, so your Mauritian friends might recommend a heart specialist when you ask about a doctor. Just explain that you only need someone who can treat common ailments like colds and coughs and who can be reached at any time.

Doctors' fees depend on their qualifications and popularity. But in general they are very reasonable. Doctors do not fill prescriptions. For this you have to go to a pharmacy. Many doctors' cabinets are adjacent to a pharmacy since they benefit each other mutually. Certain controlled drugs cannot be bought when the pharmacist is not on duty, so you might have to come back or look for another one. Many pharmacies prepare their own cough syrups and these are quite effective, having been tested on patients over the years. So in cases of mild coughing or runny noses, the pharmacist may be able to help you better than the doctor. The pharmacies in the same town take turns to open on Sunday afternoons. The Sunday newspapers advertise the ones that are on duty, or 'guard' as they call it.

If you are on long-term medication, ask your home doctor for a few months' supply to give you time to find an equivalent prescription locally. Most medicines in Mauritius are imported from Europe, mainly France and Switzerland.

Hospitals

There are four main government hospitals in the country: the Jeetoo Hospital in Port-Louis, still called Civil Hospital by most people; the Princess Margaret Orthopaedic Hospital, also called Candos Hospital, between Quatre-Bornes and Vacoas; the Sir Seewoosagur Ramgoolam National Hospital in Pamplemousses, also known as the Northern Hospital; and the Jawaharlal Nehru Hospital in Rose-Belle, the newest of the lot. There is also an excellent ENT (Ear, Nose and Throat) department in Moka. The hospitals benefit from sophisticated equipment and qualified personnel, but suffer from chronic overcrowding and the staff are worked off their feet. Treatment is free and where fees are to be paid, they tend to be minimal. This is probably where the problem lies: since hospital treatment is free, many people go there for minor ailments that can be cured through self-medication. In addition to the main hospitals, there are also treatment clinics and health centres in towns and villages. Called dispensaries, they offer non-surgical treatment for wounds and common ailments as well as vaccination services for children. Here, too, treatment and medication are free of charge, but you must be prepared to wait at least half a day before being attended to as the dispensaries are overcrowded and the staff are rather slow.

Clinics

In Mauritius, clinics refer to private hospitals. There are several in Rose-Hill, Curepipe and Port-Louis. Patients go there for surgery or medical treatment, or to visit a doctor. For post-surgery treatment and dressing of wounds, you do not have to go back to the clinic. You can make a private arrangement for a nurse from the clinic to visit you at home. Of course you have to pay them personally, but this will probably still be cheaper than going back to the clinic.

Clinics are much smaller than hospitals and the equipment not as varied and up-to-date, but service is much more personal. This comes at a price, though, because a stay in a clinic runs into the thousands of rupees. However, private medical treatment in Mauritius is still much cheaper than in most other countries. If you do need to be hospitalised, you can go to the clinic of your choice and your personal doctor will visit you there. This is not possible in a hospital: you will be seen by the hospital doctor (who might still be

your personal doctor since specialist doctors working for the government are allowed to carry on their private practice).

Safety Hazards

The highest risk of injury in the home is that of electrocution. Electricians are not licensed and sometimes wiring is done in a haphazard way. Two-pin power points at floor level pose a real danger for young children who like to poke their little fingers in whatever hole they see and socket covers are not readily available. In general, devices for child-proofing the home are not available, so it would be a good idea to pack them along if you have young children. Another electrical hazard is overhead cables that run close to the trees in your garden. Make sure that the branches touching the wires are lopped off.

It is a good idea to have everyone in the family vaccinated against tetanus and rabies before coming to Mauritius. Sometimes the pavement is littered with rusty stuff that could scratch you as you walk by. There are also more flies and insects than in other more sanitised societies, so always keep food covered.

CYCLONES

One of the most exciting (and trying) times of your stay in Mauritius will be during a cyclone. The cyclone season stretches from late November to early April, and there are several cyclones every season. The island is hit directly once every few years and the damage is extensive. When they pass by off the coast, they bring much needed water in the summer months. A cyclone arises from a combination of low pressure and high temperature. Most Mauritians know that when it is stiflingly hot and the air is very still, a cyclone is certainly hovering in the area.

Warnings

There are four cyclone warnings:

- Class I
  Little risk of strong winds. Everything goes on as usual, but schools are on standby to release the students if a Class II is announced. Radio and television announcements are

made during the regular news bulletins. A little red flag is hoisted on all government flag posts, like the police station or other government building. The weather does not seem unusual, but it might be slightly darker with light intermittent drizzles.

- Class II
  Schools are closed but offices and shops go on working as usual. Weather updates are given more frequently and people are advised to take precautions and stock up on essential supplies. There are now two red flags. It is still quite hot, but there is definitely more wind and it starts to get dark.

- Class III
  The cyclone looks set to hit the island or at least to travel within a few kilometres of the coast. Everyone is supposed to be at home and houses are secured. Cyclone bulletins are announced every half-hour and winds are strong,

Emergency Supplies

It is always useful to keep some emergency supplies at the start of the cyclone season so that you do not have to rush about gathering food and other essential items like batteries and candles when a cyclone warning is issued. Here is a short list:

- Battery-operated transistor radio and batteries (check that they are in working order as soon as a Class I is issued)
- Canned food and dried vegetables; instant noodles; bread
- Electric torch and batteries (again check them at Class I stage); propane lamp (it is brighter and can be hung overhead when having dinner); candles and matches
- Mop and lots of cloth (water can seep in through the window frames)
- Gas stove

accompanied by rain. This time there are three flags. When a cyclone reaches Class III, there will definitely be some damage to livestock and crops.

- Class IV
  The cyclone is passing over Mauritius. Very strong gales of 120 kmph and rain lashes across the whole country. By now there is probably no electricity and running water, but the radio station will continue to broadcast weather updates. Four red flags are hoisted, but there will be no one to see them. After a few hours of very fierce weather, there is a lull and everything is still: this is the 'eye' of the cyclone. Do not for a second think that it is all over. The calm lasts about an hour or so and then the 'tail' of the cyclone hits. The wind and rain direction is reversed, but the intensity is the same. The whole episode might last half a day, but the havoc and damage caused will take several weeks to clear.

- Playing cards, dominoes, Monopoly and other board games
- Lots of water

Other things to do before the cyclone hits:
- Pull down the television antenna and lay it flat on the roof the moment Class II is announced
- Make sure that all the windows and doors close securely
- Chop off the tree branches that could damage your house if they break during the cyclone
- Bring your pets into the house
- Set your freezer at the maximum temperature so that all meats are frozen hard and will take longer to spoil if there is no electricity
- Cook all perishable foods

I WAS JUST SAYING, WE'RE HAVING A CLASS FOUR CYCLONE AND SHE HUNG UP!

A blue flag at the police station denotes that the cyclone is over and people can go about their business. Offices resume work the next day or as soon as electrical supply has been re-established. Schools close for a few days or even a week or two, since they are used as refugee centres.

Cleaning Up

The damage caused by a cyclone is indescribable. Crops are flattened, electricity cables are felled to the ground, ditches overflow with water and rubbish, branches and leaves litter gardens and roads. More serious are the roofs that are blown off houses and broken walls. To make matters worse, there are no electricity and water supplies. And even when the supply of electricity has resumed, there may still be no water because the reservoir filters are choked with rubbish.

The first tasks of the authorities are to clear the roads and repair electric cables. It is no use calling the CEB or your local council even if your household rubbish has not been removed for more than a week because they are doing the best they can. You can help by clearing your garden and stacking all the branches and other rubbish in one corner near the gate so that, when the rubbish collectors call at your house, they can remove everything as swiftly as possible.

Your house might also be in a mess if water has seeped in. Open all the windows and doors and clean up as best you can. The CWA sends out trucks to distribute water; find out where they are stationed and bring your biggest containers.

If you have not suffered much damage to your property, you might want to help others clean up. Go to the nearest school or social centre and volunteer your help. It will always be gratefully accepted.

CULTURE SHOCK

Wherever you come from, Mauritius will offer something familiar, be it in the population make-up, food or people's attitudes. However, it will never be the same as home. So you might not feel culture shock right from the beginning because you will be concentrating on the few familiar things and enjoying the novelty of the unfamiliar.

It might be a few months later that culture shock will kick in. It could be in the form of a general feeling of depression or homesickness, or in a feeling of frustration over the different way things work here. Whatever it is, the moment you do not feel comfortable or are irked by some niggling feeling, it is culture shock. The thing to avoid is repressing your feelings. It is perfectly all right to be irritated by the laid-back attitude of your colleagues or by the sound of Creole or French wherever you go.

However, do not go ranting and raving in front of your Mauritian friends. You might not find them understanding enough because the idea of culture shock is alien to them. They sincerely believe that their island is the best place to live on earth and would not understand why you are not enjoying yourself. Give them an idea that you are not quite used to living in Mauritius yet and take part in local activities. Do not shut yourself off from Mauritian society. Ease yourself into Mauritian living by visiting with friends or going to the beach. But always make time for yourself, both at home and in the office, when you can set things in perspective and be critical of certain attitudes and behaviour.

A TASTE OF MAURITIUS

'I'll bet what motivated the British to colonise so much of the world is that they were just looking for a decent meal.'
—Martha Harrison

TALK FOOD TO ANY MAURITIAN and their eyes will light up. Their forefathers came from countries with strong culinary traditions and all Mauritians take pride in their ancestral cuisine while enjoying typical Mauritian dishes.

ETHNIC CUISINES

Ethnic cuisines in Mauritius refer to Asian food, mainly Chinese, Indian and Muslim. Most Asian families eat their own food at home, but not exclusively. A curry would be present at the Chinese dinner table on a regular basis, and the Indian family would try frying some rice once in a while. And instant noodles can be found in the kitchen cupboard of every family in the country.

Chinese Food

Chinese food is characterised by the use of fresh meats and vegetables and of sauces, like soy sauce or oyster sauce. Dishes range from the simple stir-fried greens to the elaborate shark's fin soup. Many cooks like to add some slivers of pork or chicken to their fried greens, a habit from the old days when meat was less affordable and those few slices would constitute the meat portion of the diet.

Pork features prominently in Chinese cuisine, although, for health reasons, it is much less popular these days. *Foong moon choo niouk* (literally, red braised pork) is a wonderfully fragrant stew of pork belly or brisket with sweet rice wine and a handful of red rice called *kiouk*. With a few slices of bean curd, it is hearty peasant fare, of the type that tugs at the heartstrings of Hakkas all over the world. The dish has gone out of favour with the more health-conscious young Chinese, but it can be just as delicious prepared with lean cuts of meat. One pork dish that is popular with everyone is *cha shao*, called by its Cantonese name, *char siew*, by restaurants. Much more acceptable meats to the young nowadays are chicken and beef. Steak is a great favourite and the clientele of most steak houses is predominantly Chinese. Mainly because of its scarcity and price, fish is not as frequently served on the dinner table as chicken. Duck is rarely available, and mutton or lamb is not featured in Chinese cooking because its distinctive flavour does not agree with the Chinese palate.

Hakka cooking generates minimum wastage. Bad cuts of meat are stewed or braised to produce highly flavourful dishes. Leftover rice is fried with egg, Chinese sausage and peas, and is served as a main dish. The dregs from making rice wine are collected and mixed with *kiouk* to produce *chao*. This is used to flavour clear soups or is stir-fried with beef and pickled mustard greens. Slightly sweetish, it has retained some of the taste of wine and imparts a distinctive flavour.

Rice is the staple in all Chinese homes. But most people eat only one meal of rice a day, at dinner. Breakfast is taken on the go and lunch is usually a packed sandwich in the office. Even those who can afford the time still prefer bread for lunch. Noodles cooked in soup are only taken at lunch while fried noodles can be eaten at both meals. Noodles, however, are a meal in themselves. When a family has fried noodles, they do not cook anything else. The only other dish is an accompaniment of *satini* ((*Please refer to section on Creole cuisine for more on* satini.)

Most restaurants are Chinese for the simple reason that there are more Chinese people in the restaurant business. However, if you are used to authentic Cantonese or Sichuan cuisine, you would probably be disappointed by the fare dished out at these restaurants. Only the more upmarket establishments employ chefs from China or Hong Kong and even there, dishes are adapted to suit the Mauritian palate.

Indian Food

Indians also eat rice as their staple, mainly at dinner. Other staples are a variety of pancakes, called *roti*, *farata*, *puri* or *chapati* depending on the method of cooking. They are all made of wheat flour mixed with water to form a dough. Oil or ghee may be added to the dough while kneading or in the rolling process, and the pancakes are either toasted on a griddle or deep fried in oil. Few families can afford the time and effort to make *roti* on a daily basis and it is eaten as a special treat. Of course, Indians also consume large amounts of bread, like everybody else.

Meats are usually cooked in curries, always called *masala* even though the recipe does not bear much resemblance to the Indian *masala*. A fish *masala*, for example, tastes very different from a chicken *masala* because the spices are different. Few cooks take the trouble to grind the various spices for the curry. Why bother when several brands of fragrant curry powders are available on the market ready for cooking? Goat meat, mutton, chicken and fish are all used. Religion forbids the consumption of beef and social custom has made pork also taboo. The ingredients that go into a curry, aside from the curry powder, are onions, garlic, tomatoes and chillies. Potatoes, aubergines and okra are added in to enhance the taste.

Vegetables and greens are mostly stewed with onion, ginger, garlic and chilli. *Achard* is made of shredded cabbage, carrot, beans and cauliflower together with garlic and onions. Usually translated as pickled vegetables, it is, in fact, cooked with a mixture of ground spices, mustard oil and vinegar. Crunchy and spicy, *achard* is best eaten with crusty bread. If the vegetables have been put out in the sun for a day or so prior to cooking, *achard* can keep for quite a while in a sealed jar. The same method and spices are used to make mango, hog plum, star fruit and heart of palm *achard*. Only green fruit is used and the result tends to be rather sour. Small green chillies are pickled either in vinegar or oil and eaten as a condiment.

Madras curries tend to be very hot. Another feature is the use of tamarind in various dishes, of which *rasson* is the more well-known. A hot and sour clear soup, it is reputed to cure hangovers fast.

Muslim Food

Muslims, of course, do not eat pork, but do consume beef, unlike Indians. Regular Muslim cooking is not very different from Indian food for, after all, both Muslims and Indians come from the same country. So curries and stewed vegetables are also found on the Muslim table. However, they do not eat *roti* and their only staple is rice. The *nan* bread that is baked in Muslim bakeries is more like a bun than the *nan* of northern India, which is closer to a *roti*.

Probably the Muslims' greatest contribution to the food scene is *briani*. Cooked in a huge steel pot called *deg*, this complete meal contains layers of fried onions, meat, potatoes and Basmati rice. What makes *briani* so utterly fragrant is the addition of saffron which gives a golden yellow colour to the rice and potatoes. A few strands are enough for a whole pot, fortunately, since the spice is very costly. (Mauritians actually call turmeric 'saffron' because it is a cheaper alternative; saffron itself goes by its Urdu name, *jaffran*.) Other spices that go into the dish are cloves, cinnamon and cardamom. A cool cucumber salad with green chilli and mint or a *satini* goes best with *briani*. (*Please refer to section on Creole cuisine for more on* satini.)

Kalia is a kind of rice-less briani, a stew of beef or mutton with potatoes and spices. Without the addition of saffron, the gravy is brownish rather than yellow, and it is delicious with rice. *Halim* is also spicy, but it is a thick soup of mutton, lentils and rice.

Muslim eateries are well known for their cutlets and *catless*, spicy meat patties (usually mutton) coated in bread crumbs before being dipped in beaten egg and deep fried. Cutlets are actually bigger *catless* with a small stick of bone at the end that acts as a holder. Also on sale are a variety of sweetmeats such as *rasdoula*, *gulab jamun* or *moutaye*. You might not appreciate them if you do not have a very sweet tooth.

THE MELTING POT

The food served in most Mauritian homes is now a real melting pot of various cuisines. The different communities sample each other's dishes and adapt them to suit their taste buds. If they are more used to spicy food, chilli would be added to dishes that originally do not contain it. On the other hand, some Chinese families cook curry without chilli.

Creole Cuisine

Creole food is eaten by everyone. Its influences are African, Indian and French. Onions, garlic, tomatoes (slightly smaller and more tart, they are called *pommes d'amour*—love apples—in Creole) and chillies are present in almost every dish. Ginger is also widely used. All these ingredients come together in *rougaille*—rich, aromatic and typically Mauritian. If there was such a thing as a national dish, this would certainly be a very strong contender. Plain tomato *rougaille* is served as a side dish, maybe to accompany a curry, or as a topping for steak à la Créole. Meats can also be cooked in *rougaille*: sliced beef, *snoek* (salted fish imported from South Africa), *chevrettes* (tiny freshwater shrimp found in Mauritian streams and rivers), corned beef, canned sardines or sausages.

Satini also contains chopped onions, tomatoes, chillies and coriander. Similar to Mexican salsa, it is also a side dish. But again, imaginative cooks may add leftover fried fish, corned beef or sardines to create a variety of dishes. Peanut butter *satini* makes a spicy and unusual, but delicious, sandwich spread.

Stews are called *daube* in Creole and they also contain onions, garlic, tomatoes and chillies. Any meat can be stewed, except for pork. Stews are popular because they do not require fresh meat, nor the best cuts, and they are easy to prepare. Potatoes, *chou chou* (chayote, a light green squash), cabbage, peas, carrots, aubergines or okra can all be added in to give variety and consistency.

Soups also contain the same basic ingredients. Fish bone or fish head soup is full of flavour and packs a real punch.

Greens, such as spinach, potato leaf or watercress, are also used. In Creole, the word soup refers exclusively to rice porridge. Soup, as we know it, goes by the name of *bouillon*, even if it is a thick and heavy concoction.

A fish dish that is typically Mauritian is *vindaye*. Thick slices of fish are deep fried before being coated with a ground mixture of turmeric, mustard seeds, ginger and chillies. Whole shallots and cloves of garlic are added together with some vinegar, and the dish must be left to stand for a while for the flavours to develop. Less common, but just as wonderful, is octopus *vindaye*. It is cooked with the same spices, but the octopus is cut into small pieces and blanched instead of fried.

Greens are eaten at every meal. Cooked *touffée*-style, they are tossed in hot oil with onions, garlic and chilli until all the liquid has evaporated. Sometimes meat, fish or *snoek* is added for more flavour.

Creole dishes are eaten with rice or bread. Creole cooks boil their rice in lots of water which is drained off when the rice is cooked. This method gives a slightly different taste and texture from steamed rice. Today, however, most households use an electric rice cooker and the traditional method is slowly disappearing.

Spices

Creole cooking makes use of fresh herbs as well as spices, combining French and Indian traditions. Coriander, very common in Indian and Chinese dishes, is certainly the most used herb. It goes into the preparation of everything from stews, salads and curries to soups, and is also used as a garnish. The Spanish term 'cilantro', which is favoured on the American continent, is almost unheard of in Mauritius. So, when buying this herb, you should ask for coriander, or better still, learn the Creole word; it is so much more charming: *cotomili*. The other common herbs are thyme and parsley, which are used in *rougaille*, stews and certain soups. They are so often used together that greengrocers pack them together and the compound word thyme-parsley is a distinct word in Creole.

The most commonly used spice is, of course, chilli. Mauritian cooks favour the small green variety, which is hotter and gives a real kick. Big red ones are used in curry paste and generally for long cooking processes such as braising or stewing. Big green chillies are less spicy and can be stuffed with a meat paste and fried in batter for an interesting snack. Common dried spices are cinnamon and cloves for French-based dishes like stews or pot roasts. Turmeric, cumin, fenugreek, mustard seeds and coriander seeds go into those dishes influenced by Indian cooking, such as *vindaye*.

FAST FOODS

American fast food chains are making their presence felt in Mauritius, with a McDonald's restaurant at the Harbourfront Complex in Port-Louis, and several branches of Kentucky Fried Chicken and Pizza Hut in various parts of the island. If you cannot make it to Port-Louis for a burger fix, do not fret. Several local joints have sprouted up and sell various versions of the stuff. You can even get one at the popular beaches, sold from a camper van. They are well worth trying since the local manufacturers add a twist to their patties by including chilli, onion, garlic and herbs. Burgers go by the name of beefburger rather than the more common hamburger because of the latter's association with ham, which is prohibited among

Vans offer a cheap meal on the go at the beach or at lunchtime in the city centre.

Muslims. Hot dogs, however, are a rarity because Mauritians do not think much of a sausage in a bread roll.

Local fast food on the same theme—that is, some meat stuffed in a bread roll—abounds, and most Mauritians find them much more attractive. Office canteens, camper vans and small snack bars all sell crusty bread loaves stuffed with *achard*, *vindaye* or octopus curry. You can add more kick to it by asking for some pickled chilli. Considered slightly more upmarket, because they come in a softer bread roll, are ham and roast beef sandwiches. They both go by the same name of *pains fourrés*, meaning stuffed bread. To these you can add mayonnaise, mustard or hot chilli sauce.

By far the most popular fast foods are *roti* and *dholl puri*. The former is a plain flour pancake cooked on a hot griddle while the latter is a softer pancake stuffed with mashed *dholl*, a yellow split pea, flavoured with turmeric and cumin. *Roti* is sold singly while *dholl puri*, because of its melt-in-the-mouth softness, comes in pairs. Both are eaten with a variety of condiments, including *rougaille*, *achard*, *satini*, potato curry and pickled chilli. You can have everything or you can ask the vendor to omit the chilli. These wayside delicacies are best eaten hot because they tend to harden when cold. You will find *roti* and *dholl puri* at street corners in the centre of town, sold from a glass case atop a bicycle, or in market stalls.

For flavour and price, nothing beats a couple of pairs of *dholl puri*. Many workers make it their daily lunch. A variation is the *puri*, a smaller pancake that is deep fried instead of toasted. These are usually sold in Muslim teahouses and are just as delicious.

Also sold, and cooked, at street corners are *samoussas*, flaky triangular packets with a potato curry filling, and *gâteaux piments* (chilli cakes), coin-sized balls of ground *dholl* mixed with chilli, cumin, coriander and spring onion. The latter are rather similar to the Middle Eastern falafel. The vendor crouches behind a wok filled with hot oil sitting on top of a Primus cooker and deep fries the snacks. Thin slices of potato and aubergine coated in light batter are also deep fried. These are crispy on the outside and soft on the inside, but tend to retain quite a bit of oil. *Gâteaux piments*, battered potato or aubergine in a loaf of bread make a convenient and cheap meal.

Sweet fast foods are less readily available, but you do come across them from time to time. *Gâteaux patate* are crescent-shaped pastries made from a dough of flour mixed with mashed sweet potato. These are filled with grated coconut and sugar which, when deep fried, forms a syrupy centre. When cold, they tend to become rather oily, so it's best to consume them immediately. *Macatia* are sold by vendors on bicycles. You can hear them coming by their chants of '*macatia coco-o-o*'. Small soft buns stuffed with a mixture of desiccated coconut and sugar, they make perfect tea-time snacks.

DRINKS

It is quite safe to drink water straight from the tap, except after heavy rains and cyclones. But if you are at all worried, it is best to boil it first. Bottled water is available, but really not worth the expense. The water that flows from your tap is rain water that has been filtered and made fit for human consumption. Mauritius has no water recycling facility, so you can rest assured that your tap water is the freshest possible. Mauritians consume a lot of rather unhealthy fizzy drinks, both in the home and at work or school. In a restaurant, the probability is that almost every table will have at least a Coke, Pepsi or Seven-Up. Surprisingly in a country with an abundance of tropical fruit, there is no tradition of drinking fresh fruit juice, except perhaps in the most upmarket establishments. Whatever juices are available are packed in cans or cartons, and most of them are imported.

Local drinks are sweet, cool and refreshing. The most exotic is certainly chilled *alouda* sold at roadside stalls and in the market. It is made from a base of milk and rose syrup to which are added strips of plain jelly and *tookmaria* (sweet basil seeds). Some vendors call it *la mousse* (jelly). The best *alouda* is sold in the Central Market in Port-Louis where vendors offer samples to tourists. It is advisable to go slow when you first try it, however refreshing you find the drink. On a hot summer day, it really tastes like ambrosia, but the combination of ice, milk and *tookmaria* can prove lethal for unsuspecting stomachs. A variety of *sirops* is also sold in huge fish tank-like containers. These are rather nondescript and taste just like sugared water with pink or yellow colouring. In fact, they are probably nothing more than that. Cold tamarind juice, though, is heavenly. Made from fresh tamarind and sugar or even from bottled tamarind syrup, it is sweet and tart; a definite thirst-quencher. Molasses, called *fangourin* in Creole, is another typical Mauritian drink. It is sweet and dark with a slightly burnt taste. Mistakenly referred to as cane syrup, it has somewhat fallen out of favour lately.

Beer, Wines and Spirits

There is only one brewery in Mauritius and it brews the best beer in the world. So says every Mauritian drinker and so will you after you have tasted the award-winning Phoenix and Stella. The smooth taste comes from the well-water drilled on site and the use of local sugar instead of chemicals to produce a head, making it more digestible. Of the two, Phoenix is the more popular, being cheaper and stronger in alcohol content.

The popularity of beer keeps growing because it is seen as a socially-acceptable drink (as opposed to rum). The low alcohol content makes it less intoxicating and a beer drinker would not be labelled a drunkard. (It is a totally mistaken notion, though, that you do not get drunk on beer.) A group of friends getting together over a couple of beers is almost a weekend fixture. Women and youngsters like beer because they can get a kick without being 'bad'.

Despite the all-pervasive French influence, there is no tradition of drinking wine with a meal. Mauritian wines are misleadingly labelled 'fruit wines' because they are made from grape concentrate and not fresh grapes. Thus many people believe that local wines are distilled from tropical fruits. Mauritian wines are pleasantly drinkable and inexpensive. In fact, the Tibordo label is even cheaper than a can of Coke. With better quality wines coming on the market, there is now a growing trend for sophisticated drinking, and the better-travelled hosts would certainly serve a good wine, whether local or imported, to their dinner guests.

However, the more prestigious drink is still whisky. It is served at cocktail parties and some people even take it with their meal. Whisky is not cheap and so it is reserved for celebrations. A cheap liquor is rum, served in shot glasses in seedy-looking bars. Rum-drinking has always been

associated with male drunkenness, and it is not served to guests if the hosts can afford something more expensive. However, Mauritian rum has a distinct flavour, being distilled from sugar, and the Green Island label is starting to enjoy some recognition overseas. Rum goes into most local cocktails, which are ironically considered 'high-class' drinks, whereas drinking plain rum is crude. Coco-Rico is a coconut-flavoured rum that goes very well with fruit juices, especially pineapple.

FOOD TABOOS

Most food taboos are associated with religion. Muslims do not take pork but are not that rigorous about food being halal (prepared according to Islamic precepts). Most butchers (apart from pork butchers, of course) are Muslim and they make sure that they sell halal meat. Frozen poultry is usually halal, but not all fresh poultry. Fewer Muslims eat out because

all non-Muslim restaurants are not halal, but they still go to Chinese or Creole restaurants and just order dishes that do not contain pork. Here it must be said that the women are more conservative than men. They would attend a party at a non-Muslim's house but might not consume anything other than a soft drink. Most Indians also do not consume pork in addition to beef and many Creoles also shun pork because they think that it is a 'dirty' meat since the pig is a dirty animal. The Chinese, on the other hand, eat pork but do not like mutton and goat meat.

Vegetarianism is not very popular in Mauritius, mainly because it is associated with the Maraze caste. Also, in a country where the majority of the people have been traditionally poor, now that they can afford to buy meat, they are not going to keep away from it.

Most Indians and Muslims now eat with a fork and spoon. But when they do eat with their bare hands, they use only the right side, which is considered the purer side.

FOOD SHOPPING

Most Mauritians buy meats, fruits and vegetables at the market, called *bazar* in Creole. For their other household needs, they go to the corner grocery. The latter is called *boutique* in Creole; a boutique, in the English sense of the word, is spelt *boutik*. All groceries are family-owned and run, with the children helping out during weekends and after school or work. The goods are stacked on shelves behind a counter or in locked glass cases. The shopkeeper stands behind the counter and serves the customers from there. All the purchases are put on the counter before your bill is added up. You can ask for a discount, but most prices are fixed, and even if you do get a discount, it would only be a few cents. The cash till is nothing more than a drawer in the counter. Some shops put your purchases in plastic bags, others do not or make you pay for the bag. So it is always safer to bring a bag along with you.

With the shortage of labour, many shops have been renovated to be self-service style. These usually carry a larger range of goods and might have a deep freezer with meats and ice cream. Such self-service shops call themselves supermarkets, to set them apart from the *boutiques*. However, real supermarkets are also present, and their numbers are growing as more and more franchises and local enterprises come onto the scene.

Bazars

Every town and large village has a market in a very central location. In the suburbs, you can go to the *ti bazar*, a mini-market selling vegetables and a limited selection of meats. Not all markets open every day. Some trade on one or two days of the week only. These are called *foires* (fairs), but function just like any other market.

Most *bazars* are built on an open concept, with a roof but only iron bars on the sides. The meat section is separate from the rest of the market and is housed in a concrete building, for hygiene reasons. Because of religious sensitivities, pork is sold in a separate annex, with its own door. The whole interior is tiled and the meats are laid out on sparkling clean counters or hang from hooks in front of the butcher. You can choose the exact piece you want or you can ask the butcher to do it for you. Prices for the various cuts are standard throughout the market, but might vary from town to town. All prices are stated on a board near the office. Butchers do not dress the meat for you; if you want them to do so, you have to give very precise instructions and watch them do it. And you must be prepared to tip them generously.

At some markets, chicken is sold live and slaughtered and cleaned on the spot. Or you can take it home live and kill it yourself. The chickens are sold by weight and the price is that of the live animal, feathers and giblets included.

Fish is usually sold whole, except for really big ones like tuna or shark which are cut into pieces. You take the fish home as it is, with scales and everything. If you want the fishmonger to gut it and remove the scales, you have to pay a small fee. Even then you still have to do some more cleaning at home.

The fruit and vegetable area is a joyful sight to behold. The produce is stacked up high on both sides of the aisles with

Many market vendors still make use of old-fashioned scales (above). At the Port-Louis market (below), the pork section, on the left, is separated from the other meats by a wide alley.

one vendor sitting on top and another one standing in front of the stall showing off the assorted vegetables. Vegetable sellers are divided into two types: those selling greens and smaller vegetables, such as lettuce and herbs; and those selling potatoes, onions and cauliflower. It is hard to resist the freshness and vibrancy of the vegetables: tomatoes are red and plump, peppers green and shiny, and pumpkin golden and round. Bargaining is acceptable, but if the seller does not budge even when you pretend to leave, then it means you will not get a better price.

Fruit stalls are usually right in front of the market gates. All manner of tropical fruits create a riot of colours: golden pineapples, crimson litchis, yellow mangoes. Temperate fruits such as apples, oranges or grapes are also on sale, imported from South Africa or Australia.

In a separate aisle are dry goods stalls selling curry powders, tamarind paste, coconut and salted fish. The aromas can be rather pungent and it would be wise to avoid this section if you have nothing to buy there, especially when you have young children in tow. Elsewhere in the market is the bread and cooked food section. Golden crusty loaves are delivered twice a day and the best times to buy bread are around 7:00 am and 2:00 pm. The typical Mauritian loaf is the *maison* (house), a crusty round loaf with a slit in the middle. Sandwich loaves, called *moule* (mould) in Creole or *corbillard* (hearse!) in slang, are long and big and also crusty. Soft sliced bread is now more readily available, as are French baguettes. Next to the breads are *roti* and *gâteaux piments* sellers, and it is quite common to see workers buying their bread and stuffing it with the fried snacks before going to work.

The Port-Louis *bazar* is the biggest in the country and it offers a large variety of goods, such as tourist souvenirs, clothes and lottery tickets. A fascinating section is that selling medicinal herbs. The vendors have prescriptions to cure everything under the sun, from diabetes to 'evil wind'. Do not dismiss them as worthless because many of the remedies do work.

Bazars come under the purview of municipal councils. So, if you witness any unhygienic practices, you should report it to the Market Department of your town or village council or write to the mayor.

Supermarkets

Supermarket shopping is never as exciting as in the *bazar*. Fruits and vegetables look like they have been sitting on the shelves for days and pre-packaged meats are dull and unappetising. However, they carry a much wider range of household products than the corner *boutique* and their frozen and deli sections are very well stocked. Some supermarkets also have clothing and book departments.

The opening of the French franchise Continent (now renamed Jumbo Score) in Phoenix a decade ago has changed the way Mauritian families shop. A trip to the supermarket has now become a regular weekend or evening outing. Mauritians welcome the idea of being able to browse and touch the goods without feeling obliged to buy anything. Browsing is certainly not possible at the corner grocery.

Every town has a supermarket of some sort and a few self-serve stores. You can actually find all the common items of daily use at your local *boutique*, but perhaps of

Food is not always bought at the supermarket. Adults and children join in the the fun of picking *tec-tec,* a tiny clam which makes a wonderfully tasty soup.

a different brand than what you are used to back home. But you might find the air-conditioned supermarkets with piped-in music more comfortable and if you are looking for some specialty goods, a trip to Jumbo Score or Super U is never too far.

Weights and Measures

Mauritius follows the metric system, but it is hard for a former British colony to shake off the imperial measures. Foodstuff is officially sold by the kilo, but most market vendors and shopkeepers, as well as customers, still think in terms of pounds. Prices are quoted in half kilos because half a kilo equals roughly one pound. So you can ask for meats and produce in either pounds or kilos; the seller will make the necessary calculations.

The metric system is more entrenched when it comes to measures. Liquids are sold by the litre, but motorists still buy gallons of petrol even though the gauge is in litres. Speed limits and road distances are indicated in kilometres, but drivers refer to miles. This is changing, though, as new cars come with metric speedometers. But the term '100 miles per hour' as a measure of great speed has stuck in the Mauritian language. Feet and yards are used for building materials, but fabric is measured in metres. Clothes and shoe sizes follow French measurements, but some manufacturers, especially of T-shirts, also use S, M, L and XL sizes. To know which one you are, just compare yourself with the majority of Mauritians.

EATING OUT

Compared to 'foodie' societies like Hong Kong or Singapore, Mauritians do not eat out much. Food is sold every few metres in town centres, but these vendors cater mainly to lunch time crowds or people having a snack on their way home from work. One whole family going out for dinner is rare. People go to a restaurant on special occasions, or when they have been unable to cook dinner through exceptional circumstances. Young working couples who do not have the time or inclination to prepare their own dinner usually eat with the parents before going home.

But, of course, habits are changing. Receiving one's salary at the end of the week or month is cause for celebration and restaurants are often packed on pay day. Greater affluence and the proliferation of good restaurants make people more inclined to go out for dinner. There is a wide spectrum of eating places where you can have a good meal cheaply or bust your whole pay packet in one evening. Most of them are concentrated in towns or in the area around Grand Baie. Hotel restaurants and coffee houses are not open to the public. You would not want to go there, anyway, because they tend to charge 'exclusive' tourist prices for rather bland fare.

Restaurants

Most restaurants are in town, mainly in Port-Louis, Curepipe and Quatre Bornes. The resort village of Grand Baie has more restaurants per square kilometre than anywhere else in the country. Restaurants range from little establishments with checked table cloths to gastronomic palaces serving gourmet fare in high-class surroundings (and charging high-class prices).

Lunchtime in a resort hotel
is relaxed and casual.

Western eateries fall into two broad categories: French restaurants and steakhouses, with the latter being more casual in setting and service than the French restaurants. There has been a proliferation of such establishments lately, but most of them are situated in the towns and in Grand Baie. With their generous portions and well-marinated meats, steakhouses are popular family restaurants. Standards vary, but in general, you can't go very wrong with good quality fresh meat.

There are surprisingly few Indian restaurants in a country where the majority of the population is Indian. On the other hand, it is not that surprising since, when Indians go out to eat, they would rather sample foods other than what they get at home. Indian restaurants in Mauritius do not usually serve home-style food. Rather, they dish out a selection of regional cuisines, including tandoori chicken and mulligatawny soup. The food is quite authentic, service is good and prices are reasonable.

Creole restaurants are unfortunately not easy to come by. But when you do come across one, it is usually well worth it. The most well-known is La Cambuse which claims to 'serve Creole meals in the atmosphere of old Port-Louis'. In general,

The restaurant at Domaine du Chasseur is nestled among lush vegetation and offers a great view of the area.

you can still get Creole dishes such as venison steak, hare *salmi* (stew) or turtle curry in some Chinese restaurants and other eateries.

By far the most popular are Chinese restaurants. You will find at least one or two good ones in any town, with a wide range of prices. Those with prices in the high end tend to specialise in Cantonese or Sichuan cuisine. The rest serve the usual sweet-and-sour dishes and vegetable *chop suey*. If you are used to fine Chinese food, you might find them not authentic at all, but they are probably the cheapest restaurants in the country. Several restaurants in Port-Louis and Happy Valley in Quatre Bornes serve *dim sum* for lunch on weekends. These tend to be very popular and it is advisable to make a reservation. For dinner at a run-of-the-mill restaurant, it is not necessary to book a table in advance.

A Note About Water

If you want mineral water with your meal, you must specify that it is mineral water that you want and not bottled water. Many Mauritians believe that once water is bottled, it becomes mineral water. Whatever the local brands of bottled water may claim, they are only that: bottled water. In order to avoid any unpleasantness, it would be advisable to state clearly to the person serving you that you do not want bottled water, but mineral water like Perrier or Evian. (Incidentally, not many establishments carry mineral water, and a request for plain tap water might be met with some surprised stares.)

Cafés

If you are invited to go to a café with a Mauritian friend, do not expect pavement tables with parasols and espresso coffee. The local café is nothing more than a few basic tables in a bare room with the owner cooking at the back. Instead of sandwiches, you will eat noodles, *wan ton* or *bol renversé* (rice, meat and vegetables in a thick gravy) and sip fizzy soft drinks straight from the bottle. Noodles can either be 'naked' (plain boiled with a bit of oil) or covered with a meat sauce. 'Naked' noodles are the cheapest and surprisingly good.

Cafés usually open only during the day and are packed at lunch time. Some cafés are licensed to sell liquor and those tend to attract mainly a drinking clientele but they are the only cafés open at night.

Pubs and Bars

The concept of the pub is still rather new and nothing like the British pub. Patrons either sit at the bar counter or around small tables. Beer, rum and other liquor are available, but food-wise, you will not get anything more than fried snacks like *samoussas* or spring rolls.

The main drinking holes are bars. These are basic and cater mostly to the hard-core drinker. Many are tucked away in the back room of the corner *boutique* and do not sell any accompaniment to the drinks other than peanuts or slices of pickled lime! Patrons usually stop by for a few tots of rum on their way home from work. You should note that these bars are not licensed and you might get into trouble having a few drinks there. The licensed bars have an aluminium covered counter and the barman pours the drinks from there. You pick up your drink and consume it at one of the tables arranged haphazardly around the room. The barman notes down your orders and you pay as you leave. Here, there is a wider variety of food and one can actually fill oneself with the tapas-style dishes. These are called *gajacks* and range from braised eggs to fried beef. Most bars attract rather unsavoury characters and the only women are those working there, in general the owner's burly wife.

The snack bar is more like the conventional café. Some have pavement tables, but are not too popular because of the hot sun. As their name implies, snack bars offer quick meals of noodles or toasted sandwiches. A glass case in front contains pastries that range from the totally forgettable to delicious cakes. Many patrons come in just for a cold drink, a juice or a milk shake. Snack bars are plentiful around bus stations and in shopping centres. Newer establishments are getting more sophisticated with espresso machines and jukeboxes.

Tea Hotels

Muslim-owned eating places are called *lotel di té* in Creole, literally 'tea hotels.' (In fact, the word 'hotel' in Creole is used to mean a guest house as well as any eating place.) The main beverage, of course, is tea. Fragrant and frothy from being poured from one jug into another, they make a trip to the teahouse worthwhile. If you do not take sugar, make sure you point it out clearly because it is assumed that everybody likes their tea sweetened. And everybody takes it with milk too. You can also have cold drinks, including *alouda*, but no liquor is served.

Hot and cold meals are on offer. The usual hot choices are *briani*, or rice with *kalia* or curry. But the speciality of the teahouse must be *catless* and cutlets. You can eat it on its own or with a loaf of bread. When the meat patties come out hot from the kitchen, they make a wonderful meal stuffed in a crusty loaf. Another attraction of teahouses is their long opening hours. Some of those in Port-Louis are even open 24 hours. When hunger pangs grip you after a night out, head for the teahouse—there will still be hot cutlets and curries.

Roadside Dining

Formerly limited to Port-Louis' Chinatown, roadside dining has spread to every town and some villages as well. Unlike the *roti* and *dholl puri* that are wrapped in a paper bag, hawkers offer fried noodles, *briani* or *halim* on plates and in bowls, which you eat standing or sitting on a wooden crate. A much cheaper option than cafés, these food stalls offer something more substantial than pancakes at a slightly higher price. Business is best at lunchtime and after office hours. But some hawkers remain open well into the night, especially those outside nightclubs or gaming houses. You will also find them outside reception halls when there are weddings.

Eating by the roadside can be a fun and novel experience, but do remember that such hawkers do not have running water and proper dishwashing facilities. The Mauritian stomach is used to whatever germs might be present, but it is advisable not to try too much too soon.

Tipping

Although most restaurants include a service charge, the waiting staff still expect a tip from you. Most people generally leave the change on the table, but if you have received impeccable service, by all means leave a more generous tip. As a rule, though, it is very rare for anyone to tip more than 10 per cent. If you intend to be a regular patron and would like a certain level of friendliness, you should try to leave something for the waiters. But do not overtip because they will come to expect a big tip and will be very disappointed when you leave less. Cafés and pubs do not expect a tip, unless they are located in more touristy areas, like at the beach.

In general, Mauritius is not a tipping society. You do not need to give anything to your hairdresser or taxi driver. In fact they will find it very odd if you do. If you are really happy with your regular hairdresser, a small gift of food (a pastry from your country or a bar of chocolate) will be greatly appreciated.

Table Manners

Although being of predominantly Asian descent, Mauritians display more Western-oriented table manners. Most families use a spoon and fork for eating since the staple is rice. Use the spoon to scoop up a small amount of rice and meat and vegetables, helping yourself with the fork if need be, and bring it up to your mouth. You should always keep both utensils in your hands. Eating with one hand only is considered sloppy. Also do not put your elbows on the table while holding your spoon and fork. If you want to use your hands while conversing during a meal, lay the utensils down on the plate first. But, after you have finished eating or while waiting for dessert, do not put your hands in your lap. Just leave them on the table, with your wrists resting lightly on the edge of the table. The same rules apply if you are given a fork and knife, but of course, you use the fork to scoop the rice up, helping yourself with the knife.

If you are given a set of cutlery, then you should never use your hands to eat. Use your spoon to scrape as much meat as possible off the chicken bone, but if you cannot clean it completely, just let the few scraps go to waste. If you are eating bread or *roti*, then break it off with your hands and hold bite-size pieces in your hand to soak up the sauce from the plate. Do not put pieces of meat with bone into your mouth and spit out the bone later. Hold it with the spoon or fork and eat around the bone. If you do get a small piece of fish bone or pungent herb in your mouth, then hold it between your teeth and discreetly remove it with your fingers. Bend your head and tilt it to the side while doing so. Try to eat up everything that has been put on your plate. Leaving food shows that you did not enjoy your meal.

Conversation flows freely during a meal, but never open your mouth while there is food inside. Swallow first before making your point.

Chewing loudly is a definite no-no as well as stuffing a lot of food into your mouth. Eat at a moderate pace because eating fast might give the idea that you are a glutton. It is also considered rude to slurp your soup or any other drink. If the soup is too hot, you can blow gently onto each spoonful, but without making any noise. Do not stir it with the spoon to cool it down. And do not drink your soup directly from the bowl, unless it is at a roadside stall. If you are seized by a fit of coughing or need to sneeze, cover your mouth and nose with your napkin or with both hands and turn your head away from the table and the other diners. Do the same if you need to blow your nose. The height of impropriety is to burp during or after a meal. However, if the unfamiliar food causes you to belch, apologise immediately. Your dining companions will look embarrassed for a while, but do not take it to heart.

Throughout the meal, sit up straight in your chair. After the meal is over, it is okay to slouch slightly. While eating or conversing at the table, keep your elbows and arms close to your sides. Do not spread yourself out. Crossing your legs or shaking a leg is also considered bad form.

ENTERTAINING

As soon as you arrive in Mauritius, you will be bombarded with invitations to dinner or to visit. It is the local custom to treat foreign friends or acquaintances to dinner and Mauritians just love to have foreign guests. On the one hand, they really want to know about you, and on the other, they are proud to show off their house and cuisine.

Having Dinner

It is very important to turn up for dinner if you have accepted the invitation. Even if you are feeling slightly under the weather, you should still make the effort. Your hosts will have invited other friends and they would be extremely disappointed (not to mention lose face in front of their friends) if you cancel at the last minute. You are the guest of honour and everything has been arranged with you in mind. Even if the dinner party is to celebrate your host's birthday, you will still be a very important guest and the focus of much attention. Refusing a person's invitations repeatedly shows that you have no respect for them and would antagonise them. If the dinner clashes with your schedule, suggest another date when you will be free. Show that you are pleased by the invitation and are eager to visit your new friend.

Most dinner invitations are for 7:00–7:30 pm and the start of the meal might be half an hour to one hour later. Always bring a gift, some flowers, a decorative piece for the house or chocolates. Never suggest that you bring a dish or drinks: you are implying that your hosts cannot afford the expense or that you are suspicious of their culinary talents. Pre-dinner drinks are served with some local *gajacks*, *samoussas* or chicken croquettes. If you have not finished your drink by the time dinner is served, bring it to the table with you. Leaving it and starting on a fresh one at the table is considered wasteful.

There is no particular seating arrangement, but in general, your host and hostess sit at both ends of the table. (Mauritians rarely entertain buffet-style.) If it is a round table, your hostess would probably sit nearest the kitchen door. It is quite all right for a husband and wife to sit next to each other. However, do not plonk yourself down in the seat of your choice; wait for your hosts to suggest where you should sit. If they tell you to sit anywhere you like, then take your cue from the other guests. Wait for them to move towards their chairs and take the vacant ones.

Table setting is simplicity itself: one dinner plate with a fork and spoon or knife next to it and a glass in front. The fork is always to the left of the plate and the knife or spoon on the right-hand side. If you are left-handed, you just switch the two when you start eating. There is no difference between soup or rice spoon; you use the same one for both. Your napkin or a paper serviette might be tucked into the glass or folded under the cutlery. Some Chinese families might set bowls and chopsticks. Don't worry, they will make it a point to teach you how to use them. Try it; it's fun. For the serious business of eating, use the spoon provided.

All the dishes will be on the table by the time you sit down, and the rice will already be on your plate. If you think you cannot finish it, ask your hosts to return some to the pot. Soup will also be sitting on the table, served in individual bowls. You do not start with the soup; you just drink it while eating your rice. If your hosts are serving *plat au pain* (a dish that is eaten with bread instead of rice), then the dinner plate will be empty and the bread (usually baguettes) cut into thick slices on a platter or basket at the side of the table. Do not ask for butter to go with your bread because it will alter the taste of the dish. A Mauritian meal does not have distinct courses. At the start, all the dishes are passed around for you to help yourself. Do not take too much because you are expected to help yourself to more during the course of the dinner. Take one spoon of everything, mix it with your rice and start eating. When you have finished the meats and vegetables but still have rice, just take more of the dish you like. Try to clean up your plate by mixing the gravies thoroughly with the rice, unless they are too spicy for your taste.

Dessert is not usually taken at the table. You adjourn to the living room and your hostess will bring out little cups of ice-cream or flan. The more sophisticated host would offer some liqueur.

A variety of drinks are served with dinner, wine, beer, whisky, rum, fruit juices or colas. Water is not usually served. If you want to have water, say that the food is rather spicy and you need water to wash it down. Coffee is almost never offered after dinner. You go on drinking whatever you started with. Perhaps when the party is drawing to an end, your hosts might suggest a cup of coffee or tea as a nightcap before you leave. Do not stay any later than 10:00 pm–11:00 pm.

Entertaining Mauritian Friends

Your Mauritian friends do not expect you to reciprocate their dinner invitations. And they do not keep track of who went to whose house last. However, they will be delighted to be invited by you. For one thing, they are curious about your house and how you live. And, secondly, they feel honoured to be asked to your house. If you invite them, it means you respect them and consider them your friends.

Do not serve pre-dinner drinks with potato chips or peanuts only. This gives an impression of being cheap. Your snacks should be more substantial, with some meat in them. There are a number of frozen *samoussas* or *vol-au-vent* on sale in most supermarkets. These are easy to cook and always popular.

Even if your custom is to have the various courses served one after the other, do not confuse your guests by setting an array of cutlery in front of them. Keep it to one fork, knife and spoon. The same with glasses: one will do. Dessert spoons can always be brought out later. As for seating arrangements, try not to break up couples, especially if you are not familiar with one of them. The unfamiliar spouse will feel rather awkward to be seated next to total strangers for one or two hours. Remember not to serve pork and liquor to Muslim guests. However, you and the other guests can go on drinking. If you are serving a buffet and one or two dishes contain pork, tell your Muslim guests about it so that they can avoid those dishes.

The food most of your friends would like you to serve is, of course, your own cuisine. However, try to prepare only those dishes that are slightly similar to Mauritian cooking.

If there is a dish that you feel would be alien to your friends, even if it is your national dish, forget it. But you can tell your guests about it.

Unless your religion forbids it, you should offer hard liquor to your guests, not just beer, and even if you yourself are a teetotaller. Whether they take it or not does not matter. To entertain properly, one must bring out a bottle of whisky or rum.

Restaurants

The custom of inviting friends to restaurants is slowly making its way here. Somehow taking someone to a restaurant instead of having them at home smacks of insincerity, unless your friends want to make you taste a speciality at a particular eating place they have been impressed with. Even then, you will still be invited to the house for drinks first, and perhaps coffee afterwards.

If you are uncomfortable about having guests at home and still wish to reciprocate your friends' hospitality, then by all means take them to a restaurant. Tell them that you want to discover new eating places and ask them to suggest somewhere they like. But make it very clear that it is your treat and make all the arrangements by yourself, like booking a table and deciding on the time.

Come for a Drink

When someone asks you to come for a drink, it is much more than a drink that they will be offering you. An invitation to a drink is almost equivalent to a dinner invitation. It is usually in mid- or late afternoon and the drinking session will drag on until dinner. In addition to drinks (that is, beer, rum or whisky), a whole array of snacks will be prepared and you can really fill yourself up on them without having to eat dinner. Even if the invitation is made on the spur of the moment, your host will quickly whip up something delicious to go with your drinks.

Now, when you are invited to have a drink, it is all right to bring some of your own. If you are really partial to a particular brand or a particular liquor, bring some so that you can share your appreciation with your friend. Maybe they will discover that they like it too and you will have one more thing in common.

ENJOYING MAURITIUS

'The happiest people don't necessarily have the best of everything. They just make the best of everything.'
—Anonymous

FUN IN THE SUN

Before coming to Mauritius, you will have read brochures claiming that it is a place where the fun never ends. Its reputation as a world class tourist resort has also sharpened your appetite for having fun—and you will certainly not be disappointed. Having fun could be the motto of the Mauritian people. Nowhere will you find a population so bent on enjoying themselves.

BEACH CULTURE

The best beaches are in the northern part of the country. However, these tend to be crowded, but then also, they offer more amenities and creature comforts for the beach-goer. If you want a quiet time, head for the less popular places like La Prairie on the west coast or Pointe d'Esny in the south-east. And if you drive around, you can still find secluded stretches of sand that come close to the idyllic image hawked by the Tourism Office.

However, Mauritius has not developed the type of beach culture associated with places like Hawaii or Australia's Gold Coast. You will not see beautiful people showing off their well-toned bodies in skimpy swimsuits and you might attract a few curious stares if you do. There are a few beach bums, but there are enough hotels to offer most of them gainful employment as water sports instructors or boathouse helpers.

Facilities are very basic even at popular beaches like Flic-en-Flac. At least this one has a rescue centre!

It is safe to swim off most beaches, except for some places in the south. If you see a sign warning that swimming is dangerous, do not ignore it. And even if there is no sign, but the water looks choppy, be very careful about going in. Unfortunately, some of these signs are not properly maintained and there have been cases of drowning at beaches where the warning sign has broken off. Non-life-threatening hazards are the sea urchins that lurk along the sea bed, especially along the west coast. They can inflict nasty cuts, and you might need surgery if one of the spines breaks off and gets lodged in your foot. Watch out also for sea cucumbers—when stepped on, it releases a kind of gooey substance that causes a rash.

Picnics

Most people with a car go to the beach for only the afternoon, leaving after lunch and coming back home before dinner. Taking the bus means setting off earlier, like mid-morning, and leaving the beach at around 5:00 pm. You can have a really hassle-free outing if you choose a place like Grand Baie or Péreybère. You park your car, walk a few steps and you

Sea, sun and sand: that's what most tourists come to Mauritius for.

are already frolicking in the sand. Hungry or thirsty? There are several food and drink vendors in the car park, and a few restaurants a short walk away. Washing facilities may not be up to scratch, but most people just allow their swimsuits to dry on themselves before making their way home. With young children, it is advisable to bring a container of fresh water, and perhaps their favourite biscuits. Do not forget an adequate sunblock cream, with an SPF (sun protection factor) of at least 15. Other essentials are a couple of towels, a beach mat or one of those beautiful *pareos* on sale in all tourist shops, and a swimsuit, of course. Topless sunbathing (for women) is not outlawed (at least there are no signs saying so), but it does show a blatant lack of respect for the locals who are mostly conservative. Wearing really skimpy swimsuits is also not advisable, for both men and women.

If you choose to just drive about in search of that deserted stretch of beach, then you should definitely come better prepared, even with a first-aid kit. You can take the opportunity to lay on a lavish picnic lunch, but always

Fair-skinned people invariably get accosted by hawkers selling souvenirs.

remember to bring plenty of fresh water to wash up and plastic bags for your litter. Secluded places rarely come with bins and it will certainly not do to leave your rubbish behind. Beachside barbecues are not part of the local beach culture because of the poor washing facilities. In any case, there are no barbecue pits, and if you want to have a barbecue, you have to bring your own set, or dig a hole in the sand, as some groups of students do. You would not want to consider this option, though, because it really messes up the beach.

Camping

There are very few camping sites in Mauritius, and all of them are located near beaches. This is unfortunate because Mauritius, having such good weather and no dangerous animals, actually offers many ideal places for camping, especially in the unprospected interior. Actually, only Boy Scouts and Girl Guides and school groups use the camping grounds. The rest of the population just pitches a tent among the casuarina trees on the beach and makes do with whatever facilities are available. In any case, a camping trip never lasts more than one or two nights. If you intend to spend a night on the beach, be sure to bring some warm clothing. It can get quite windy and chilly during the night.

If you are invited to go camping with some Mauritian friends, there is no need to prepare your sleeping bag or torch light. They are only inviting you to spend a few days in a house by the beach. You do not have to bring anything except your personal effects since the house will be completely furnished. Even though the beach is only an hour's drive away, at most, Mauritians still like to rent a house for a few days and have a more relaxed lifestyle, without fixed schedules and duties. In fact, many people treat this as their annual holiday since not everyone has the means to travel overseas.

Water Sports

All types of water sports can be practised in Mauritius, from the lazy pedal-boats to the more demanding water-skiing or scuba diving. If you practise a sport that requires bulky equipment, like windsurfing, it might be a good idea to bring your own. Of course you can buy it here, but the choice is limited and price rather steep. For items like fins or masks, do not bother, they are easily available, even from ordinary shops.

Scuba diving is one sport that is developing fast and for good reason—the waters around the reef offer endless opportunities to watch all types of fish and corals, some very rare. There are several diving schools located in various regions, most of them affiliated to the Mauritian Scuba Diving Association. All instructors are highly qualified, making scuba diving one of the safest and most fascinating sports. You will need a light wetsuit, and your own mask and fins. Bottles are provided by the club.

Sailing

There is only one sailing club in Mauritius, the Grand Baie Yacht Club. It offers temporary membership to visitors. Apart from sailing, members can also practise water-skiing. The Mauritius Yacht Charters Ltd rents out boats, but it tends to be quite expensive. The marina at Caudan Waterfront offers anchorage to sailors from all over the world. You can also take a harbour cruise from there.

Fishing

Mauritius is deservedly well known for big game fishing. For many years it held the world record for the blue marlin, one of the most fierce battlers of the deep. Marlins, blue and black, are the prized catch, because of the struggle they put up. Other fish usually caught are tuna, bonito, dorado (a type of dolphin), barracuda and shark of the hammerhead variety. Strictly speaking, the fishing season is from October to March, but it can be extended from September to May. It is advisable to book a boat well in advance at the height of the season since many visitors come to Mauritius at that time expressly for big game fishing. The best places for hooking a catch are off the western coast of the country. There are fishing centres at La Pirogue and Le Paradis hotels and a

The black marlin is a prized catch for any deep sea angler.

BEACHCOMBER
FISHING CLUB

BOAT	CHALLENGER 1
ANGLER	M. KINGDON
FISH	BLACK MARLIN
WEIGHT	500 LBS
TACKLE	130
SKIPPER	ANTONIO
DATE	4-10-9

fishing club at Black River. The fleets are modern and well maintained, with experienced crew who know where the fish are and how to handle the boat to your best advantage. In late afternoon, when the boats start to return to the centre, the crowd at the jetty eagerly tries to catch sight of the little black flag that denotes which boat is coming back with a marlin. As soon as the fish are unloaded, they are weighed and the angler's name and weight of the fish noted on a blackboard. You then get your picture taken next to the board and your catch. Anyone who has caught a marlin will certainly treasure the memory for the rest of their lives. However, the angler does not get to keep any of the catch. It goes to the club, which shares it with the skipper.

If you are not into such athletic (and expensive) pursuits, you can still partake of the joys of sea fishing at a much cheaper price. There are fishermen in the areas around Le Morne or Black River who will take you out in their motor boats, either within the lagoon or near the reefs. To get in touch with one of them, just ask at the local *boutique*; your man might be in there having a drink or somebody will know someone with a boat willing to go out with you during the weekend. You negotiate the fee on the spot, but let him advise you on when is the best time to go. If the weather is not too good, you will have to wait until the next weekend. If you do not

Underwater fishing is strictly prohibited. If you are found with harpoons or guns, you will face a heavy fine.

have your own equipment, your fishing partner can provide it. You bring along the drinks (beer or rum) and maybe a snack or two, and you divide the catch evenly between you or make some other arrangement.

The Outer Islands

Dotting the sea around Mauritius are several little islands that are great picnic or nature watching places. The only one that is commercially exploited is Ile aux Cerfs off the eastern coast near Trou d'Eau Douce. A regular boat service run by the Touessrok Hotel ferries visitors to the island; or you can ask an independent boatman to take you there. The best part of the beach is taken over by the hotel, which operates a boathouse and several restaurants. The various amenities are open to the public, except for the beach parasols. Technically, non-hotel guests are not allowed to sit in their shade. A stunning golf course is also open to paying customers. The rest of the island is worth visiting for its rustic charm and roaming deer and other animals.

The north coast has a few islands that are good for picnics and a quiet day away from it all. You can charter a small boat with an outboard motor from an independent operator at Cap Malheureux. It is not advisable to ask the boatman to go off and come back for you at an appointed time. Since you are likely to be a one-off customer, he might take another group of picnickers to another island and just forget about you.

Round, Flat and Serpent Islands in the north are nature reserves and thus not easy to visit. You need a permit but it is worth the effort since they support rare species of flora and fauna which have evolved in isolation away from human disturbance. Some of these species are unique or on the brink of extinction. A few other islands are classified as nature reserves, but they present much less interest than the three in the north.

OUTDOOR FUN

You can enjoy outdoor activities almost year round thanks to the wonderful climate. But we cannot really talk of the 'great outdoors' here since Mauritius is really a very small place with not much variety in landscape.

Sports

Mauritians describe themselves as a sports-crazy people, but only as spectators. Most adults do not practise any form of sport, except for the occasional dip in the sea. But if you are a sport enthusiast, you can still practise your favourite sport, although you might have to look around for the facilities.

The major sport in Mauritius is football. There is no professional league, but some of the well-known clubs display skills that are above amateur standard. You will certainly find an amateur club in your area that meets for a game every Sunday morning. Or you can join a group of friends who have the use of the local school's pitch for a free game. You will be playing with children, grandfathers and people of all shapes and sizes. Tempers flare, you come home all bruised, but everybody has a good time. In Mauritius, football is a game strictly for men. Women and girls are accepted for casual ball-playing at the beach, but not in clubs.

Basketball and volleyball are also played in clubs, with tournaments at the national level. Most basketball clubs are in Port-Louis and the game attracts mostly Chinese players. Volleyball, on the other hand, is dominated by the Creole community and the clubs are in the plateau towns. If you want to play either game, just join one of the clubs.

Tennis is seen as a rather high-class game because of the investment in a racquet and other gear. Few courts are available, mainly in hotels and at the tennis clubs in Port-Louis and Rose-Hill. The Gymkhana in Vacoas also has courts.

Golf is enjoying greater popularity with the opening of new courses and the staging of several international tournaments during the year. The game is by no means cheap, but the course fees and club membership fees seem derisory when compared to countries like Japan or Singapore. If you live in town, it is well worth becoming a member of the Gymkhana Club; it has the only golf course in town and offers temporary membership. Even its ordinary membership fee is not high, but it has little investment value. Other golf clubs are located in the east and south of the island. They are more challenging than the Gymkhana, but the fees are much higher. A few hotels also run golf courses, mostly nine holes. The courses are not open to walk-in players.

Hiking

Not much forest remains, and those that have survived, in the area around the Black River Gorge, are now gazetted as nature reserves. You can explore them on your own, but the lack of proper trails and signboards makes this difficult. However, you do not need a guide per se, just a friend who has been there a few times before. In theory, you need to obtain permission from the Forestry Department and are not allowed in a nature reserve between 6:00 pm and 6:00 am.

But, as long as you exercise environmental care, you need not worry too much about such formalities.

The most popular hiking area is the Macchabée-Bel Ombre Reserve. The largest nature reserve, it comprises Macchabée, Petrin, Plaine Champagne, Bel Ombre and Montagne Cocotte forests. In addition to the challenge of the hike, you are rewarded by the breathtaking view of the Black River Gorge and several waterfalls. Certain parts are difficult, but you do not have to be an athlete to negotiate the paths. What you need are good walking shoes and perhaps a walking stick. Remember to bring drinking water as the water in the streams may not be fit for consumption. A raincoat is also necessary during the cooler months in the area around Plaine Champagne. If you are going to end your hike at a different place from where you started, it is a good idea to ask a friend to drive there and wait for you. Public transport to the nature reserves is extremely limited.

For those in search of more thrills, there are several mountains beckoning to be climbed. Again, do not attempt any climbing on your own; get a guide, for the first time at least. The different mountains present varying levels of difficulty, from the tall but gentle Black River Mountain to the steep Pieter Both. Pouce is popular with beginners because only the tip is steep and this can be bypassed; you climb right over the mountain and take the bus home on the other side.

Lightning is a serious hazard when mountain climbing; always check the weather forecast before you set off.

Nature Observation

The best places for observing the endemic flora of Mauritius are, ironically, the botanical gardens in Pamplemousses and Curepipe. Pamplemousses, in particular, has specimens of almost everything that grows on Mauritian soil. The nature reserves, on the other hand, present the advantage of seeing the trees and plants in their natural habitat. Several rare trees (ebony, teak, colophane and tambalacoque) can be seen growing to impressive dimensions. Epiphytes thrive in the damp forests, especially tree orchids.

As for animals, deer, monkeys and mongooses can be spied in the forests. If you are driving around undeveloped areas, you can come across the odd hare or wild pig. Birds can be observed anywhere; rare species can even be seen in towns sometimes. The Mauritian kestrel and pink pigeon, that are threatened with extinction, can sometimes be spotted in the Black River forests.

The outer islands present innumerable occasions for observing birds, snakes and lizards, some of which are highly endangered.

Guava Picking

One of the favourite outings during the guava season (April to August) is to Plaine Champagne. This is a local variety, with small red fruits that resemble berries. The flesh is soft, almost gooey, with rather big seeds. Called *goyaves de Chine* (Chinese guava), they have no similarity at all with the regular guava when it comes to taste. These small guavas have a tart sweetness that tickles the taste buds. They make great preserves that are wonderful on toast. Guava sherbet is one of the best in the world. The fruits grow on low bushes lining the road from Mare aux Vacoas reservoir to Chamarel. You park your car by the roadside and start picking the guavas. If you venture into the bushes, you will be rewarded with bigger and juicier fruits.

A trip to Plaine Champagne is more than just picking guavas for preserves. The air at this altitude is brisk and invigorating. You can drive to the viewpoint for a fantastic view of the gorge, and there are a few picnic areas for lunch. Another highlight is a visit to Grand Bassin, the awesome lake held sacred by the local Hindus.

Island Hopping

Mauritius is a good starting point for short trips to the neighbouring islands. The local air carrier schedules several flights a day to Reunion, Rodrigues and the Seychelles.

For something completely different from Mauritius, hop on a 30-minute flight to Reunion. Although called the sister island, it is both physically and culturally different. For one thing, they speak only French there. The majority of the population is Creole and the lifestyle is more liberal (after all, they are French). Reunion offers slightly more upmarket shopping than Mauritius, but at French prices plus cost of freight. In terms of scenery, Reunion is very diverse. There are few sandy beaches, much of the coastline being flanked by abrupt cliffs. The high relief in the interior makes for inaccessible mountains and caldeira, offering a great challenge to the hiker. It snows in the Cilaos area during the winter months and the active volcano of La Fournaise erupts regularly, sending flows of lava down to the sea. There is much contrast between the European style towns and the 'third world' interior.

Also a short hop away are the Seychelles islands. Apart from the expensive resorts which are not much different from the ones in Mauritius, there is not much to experience. The Seychelles' claim to fame is the *coco de mer*, locally called *coco fesse* for its resemblance to a certain part of the human anatomy.

Madagascar, the 'big island' of the Indian Ocean, is further away but makes for a fascinating trip. You will probably need more than a few days to take in everything the country has to offer. Tourist facilities are not brilliant, thanks to the decades of socialist style government. The primary forests, despite being cleared at an alarming rate, are of utmost ecological importance. Madagascar has the highest number of endemic orchids in the world and the lemur, a furry monkey, can only be found here. As for the people, there are several hypotheses about their origin, one of the most interesting being that they descend from South-east Asian Malays who are in turn descended from Polynesians sailing west. Witchcraft is still widely practised and the local version is said to be one of the most potent in the world.

Rodrigues is another place worth visiting. (*Please refer to* Chapter Two: 'Mauritius Welcome You', *page 37.*)

What is lacking is the structure for taking cruises around the islands of the Indian Ocean. At the moment, you have to make independent arrangements to visit them separately.

Treasure Hunting

The word 'treasure' always brings a twinkle to the eye of the Mauritian. Legend has it that Robert Surcouf, the most famous of the corsairs, did not hand over all his booty to the French colonial administration and that he buried a fabulous treasure that is only waiting to be discovered. Many Mauritians dream of finding a treasure, but it remains just a dream. There is a little known treasure hunting society and its activities are shrouded in mystery because anybody who actually believes in treasures is considered a lunatic. If you are bitten by the treasure hunting bug, do not pay a fortune for a map. (If the map were genuine, the seller would have unearthed the treasure themselves.) It is better to take up scuba diving and explore the sunken old ships. You may come across an untouched one. There are certainly many wrecks lying on the sea bed surrounding the island, but so far, nothing of value has ever been salvaged.

THE ARTS

Unfortunately for the culture buff, the arts scene in Mauritius is far from vibrant. The performing arts, in particular, suffer sorely from lack of funding and expertise. If you are an artist or have artistic inclinations, you will find much in Mauritius to draw upon for inspiration. However, appreciation will not be so forthcoming. And get yourself a day job; you cannot make a living as an artist in Mauritius.

The Museums

There are only two museums in Mauritius, one in Port-Louis that deals with natural history, and the naval or historical museum in Mahebourg. Both of them are free and are open every day. In addition, there are a few memorial museums, of which the most interesting is La Nef, the former house of poet Robert Edward Hart at Souillac. Built out of coral, it stands on a bleak stretch of beach facing the sea and contains a collection of the poet's memorabilia. Entrance is free and the museum is open every day except Tuesdays and public holidays.

The Natural History Museum houses a small collection of stuffed animals and birds, of which the most intriguing is a reconstruction of the dodo. Apart from the dodo that is kept in a glass case, the other animals are displayed in the open with the birds hanging from strings overhead. You get a funny feeling walking among musty smelling manatees and sharks and looking up to see an albatross in full flight. There is also an interesting collection of shells. The library, with over 50,000 volumes and housed in the same building, is open to researchers of the Mascarenes archipelago.

The Naval and Historical Museum is located in a beautiful old house built in the 18th century. Dedicated to the epic Battle of Grand Port, it displays an interesting collection of naval relics, including cannons, anchors, sailors' crockery and even an old biscuit distributed to the sailors as rations. Other exhibits feature French colonial furniture, including the bed of Mahé de Labourdonnais, French East India Company dinnerware, old maps, stamps, coins and paintings. The museum offers a wonderful lesson in colonial history and gives an insight into the customs and living conditions of the first Mauritians.

There are two art galleries, the Galerie d'Art de Port-Louis behind the Mauritius Institute and the Galerie Max Boullé in the building adjoining the Rose-Hill town hall. Both feature works by local artists but do not have a permanent exhibit. Quality is uneven. As for commercial galleries, two in Grand Baie are worth a visit: those of painters Henri Coombes and Helene de Senneville.

Local Artistic Expression

The *séga* is of course the typical Mauritian song and dance. Fusing this traditional heritage with the West Indian reggae, local rasta groups have come up with a new genre, the *seggae*. While retaining the West Indian rhythm, the *seggae* uses Creole lyrics and *séga* instruments, like the triangle and maravane. Unlike the *séga* which can be humorous or ribald, *seggae* lyrics explore serious issues like social inequality and corruption. The popularity of this new musical form has now grown beyond Mauritian shores and *seggae* has new followers in the neighbouring islands, especially in Reunion.

Rasta groups are the only ones to stage regular concerts in the country. They usually perform to sell-out crowds of youths who watch them for the music and not because they believe in the rasta way of life. If you do not want to wait to catch them in concert, check out the few nightclubs in Rose-Hill or Curepipe. Some groups also perform as guest artistes in the hotels.

Because the rhythm is purely West Indian, *seggae* is danced with the moderate shuffling steps of reggae rather than the eroticism and wild abandon of the séga.

The Performing Arts

The Mahatma Gandhi Institute and the Chinese Cultural Centre are doing much in the teaching of Indian and Chinese music and dance. A small but growing group of exponents is emerging. Combining technical mastery of their art with innate talent, they are keeping alive their cultural tradition. Performances are open to the public and staged at the Institute or Cultural Centre. Anybody can enrol in the classes, irrespective of cultural background. The Indira Gandhi Centre for Indian Culture, which is the cultural arm of the Indian High Commission, offers classes in Indian performing arts and yoga. Students as well as local artists have an opportunity to showcase their talents in monthly cultural shows. The centre also brings in artists and performers from India on a regular basis.

It is the Western performing arts that are sorely lacking. Locally there are very few ballet and music teachers and certainly no centralised schools like those mentioned above. To catch a ballet or a classical concert, you have to wait for foreign visiting groups brought in by the British Council or the Centre Culturel Charles Baudelaire. Such visits are very few and far between and you can go a few years without watching a play. Performances that are brought in cater very much to traditional tastes, such as *Swan Lake* or *Carmen*. Plays are always those that feature on the school syllabus, so you will invariably watch Shakespeare or Molière. A few local plays in Creole are staged now and then, but their appeal is limited.

As for 'highbrow' performances such as opera, you can forget it. Once in a while, a commercial venture brings in an operetta troupe from France for a couple of performances, but the costs of production are such that it is not a profitable activity. Gone are the days when the 'lyrical season' of Lopez operettas would see gentlemen in their tuxedos and ladies decked in their best finery mingling in the lobby of the Plaza Theatre.

Pop concerts are also rare. Apart from the rasta gigs, a few town councils may organise a 'variety show' in front of the town hall to celebrate a certain event, Republic Day or the New Year. Mauritian singers and musicians are very talented, but they lack the infrastructure to improve themselves and to be viable commercially. To do so, they have to leave the country and try their luck in France or Germany. Some have been fairly successful in their country of adoption. Foreign acts, mainly French, might stop by for a single concert after a tour of Reunion.

Movies

Cinema is cheap in Mauritius, but there is not much variety. The ABC in Rose-Hill and Caudan in Port-Louis are multiplexes with comfortable seats and good quality projectors. They screen the latest releases from Hollywood and France as well as Bollywood, albeit with a few months' delay. All English movies are dubbed in French. If you want to watch the original version, try the video store.

The other cinemas in the country are roach-infested old shacks that pay no attention to the spectator's comfort, or safety. They usually screen pornographic flicks that have escaped the censors' scissors. Respectable ones show Indian films, but these tend to be in the rural areas.

GAMBLING

One of the most popular pastimes of the Mauritian people is gambling. Some concerned persons, among them several members of the clergy, have warned that gambling is the cancer of Mauritian society slowly eating away their values together with their money.

The Races

Horse races have been held in Mauritius since 1812, at the Champ de Mars race track, the oldest in the southern hemisphere. The racing season stretches from May to November and races are staged almost every Saturday or

Sunday. The most important meet is the Maiden Cup, in which horses run two rounds instead of the usual one or one and a half, thus making it a test of endurance as well as speed.

The Champ de Mars comprises the race track itself, a grandstand on one side of the track and an arena surrounded by the track. Entrance to the arena is free and it looks like a giant fairground with food and games stalls and even some fairground rides for children. You can drive your car right into the arena and let the kids run about while catching a glimpse of the horses as they thunder by. A few bookmakers operate among the other stalls to cater to those punters in the arena. A larger number can be found within the grandstand area for which tickets are required. Serious punters prefer to pay to get into the grandstand so that they can gauge the horses going through their paces before the race. The crowds at the bookies' stalls are several persons deep. Do not be surprised to see your office 'boy' burning his pay packet in a single day here.

Betting operates on the tote system, and much of the betting is done on the basis of a tip from a 'reliable' source, such as a stable hand or jockey. Tips are called *tuyaux* (pipes) in Creole and most of them are unfortunately leaky. By the end of the week, when the official racing fixtures are published, your office will be abuzz with tips and speculation. There is certainly nothing wrong in venturing a few rupees, especially when some colleagues are certain of the reliability of their tip. But beware those colleagues whose life is ruled by the races. You will spot them easily, those who can talk of nothing but the races on Friday and who come in depressed on Monday. They will soon be asking you for loans to fuel their addiction or offering to place bets on your behalf.

Casinos
Since the first casino opened in Curepipe in the 1970s, there has been no looking back on big time gambling in Mauritius. Today, aside from the few casinos located in beach resorts and the original Casino de Maurice in Curepipe,

you can try your luck at several establishments scattered all over the country. They are all operated by Casinos of Mauritius. Opening times are around 8:00–9:00 pm on weekdays and early afternoon on Sundays and public holidays. Closing times vary; if a big time gambler wants to continue into the wee hours of the morning, the manager has the discretion to keep the casino open. Entrance is free.

The usual games are roulette and blackjack, with stakes starting quite low. All gaming tables have a maximum limit, except for those reserved for a few regular patrons. All casinos also have a collection of slot machines ranging from the conventional fruit machine to poker games. Dress code is not strict, but shorts and sandals are definitely not acceptable. Persons who appear under-aged are denied access to the gambling room, and are directed to the slot machines instead. However, a mild protest and a calm statement that you are above 18 are sufficient for the security personnel to wave you in with their apologies.

If you are not a seasoned gambler, it is safer to keep away from those tables with serious looking locals placing heavy bets. You may be blamed for any loss they incur, especially if they were on a winning streak before you joined in. However, nothing untoward will happen to you, except for a few jibes about 'stupid foreigners' and some killer stares.

Casinos are usually crowded on weekends and around the Chinese New Year period—most patrons are Chinese. The ones located in beach hotels attract more well heeled customers since they are not easily accessible by public transport and patrons need a privilege card to get in. The crowd at the Curepipe casino is more varied in terms of cultural background and income level. Here again, many of the patrons can ill-afford to lose a single rupee.

Although highly addictive, casino gambling touches a small portion of the population. For this reason, the government will not stop issuing permits to hotels intending to open a casino.

Dominoes

For the less wealthy, there are several gambling houses in Port-Louis and the other towns offering games with intriguing names like Big-Small and Van Lak. Many are actually fronts for drug dealing and attract much low life.

Given the Mauritian's inclinations towards gambling, every occasion is good to wager a bet. A ubiquitous sight in the villages is the group of men gathered under a big banyan tree by the roadside intent on a game of dominoes or cards. Winnings and losses range from a couple of rupees to about a hundred. The players are backed by a few onlookers who lend much excitement to the game.

You will surely be invited by friends to join in their friendly card or domino games. If the stakes are not high, why not? Just make sure that you know all the rules of the game; otherwise, some of the players might blame you for their losses. If you think that gambling in any form is a serious evil, there is no need to adopt a censorious tone. Just decline politely, and do not try to convert your friends to your way of thinking.

CLUBS

Wherever you live, there is bound to be a club nearby. It may not be what you are used to back home and you may not even consider it a club, but it provides a room for playing cards, darts, carrom (a board game similar to pool) and dominoes, and for general socialising. In addition, the club organises friendly football matches. Social centres function in much the same way, but also provide structured classes for new mothers, young girls or old age pensioners. Local clubs have a small joining fee and a nominal monthly subscription. However, they do not provide jerseys for football matches or other gear.

If you are looking for a 'real' club with clubhouse and recreational activities, try the Gymkhana (there is one in Port-Louis and another at Vacoas). Membership fees are low and facilities are adequate. There are a few other clubs, but membership is very much divided along ethnic lines.

THE NIGHT LIFE

If you walk about town after 7:00 pm, you will be forgiven for thinking that there is no night life in Mauritius, and it is true to some extent because most people spend their evenings at home or at a friend's house. The roads are virtually deserted after the shops have closed and the whole country seems to have gone to sleep.

In the urban areas, the whole night scene is limited to a few discos, one multiplex cinema, several restaurants that close around 10:00 pm, and taverns that draw a mainly hard-drinking crowd of middle-aged men. The villages only have the local tavern.

If you are looking for lively night life, then you should head for Grand Baie. With its restaurants, pubs and discos, it is the closest to an entertainment strip in Mauritius. You can have good, clean fun, but if it is entertainment of a seedy nature that you are looking for, Grand Baie also caters to such tastes. But be warned that AIDS has been present for several years now and that there is no proper screening for sexually transmitted diseases. In addition to such health hazards, you might also be the victim of the ire of the local population who try to take action against the seedy reputation of their village from time to time.

If you still do not know what to do with your evenings, the casinos are open well into the night. However, one short visit can burn a big hole in your pocket.

FESTIVALS

With so many different communities living on the island, the festivals celebrated by Mauritians are both colourful and varied. Most festivals are celebrated very publicly, but there are some that are celebrated among the family only. In such cases, to be invited to participate in the festivities is a great honour. However, not all festivals are public holidays. When a certain community celebrates a festival that is not a public holiday, many members of the community take leave from work.

Dates of Major Festivals

New Year	1 January
Thai Poosam Kavadee	2 January
Abolition of slavery	1 February
Chinese New Year	January/February
Holi	March
Easter	March/April
National Day	12 March
Ougadi	March/April
Labour Day	1 May
Feast of the Holy Virgin (Assumption)	15 August
Rakhi	August
Ganesh Chaturthi	August/September
Père Laval	9 September
Divali	October
All Saints Day	1 November
Arrival of the First Indentured Labourers	2 November
Ganga Asnan	November
Eid-Ul-Fitr	Moveable
Christmas	25 December

New Year

Previously celebrated on a big scale by the Creoles only, the New Year is now a day of rejoicing for all Mauritians. Celebrations start on New Year's Eve with many companies holding their end-of-year party in the morning and employees going home after lunch, some in a rather tipsy state. Some meet at a friend's place to continue their libations, others hit the shops for some last minute gift shopping. Groceries and supermarkets are thronged with people stocking up on liquor and food. Most people celebrate the New Year at home with a sumptuous dinner. There is no particular dish that is served country-wide, each family cooking their favourite food, be it shark's fin soup, roast beef or chicken curry. Hotels and restaurants tend to feature seafood (lobster is a favourite) or game fowl such as pheasant. If you are invited to a friend's house for the New Year's Eve dinner, a bottle of champagne and some after-dinner chocolates would be greatly appreciated. In the case of a teetotaller family, the chocolates would still be fine, but you might wish to add some flowers and a cake.

Dinner is followed by dancing into the wee hours of the morning at a disco or some other dancing party. At the stroke of midnight, the firecrackers start popping, party-goers sing 'Auld Lang Syne' and champagne is drunk. Almost every household, irrespective of ethnic origin, joins in the firecracker-letting. This goes on for at least a full minute and during this time, all the neighbourhood dogs are scared stiff and howl non-stop. If you have young children who have never heard firecrackers before, it is a good idea to remain close to them in case your neighbour decides to let off some crackers at close range.

New Year's Day itself is spent recuperating from the previous night's exertions for some and in further merrymaking for others. Most churches hold a service and people go visiting each other and exchanging gifts. If you hold a managerial post in your organisation, some of your staff might come to give you and your family their New Year greetings. They usually do so in the morning, so check with colleagues whether this custom is practised in your company and wait for them to turn up. It is customary to serve some light refreshment and if you have some typical New Year cake from your country, they will feel very honoured to be offered some. Some of your staff would bring presents and if you feel uncomfortable with this, let the word out around the office well before the day itself. You do not have to reciprocate with the presents.

The festive feeling lingers into the next day as it is another public holiday, the Tamil festival of Kavadee. For the Creoles however, the New Year merrymaking does not end until 8 January, called *le roi boire* (literally, 'king of drinks'). As its name suggests, this is one last bash when they indulge in heavy drinking. Many workers may not turn up for work.

Thai Poosam Kavadee

Although Thai Poosam Kavadee can be celebrated any time in January or February, the official public holiday is on 2 January. The main Tamil temples hold a Kavadee procession followed by fire-walking on the temple grounds.

Thai Poosam is dedicated to Muruga, the favourite deity of the Tamils. The ten days preceding the festival are considered to be sacred and devotees fast for the whole period. A thorough bath is essential and they eat only vegetarian meals prepared at home. Every day they go to the *kovil* (temple) with offerings of coconut, fruits, camphor, oil and incense. After washing and decorating the deity, they start the worship, first with silent prayers, then with loud hymns punctuated with shouts of 'Arohara' (meaning 'Glory to God').

The Kavadee is an arch-shaped wooden structure which the devotee carries on the shoulders as a sign of penance. It is decorated with flowers and leaves, some with very elaborate designs. On the day of the ceremony, the priest pours some milk into two small brass pots which are tied to each end of the Kavadee. The procession starts from a river where the purification rites are carried out and winds its way through the town or village to the temple. At the end of the procession, the milk is poured onto the deity and some of it is collected and drunk by the devotees. The fact that it has remained fresh despite the summer heat is taken as a sign of Muruga's greatness.

The most spectacular aspect of a Kavadee procession are the acts of self-mortification which the devotees indulge in. In addition to carrying the heavy Kavadee, they pierce various parts of their bodies with tiny needles. In some cases, the whole torso and back are covered with the needles, like a chain mail. The fire-walking is another exhibition of penance and piety. A large pit is filled with 15 centimetres of glowing embers. Led by the temple priest, the devotees walk across this pit in single file to the sound of Aroharas from the onlookers. The fire-walking leaves no scar on the soles of the devotees. It is said that if the ten-day fast has not been properly performed, the person will bleed when being pierced and will get burnt on the coals.

Being a Spectator

The Kavadee procession can be observed along its route from the river to the temple. On the day of Thai Poosam, several processions are held in the major towns, Port-Louis and Rose-Hill in particular. If you are interested, try to find out the route and station yourself along the pavement with the other townspeople. You can also watch the fire-walking in the temple grounds. The one in Rose-Hill has chairs laid out for spectators around the smouldering pit, but you have to pay a small fee. Cameras and video cameras are also allowed.

Chinese New Year

Officially known as the Spring Festival, Chinese New Year falls sometime in late January or February. Only the first day of the New Year is a public holiday, although many Chinese workers take leave on the second and third day. As a rule, children do not go to school on the second day. Shops and other small businesses owned by Chinese close for at least three days, even a whole week in some cases.

Preparations for the new year start a fortnight or a week before with the thorough cleaning of the house and the making of New Year cakes. These are actually fried pieces of dough containing sesame seeds and purchased prawn or fish crackers. Every family gets together to make these cakes. One cake which is not made at home is the *gâteau la cire* (literally, 'wax cake'), an extremely sweet and sticky pudding made with glutinous rice flour and brown sugar and flavoured with orange peel. In the Hakka dialect, it is called *diam pan*, meaning, aptly, 'sweet pudding'. New Year cakes are consumed by the family during the two weeks that the festivities last and are distributed to friends and neighbours, with *gâteau la cire* being a hot favourite.

The festivities start on New Year's Eve with the reunion dinner when the extended family gathers for the best meal of the year. The older folks make offerings of incense and food to the sky god in the morning and complete the ritual with some firecrackers. Remember it is a great honour for you to be invited to a reunion dinner because traditionally this is for the family only. You are not expected to bring any present, but a bottle of liquor (the Chinese prefer whisky) and some sweets for the children will be appreciated. After the dinner, the adults give *foong pao* (red packets containing money) to the younger ones. You do not have to give any to your Chinese friends' children if you visit them, but they will give one to your children. It's meant to bring good luck and is not strictly speaking a gift. The evening is spent drinking, playing mahjong or cards, and firing crackers for the children. Many young and not so young people round off the evening at a dancing party, with a countdown and letting of firecrackers.

On New Year's Day itself, all Chinese households let off firecrackers at different times of the morning depending on when they wake up. The red residue of the crackers is not swept away because it brings good luck. Many households also do not sweep the floor on the first day of New Year for fear of sweeping away all the good fortune enjoyed during the previous year. Some families go vegetarian on this day. One pragmatic aspect of the Chinese community is that they would offer incense at the temple before going to the church for the New Year service.

In addition to visiting relatives and friends, it has become customary to go to the beach for a picnic. This makes sense as you get to meet more people this way. Food-wise, the picnic might consist of a pot of curry or *briani*; rarely is any Chinese food consumed at the beach. And, of course, gambling takes place here too.

Merrymaking (and gambling) goes on for the whole fortnight culminating in another reunion dinner at *niat pan* (half month). One card game that is played during this period is called *van lak* (a form of blackjack). It is popular because many people can play it and even young children can join in because it is so simple. In the last few years and with growing affluence, many families have chosen to spend the New Year holidays at a resort hotel, thus avoiding the hassle of cooking for a large number of people and cleaning up after them. The other advantage is that some hotels have a casino and the adults can gamble the night away. Many hotels have specials during the Chinese New Year period but you should book well in advance because rooms are limited.

Maha Shivaratri

One of the most popular Hindu festivals in Mauritius, the procession to Grand Bassin in the Plaine Champagne area is a colourful sight that gives the other communities a glimpse of the fervour and devotion of Hindus. Maha Shivaratri is dedicated to Shiva, who is also known as the upholder of the Ganges River. To the Hindus, Grand Bassin is the reproduction of the Ganges in Mauritius, and they call it Ganga Talao, the Lake of the Ganges.

Preparations for the festival start weeks ahead, including at least one whole week of fasting. Three days before the festival, devotees from all over the island start on their pilgrimage to Grand Bassin. Dressed in white and in small groups, men, women and children travel on foot, a journey that sometimes covers 50 km (31.1 miles). They all carry a small bottle and some carry structures (known as *kanwars*) made of bamboo and decorated with white paper, colourful streamers, mirrors and tinkling bells. Some of these *kanwars* are real masterpieces and so huge that they require several men to carry.

When they reach Grand Bassin, the pilgrims proceed to say prayers at the various shrines built around the lake. Every night, mass prayer sessions take place in the immense hall of the temple. The atmosphere is one of fervour and devotion. After saying their prayers and filling their bottles with the sacred lake water, the pilgrims slowly make their way back home, still on foot. The *kanwars* are left on the banks of the lake. The water is brought to the local temple to be poured over the Shiva Lingam, the stone symbol representing Shiva.

Holi

A harvest festival in India, Holi has lost its agrarian significance in Mauritius and is now mainly confined to those villages with a strong Indian presence. What remains is the joyful throwing of coloured powder or water at one's friends and acquaintances, accompanied by vigorous singing. *Melas* (meetings) are organised in various parts of the island where some speakers try to spread a social message and the crowds have fun singing and dancing. Sometimes the crowds are unwittingly forced to listen to an electoral harangue by politicians taking advantage of the *mela*.

In the evening, after a thorough scrubbing, friends embrace each other and children pay respect to their elders. Sweetmeats are also exchanged.

Take It In Your Stride

Holi is characterised by red because it is the colour of joy for Hindus. If you get hit by a balloon filled with coloured water or some red powder while walking or travelling in a village, do not kick up a fuss. You may be annoyed that your pristine white shirt is utterly ruined, but no malice was meant and you should take it in the spirit of the festival. Generally people do not throw colour at strangers, only when they see friends or someone who is visibly also celebrating.

Eid-ul-Fitr

This Muslim festival takes place on the 29th night of the fasting month of Ramadan. A group of religious people take a boat out into the open sea to search the sky for the first sign of the new moon. If they do not see it, then the fast continues. If the moon appears, however, the fast ends immediately and the next day is Eid-ul-Fitr, popularly called Eid. The government sets aside a provisional date for the public holiday and the whole population tunes in to the news on the previous evening to check if the moon has appeared or not. Sirens also blare from the top of every mosque. It is a rather archaic method of determining a holiday, but it does make for some suspense and excitement.

Eid marks the end of a whole month of penance and communion with the divine. In the morning, every Muslim puts on elegant new clothes and the whole family sits down to a breakfast of *sheer korma* or *sewaiye*, a special Eid preparation of milk, vermicelli, sugar, nuts and flavourings.

The men then congregate at the mosque for the most important prayers of the year. After prayers, many families make their way to the cemetery to pay respects to the dead. The rest of the day is spent visiting friends and relatives to exchange greetings. Children receive gifts of money from their parents and relatives. This is a day for the family and most Muslim families entertain their friends and guests at home. Generally only Muslim friends are invited. However, they do give out sweetmeats and cakes to neighbours and friends of the other communities. Muslims greet each other with 'Eid Mubarak', Urdu for 'The blessings of Eid be with you'. It is quite all right for you to offer the greeting to Muslim neighbours or friends you encounter during the day.

Eid is not Eid to a Mauritian Muslim without *briani*, and every family prepares it by the *deg*-full. (*Deg* is the big brass pot used for cooking *briani* over a slow wood fire.) Some of your Muslim neighbours or friends might bring some *briani* over to your house. It is a real treat and you should show your appreciation profusely. You do not have to give anything in return; just offer them some of your own delicacies when you celebrate your next holiday.

Easter
Prior to celebrating Easter, the Catholic community observes a 40-day fast beginning on Ash Wednesday. As this day is

not a public holiday, the churches hold the service very early in the morning so that their parishioners can attend mass before going to work. If you see colleagues with some greyish stuff on their forehead, do not offer to wipe off the 'dirt'. It is merely the ash that the priest smeared on their forehead during the service. The more pious Catholics fast for the whole of the period of Lent, but most people only fast on Fridays or just Good Friday. Restaurants see a substantial dip in business during this time.

During Lent, Catholics attend what they call 40 *heures* (40 hours). The monstrance, which represents God's spirit, is exhibited at 40 different churches, one a day, ending at the Saint Louis Cathedral. Devotees try to follow the monstrance wherever it goes and pray there for an hour each time, thus making up the 40 hours.

Checking the Schedule

Check with your parish priest if there will be an exhibition in your local church, and if you want to know where to go each day, look up the schedule in *La Vie Catholique*, the weekly publication of the Catholic Church. The Catholic Church also publishes the complete time table in a small booklet. Some parishes organise pilgrimages to visit the monstrance during weekends.

Holy Week itself is a quiet affair, with evening services starting on Holy Thursday when the events of the Last Supper are re-enacted. Some parishes organise a single service for all their churches at a place that can accommodate more people. Despite the carnival atmosphere, the piety and devotion of those present is almost palpable. Evening services are held on Good Friday and Holy Saturday as well. And, of course, the Easter morning service is one of the most joyous of the year. Many families return home from the Saturday service to a real feast, not only to mark the joyousness of the occasion, but also as a relief after 40 days of fasting.

After the morning service on Easter Sunday, many Mauritians go to the beach for a picnic. Good food and plenty of liquor are packed and it is a day of fun for all. Getting drunk at Easter is almost part of the tradition for some. You can experience the Creole folklore at the popular beaches like Flic-en-Flac, Blue Bay or Mon Choisy when friends and relatives come together for impromptu *séga* sessions or games of cards and dominoes.

Chocolate Easter eggs are given to children, much in the same way as toys are given at Christmas. However, most of the Easter traditions of Christian countries, like egg hunts or Easter bunnies, are absent.

Rakhi

Raksha Bandhan, or Rakhi, is a celebration of sisterly love. The *rakhi* itself is a colourful wristlet trimmed with silver and gold threads, shaped a bit like a watch. Hindu girls and women tie the *rakhi* to their brother's right wrist and feed him a piece of Indian sweet while praying for his happiness and success. He, on his part, promises to protect her till death and gives her money as a token of his affection. The *rakhi* is worn whole day long.

For days before the festival, you will see shops and street stalls laden with the colourful wristlets. If you do take a liking to them, you can buy and keep them as souvenirs. You will not be offending anyone. However, it is not in very good taste to buy one and wear it yourself, especially if you are a woman. *Rakhi*-giving is not confined to blood sisters and brothers only. A woman friend might give you a *rakhi* and you should treat it as an honour. You are her '*rakhi* brother'. But don't worry; she does not expect you to pledge to protect her all your life. If you feel self-conscious wearing a colourful bauble on your wrist, gently explain to your friend that you are not used to it but that you will treasure this expression of her affection.

Feast of the Holy Virgin

Assumption is called *La Vierge* (the Holy Virgin) in Mauritius. Even though it is not a public holiday, it is celebrated by the whole Catholic community, especially the Creoles. The church service is well attended and some people take leave from work in order to celebrate. A week or so before the festival, bakeries start to market their 'Marie' or 'Virgin cakes'. This is a plain butter cake with white and blue icing (colours of the Virgin Mary) made special by the addition of a small figure of the Virgin Mary made with icing sugar. This cake is eaten after a good dinner complete with liquor, 'Marie cakes' are also sold by hawkers near markets and bus terminals. Bringing a rather irreverent flavour to the festival, these hawkers tell their customers to come and get their 'Marie', especially if they do not have a *mari* (husband)! Many families go to the beach for a picnic on that day.

Père Laval

Père Laval, the French priest who came to minister to the downtrodden slaves, is venerated by the Catholics and some non-Catholics as a saint who can perform miracles. Every day of the week, especially on Fridays and weekends, many devotees come to say prayers and invoke his help at his tomb in Sainte-Croix. The anniversary of his death on 9 September is commemorated with prayers and church services. On the eve, throngs of men, women and children make their way to Sainte-Croix on foot. Most of them leave home in the late afternoon or early evening, depending on the distance they have to cover. The procession from Mahebourg, at the other end of the island, is more than a hundred strong and is preceded by the bearer of a wooden crucifix. After saying their prayers at the tomb of Père Laval, the pilgrims attend one of the many services conducted in the church next door. Buses run exceptionally late that night so that the pilgrims do not have to trudge their way back home in the middle of the night.

If you live along any one of the main roads leading to Sainte-Croix, it would be a good gesture to leave a few pitchers of water and some paper cups on a table on the pavement outside your house so that the pilgrims can refresh themselves. And if you want to experience the spirit of devotion, the best way is to take a bus to Sainte-Croix and walk to the shrine. Despite the carnival atmosphere generated by the food vendors and sellers of candles and

Services are conducted in the Sainte-Croix church (above), but it is the tomb of Père Laval (below) that attracts the biggest crowds, especially among non-Christians. Devotees bring flowers and candles which they leave behind.

religious imagery, the fervour and piety of all those present is genuine.

Divali

The most important festival of the Hindu community, Divali celebrates the victory of good over evil as symbolised by the brightness of thousands of little oil lamps in the night. It is customary for Indian families to distribute cakes and sweets to neighbours and friends. Some of them have been prepared at home and others purchased. When you receive them, wish the giver 'Happy Divali'. The cakes and sweets are delicious and are best eaten on the day itself.

Indian families generally do not invite friends to celebrate Divali with them because they are all busy preparing for the evening. The little earthen oil lamps are arranged in rows along the path leading to the house and wicks are trimmed. A good luck pattern is also drawn outside the front door with coloured powders. The whole family gathers to say prayers to the goddess of wealth and offers fruits, flowers and sweets. The children's foreheads are daubed with red powder. Children love Divali because they get new clothes, sometimes even gifts of money, and are allowed to play with firecrackers and fireworks.

Many families have opted for the convenience of electric multi-coloured lights and Indian houses look really pretty with so many lights shining everywhere, even on the television antenna! A car ride on Divali night has become almost a ritual for children. Bonne Terre near Vacoas and the village of Triolet are good places to visit.

Ganga Asnan

A day to worship the sacred Ganges River, Ganga Asnan is celebrated at the beach in Mauritius. All Hindus take a bath at home first before proceeding to bathe in the sea, a form of cleansing the body before offering it to the Goddess Ganga. As many Indian women and some men are still very modest about their bodies, they go into the sea fully-clothed. Places with a wide stretch of beach, like Mon Choisy, Belle Mare or Flic-en-Flac, are most popular. After a dip in the sea, offerings of fruits, flowers and milk are made. The devotees also send out burning camphor and sandalwood on betel leaves, like many little floating boats of light in the sea.

Today most of the spiritual significance of the festival—cleansing oneself of sin and renewing the bond with nature—has been lost and Ganga Asnan for a lot of young people is just an opportunity to go to the beach for a picnic and some merrymaking. Because of the offerings and the sheer number of picnickers, the beaches tend to get cluttered with litter. The sea also is not that clean as the betel leaves get washed away. So, if you are very particular about the cleanliness of the beach, it might be a good idea to keep away from it on Ganga Asnan.

Christmas

No longer restricted to the Christian community, Christmas is now a day of merrymaking and gift-giving for the whole population. Some Christmas traditions like the tree and Santa Claus, called Father Christmas in Mauritius, have even been adopted by the other communities.

You will know Christmas is near when you see toys appearing in the stores, even your corner grocery. In general,

toys are not sold at other times of the year. A week or so before Christmas, trees come on sale near markets and churches. You can get a nice freshly cut tree for a very reasonable price. Prices hit rock bottom on Christmas Eve and some people do wait for that time to get their tree. Starting from 20 December, shops are allowed to stay open later, until midnight on the 24th. As many people do not get their year-end bonus until 24 December, shops are especially crowded that afternoon.

Christians attend midnight mass and come home to a nice supper. Others have a large dinner and go dancing afterwards. Again, people eat what they like best, and not some set traditional fare. Since Mauritius inherited its Christmas traditions from the French, turkey has never been popular but it is now gaining favour among some Mauritians. Carolling is also another 'imported' tradition, with some church groups and choirs seeing it as a means of making some money while they perform at Christmas functions or even in people's houses. Children go to bed early, leaving a window open for Father Christmas to come in. Instead of hanging stockings, Mauritian children polish their shoes and put them at the foot of the bed to receive their presents. Many write letters to Father Christmas, which they entrust to their parents to mail.

Gift-giving is very much entrenched as a Christmas tradition: children receive toys and friends give each other household items or personal items like clothing, even underwear! If you are invited to a friend's house for Christmas, remember to buy a present for your hosts in addition to toys for the children. A bottle of wine or a cake is not enough. Good gift items would be a nice set of crystal glasses, a china platter or a decorative piece for the house. It is also customary for bosses to give something, usually toiletries or chocolates, to their secretaries and for schoolchildren to buy their teachers a present before school ends.

LANGUAGE AND COMMUNICATION

CHAPTER 8

'To learn a new language is, therefore, always
a sort of spiritual adventure; it is like a journey of
discovery in which we find a new world.'
—Ernst Casirer

MAURITIANS LIKE TO SAY that they are fortunate as they know two international languages and believe that they would have no problem getting a job anywhere in the world. This is, of course, a fallacy as speaking French and English is not the most important qualification when looking for a job. And, besides, the world operates on a number of other languages as well.

THE OFFICIAL LANGUAGES

Mauritius' official languages reflect its colonial past. When the British took over the country, they were faced with a totally French-speaking population. Even today, English still remains a foreign language to almost everyone on the island. Its use as an official language is just one of the few reminders of the British administration, together with the parliamentary system of government and the school system. But, despite (and because of) its alienness, English will certainly remain the official language of the country. Being no one's ancestral language, it has a neutral and unifying effect and is acceptable to everyone. Creole, which is totally Mauritian in origin and which is spoken by everybody, is paradoxically deemed too crude to be an official language.

English, Mauritian Style

There is a French saying that people 'speak like a book' if they talk beautifully, and this is exactly how Mauritians speak

English, like a book, not because they can express themselves beautifully in the language, but because they speak 'written' English. The language has never been used in daily life and the Mauritian's knowledge of English is what they read in books, mainly school textbooks. The print medium is almost entirely French, and very few English-language movies are shown on television. One must say that the language situation is really unfair on students because school is taught in English and students have to take their exams in something that is not even their second language (third or fourth is more likely).

Most Mauritians speak English with a French accent, except for some members of the Indian community who sport an Indian accent. 'R's are grated rather than rolled and 'h's tend to disappear. 'Th' is a real stumbling block for many people because it does not exist in French. Instead you will hear 'v' or 'f' depending on the vowel following it—'eiver' or 'forough' for example. Another problem area is the pronunciation of 'ch' and 'j' sounds; many people would replace them with a 'z'. (This problem occurs in French too

because these sounds do not exist in Creole.) Mauritian English has a sing-song quality due to the use of French tones and stresses being put on the last syllable of a word and at the end of the sentence (like in French).

Vocabulary tends to be rather limited, especially in the use of synonyms, making speech rather monotonous and repetitive. Where there are several words with the same meaning, the one with a French root or connection is chosen, even if it is less commonly used. For example, the word 'legal' is preferred even when the meaning calls for 'lawful'—'legal wife' rather than 'lawful wedded wife.'

Sometimes it is Creole that influences the use of one word instead of another; 'prison' is almost always used rather than 'jail' because the Creole word is also 'prison.'

To Keep In Mind

Because English is learnt from books, Mauritian speech is very courteous with rather circuitous ways of saying things. Making use of direct words is considered blunt and discourteous. You might get impatient but it is very important for the Mauritian to use 'proper' words. It is a sign of good education and shows their knowledge of English. And it would be absolutely wrong to mistake courtesy for servility. Certain words may sound servile, only because that was the way English was spoken during colonial times. The words may be the same, but the spirit is certainly different.

The influence of American pop music and movies is readily felt in normal conversations. Young people pepper their speech with words like 'dude', 'cool' or 'OK'. The use of the word 'super', on the other hand, is essentially a French fad copied from American English. An American twang is also considered cool with the young, even among those who would claim French as their first language.

Political correctness in language has not reached Mauritian shores yet. And the influence of French, in which the masculine word takes precedence over the feminine one when they are used together, does not help either. One must say that most Mauritians are happily oblivious to gender stereotyping, even militant feminists.

So the key to conversing with a Mauritian is to use simple terms, avoiding slang and colloquial expressions. There is no need to speak too slowly because your friend will get the gist of what you are saying even if they do not understand every word. Comprehension and knowledge of English varies widely, with the more educated being able to speak it better. Those who have studied in English-speaking countries are also more fluent. However, even shopkeepers will understand your requests and will be able to make themselves understood by you, albeit in broken English and with the help of a few signs.

French

Long seen as the language of the colonisers, French now enjoys higher status and is widely spoken. There is much more creative writing in French than in any of the other languages spoken Mauritius. Every Mauritian knows at least a smattering of French, and more and more people speak it in the home as it is associated with gentility and good education. Young Asians who were not exposed to the language at home now talk French to their children when they bring up their own families. They believe that it will give them a head start when they go to school.

One characteristic of Mauritian French is that it has not evolved at the same pace as its original, especially in terms of vocabulary. The word for 'quill' (*plume*) is still used today to refer to a modern pen, while in France, the word *stylo* has been in use ever since the ballpoint pen was invented. The same holds true for 'bathing': the Mauritian takes a *bain* ('bath') rather than *douche* ('shower') even though very few houses have a bathtub! The more formal second-person pronoun *vous* is preferred to *tu*, which is reserved for children, family and close friends. Younger people might follow the French trend of addressing first-time acquaintances as *tu*, but only if they are of the same age group. Calling an elder *tu* is a sign of disrespect. Youngsters are also more likely to make use of slang. Another peculiarity, imported from Creole, is the addition of *la* to verbs to give a sense of immediacy.

The former French *colons* came from coastal areas such as Normandy or Brittany and the Mauritian accent today is reminiscent of those areas. Regionalism is also present in the vocabulary. The accent of the White Mauritian is distinctive in that 'r's are almost elided and the preceding vowel elongated, giving such pronunciations as 'Aathur' for Arthur. However, many people are acquiring a more Parisian accent with the help of French films on television and through contact with visitors from Reunion Island.

Having a working knowledge of French certainly helps, although it is not essential. For one thing, you will be able to read shop signs and save yourself the time and trouble of bumbling into different ones before finding the one with the required article. And you can have more meaningful

conversations with a larger number of people. Speaking broken French is better than none at all. No one will laugh at your attempts and, in fact, your friends and acquaintances will only be too happy to help with your pronunciation. Mauritians do feel proud of their ability to express themselves well in French and will take any opportunity to show it off.

The French Cultural Influence

The French like to make their former colonies believe that theirs was a cultural colonisation, as opposed to the British or Dutch economic colonisation. And they might very well be right, judging by the extensiveness of French influence even after more than 150 years of English rule and 40 years of independence. As most Mauritians have a better understanding of French, they are more likely to be influenced by French schools of thought. In literature as well, French writing techniques and philosophies are within easier reach of the Mauritian student. It is, of course, in the interest of the French government to have a more culturally attuned Mauritian population as the island's strategic location is as important as ever.

Hundreds of students enrol in French universities every year for a variety of reasons, mainly because they are free and admission requirements are relatively low. Nevertheless, it is a fact that the standard of teaching of fine arts and design in France is one of the finest in the world. The French government offers dozens of scholarships for studies ranging from literature to technology. These are attractive because some courses are held at the neighbouring Reunion University and the students can visit their family (or vice versa) on a regular basis.

French culture makes itself strongly felt through the Centre Culturel Charles Baudelaire, aptly named after the Symbolist poet most influenced by the islands of Mauritius and Reunion. The centre offers cultural activities such as film screenings, theatre work, group discussions and library services. The Alliance Française, on the other hand, concerns itself solely with the teaching of language. As French is taught in schools at all levels, the organisation is mainly responsible for setting language and literature exams based on a French model (French in schools is based on the British GCSE model). A few schools, both primary and secondary, make it mandatory for their students to sit for the Alliance Française exams because it gives them the opportunity to deepen their study of the language and its literature and philosophy. The most enduring literary icon of Mauritius, the romantic novel *Paul and Virginie*, was written by Frenchman Bernardin de Saint Pierre.

Low-brow French culture has also invaded Mauritian homes through the soap operas and variety programmes shown on television. French game shows have attracted quite a large following. In addition, visiting vaudeville and operetta troupes bring some witty entertainment to a population starved of quality live performances.

False Friends

False friends are those words or expressions which are etymologically similar in English and French, but with different meanings. It is useful to know what they are in order to avoid misunderstanding or, worse, offending. The following list is by no means exhaustive, but it gives a good idea of the kind of mistakes that can be made.

- *actuellement*   at the present moment
- *assurance*   insurance, but also assurance
- *bail*   land lease, not bail
- *boutique*   shop (usually grocery store)
- *confidence*   secret (n.), not confidence
- *corps*   body, not corpse
- *décevoir*   to disappoint, not to deceive
- *gentil*   nice (for person), not gentle
- *hypothèque*   mortgage, not hypothesis
- *lecture*   reading, not lecture
- *légumes*   vegetables, not legumes
- *librairie*   bookshop, not library
- *nouvelles*   news, not novels
- *proposer*   to make a suggestion, not to propose
- *récipient*   container, not recipient
- *sale*   dirty, not sale
- *son*   sound, not son

In addition, some words have a wider meaning in French than in English. Parents, for example, can refer to relatives as well as one's genetic parents. Cuisine, beside its English meaning, is also a kitchen. And you can have a drink in a café as well as drink it since the word means 'coffee'. On the other hand, French verbs denoting emotion do not carry the same intensity as in English: adorer simply means 'to like very much' whereas détester is 'to dislike'. But aimer can mean both 'to like' and 'to love'.

THE REAL MAURITIAN LANGUAGE

The language of the people, of course, is neither of those described above. Creole has evolved from the pidgin French spoken by the slaves into the national language. Everybody speaks Creole and you will find it easier to learn than French because there are so many more opportunities of hearing it in daily life. A potent unifying factor, Creole is truly a Mauritian language and it imparts a sense of identity and belonging to a culturally diverse people.

Creole used to be considered crude and even vulgar by some people. The compound term patois-Creole indicating that it is a 'second-class' language is now less commonly used because its speakers no longer feel apologetic about conversing in it. Mauritian Creole shares similarities with those of neighbouring Reunion and Seychelles islands and even with such far flung countries as Martinique and Guadeloupe in the French West Indies. This is undoubtedly because Creole came about under the same circumstances in all these islands. However, as the various countries develop further and are influenced by different factors, the languages will start to diverge.

A Language in the Making

Although we refer to Creole as the Mauritian language, it is not a language in the strict sense of the word. It is actually a patois that will evolve into a language at some point in the future.

Creole vocabulary is made up mostly of French words which are either pronounced as in the original or differently (mainly for the **ch**, **g** and **j** sounds which are all replaced by *z* and the diphthong **eu** which is rendered as *ay*). Because of its limited number of phonemes, the vocabulary tends to be restricted, with the same word having several meanings. For example, *pli* can mean 'fold' (*pli*), 'rain' (*pluie*) or 'more' (*plus*). The meanings are differentiated by the determinant used or by the lack of a determinant. In any case, the context always gives an indication to the meaning. As with any living language, Creole vocabulary is constantly increasing, with newly-coined words or words imported from other languages. The highest number of borrowings is naturally from English.

With regard to grammar and syntax, Creole diverges from French in that it simplifies grammatical structures. Gender differentiation and verb conjugation do not exist, but verb tenses are indicated by *pou* (future) and *ti* (past) and a combination of the two for the other tenses. Creole syntax is the usual 'subject + verb + object' type. Sentences tend to be simple because Creole does not have that many conjunctions for different clauses.

As it does not have a standard spelling system, you will rarely see Creole in written form. Many writers use the international phonetic system, but most Mauritians do not identify with it because they have learnt French and English phonemes only. (In this book I have tried to render the Creole sounds by English sounds that are the same or as close as possible.)

Learning Creole

Creole is not taught in schools although at the primary level, especially, teachers have to resort to the local vernacular to explain concepts and even to make pupils understand French and English literature. This means that there is no structured programme for learning the language. Your best bet is to listen and talk to people from all walks of life—the bus conductor, your domestic helper or office delivery man. If you know French, that certainly helps, but it is not essential. Creole is a very simple language, with few rules and restrictions. If you have children, they will pick it up almost from the moment you land in the country. The first words they will learn are without doubt swear words. These are colourful and give a definite flavour to the language. Learning their meanings and the intricacies involved in using them can

I LEARNED THE SWEAR WORDS FIRST

be fascinating. However, swear words in any language are meant to offend and you are strongly advised not to be too liberal with them.

There are a few phrase books purporting to teach Creole to foreigners. However, they are limited by the fact that they are mostly geared to the tourist or else are too academic to make learning enjoyable. Also, until a standard spelling system has been established, Creole will be difficult to read and learn from books.

Creole Literature

Before Independence, not much was written in Creole, unfortunately, because of the perception that the language was not 'pure' enough to convey feelings and ideas. It is sad to note that some present-day poets still feel this way. However, there is now a real flourishing, in terms of quality if not quantity, of writings using the Creole medium.

Creole writers (who can be Chinese, Indian, Creole or Muslim) look to day-to-day life for inspiration. They mostly write about what is wrong with Mauritian society and try to offer solutions. Highbrow philosophising is not their cup of tea. Most successful are poets and playwrights. The latter sometimes use actual events to weave powerful allegorical dramas. Fiction, in the form of novels and short stories, is not as popular. Again, efforts at establishing a sound Creole literature are hampered by the lack of a structured spelling system, rules of grammar and syntax.

Proverbs and Sayings

Creole proverbs and sayings point to the richness of the language and the wit and wisdom of the people. Older people pepper their conversations with figurative expressions and proverbs which originated from English or French but have been adapted locally. Creole jokes tend to be quite ribald, but are not unsuitable for polite conversation.

Riddles, called *zed mo* (playing with words) are popular with children. They help to learn words and are also the perfect medium for showing off one's cleverness. Playing riddles turns into a game of one-upmanship for many kids.

Meaningful Numbers

Variety is imparted to the language by the use of numbers to mean certain words. No one knows how these meanings came about, and new numbers get added to the list once in a while.

- two — monkey
- six — homosexual
- 15 — woman's breasts
- 32 — Chinese
- 35 — girlfriend (or, more common now, babe)
- 17 — boyfriend (but not hunk, interestingly enough)
- 40 — buttocks

Brand Names

Another feature of Creole is the use of brand names to refer to certain items. Usually they are modern conveniences and the name of the first brand to be introduced gets stuck in the minds of the people. Almost every household now has a *frigidaire* and you might be invited to someone's home for a *coca* (any fizzy soft drink). Cameras used to be called Kodak but the name has been dropped. A *kolinos* smile is nothing but a big toothy grin. Yogurt goes by the French brand, Yoplait, while *dahi* refers to the yogurt drink commonly called lassi by Indians. For a headache, a Mauritian would always take a *panadol*, even if the tablet is of a different brand. But if you hear someone say that they are *aspro* when playing gin rummy with friends, it means that they are missing only one card to win the game.

MOTHER TONGUES

Most Asians learn their mother tongue at home. Bhojpuri, the dialect of the majority Bihari group, is spoken by around 200,000 Indians. In rural areas, even young children speak it among themselves. The other Indians speak Telegu, Tamil or Marathi. Hindi, the language taught at school, is not really spoken at home because it is not the ancestral tongue of any of the ethnic groups in Mauritius. However, just as more families are switching from Creole to French, better educated Indians are dropping Bhojpuri as a home language in favour of Hindi, French or English.

Few Muslims converse in Urdu in public, or even in the home. Creole is much more widely used. Urdu is learnt at school or in the *madrassa*, but preaching in most mosques is conducted in Creole. The minority Gujarati group, however, has been more successful in retaining its language, mainly because its members (usually male) marry spouses from India. Children of these unions automatically learn their mother tongue from one parent. As for Arabic, it is taught at school and some of the preaching at the main Jummah Mosque is conducted in it, but it is nobody's mother tongue.

Hakka, the dialect of the majority Chinese group, is also declining fast. Grandparents still talk to their grandchildren in Hakka, but the latter answer in Creole. The Cantonese youth have a better knowledge of their language, but the situation is not really that much more heartening. However the presence of Hong Kong expatriates has given a boost to the language. Mandarin has been taught comprehensively in schools for more than 30 years now and more and more young people are quite fluent in it.

The African languages, of course, were lost a very long time ago.

LANGUAGE AS A STATUS SYMBOL

In a small insular and layered society like Mauritius, anything is used as an excuse to show off one's superiority, and language is one of them. What one speaks in public points to one's level of education and refinement.

Speaking French, of course, is considered the highest level of refinement. Many Creoles, Mulattos and Whites claim it as their mother tongue, even though they speak more Creole in everyday life. In general, parents speak French to their young children until the latter go to school and come back speaking Creole! French is the language of choice for polite conversations, when being introduced to strangers, in a job interview and in the classroom (with teachers, not classmates). Women tend to speak more French (being more 'refined') than men, but the latter would usually open a conversation with a newly-acquainted woman with a few words in French. Even if Creole is used overall, French words are thrown in to make the speech more 'polite'. When you want to put down somebody, you speak French or English, depending on your race. Creoles, Whites and Chinese would use French while Indians and Muslims prefer English. The Indian community traditionally had more problems pronouncing French sounds and were also more hostile to the language because their ancestors were exploited by the French planters. So English was their first choice as the language has links with India and it gave them a sense of superiority, since fewer people spoke English well. Today, this is changing; with Creole being more widespread, Indians have no difficulty learning French and several Indians have published critically-acclaimed books in French. The student population at the various French lycées in the country also shows an increasingly high percentage of Indians.

Stratification also exists among Asian languages. Indians who speak Hindi feel more refined and are better educated than those conversing in Bhojpuri. Polite conversations take place in Hindi because Bhojpuri is the language of 'uncouth' rural peasants. The Chinese who can speak Cantonese and/or Mandarin feel more fortunate because they can converse with the Hong Kongers and Taiwanese.

Speaking Creole in polite company, especially 'big' Creole (that is, without the addition of a few French words), is the height of crudeness. But it is paradoxically the language of friendship and of intimacy. And certain conversations, especially where jokes abound, would be flat and devoid of flavour in any language other than Creole.

BODY LANGUAGE

Mauritians have inherited talking with their hands from the French. Gestures accompany speech to emphasise a point or just to punctuate what is being said. However, body language tends to be more restrained than among the Mediterraneans.

Gesture	Meaning
A finger pointing to one's eye	My foot; I don't believe you.
Tapping the temple with a finger	He/She is not quite right in the head.
Making circular movements with the finger near the temple	He/She must be crazy.
A circle with thumb and index finger	Perfect!
Shrugging the shoulders	I don't know/care.
Thumb on nose and fingers outstretched	You can shove it where it fits!
Moving the hand across the throat in a slashing movement	I've been scalped.
Raising the right hand to shoulder level	I swear.
Two hands raised to shoulder level	Don't look at me.
Hands clasped together like in a prayer	I'm so sorry.

Obscene gestures abound. Thrusting one's hips forward means 'I urinate on you!' whereas drilling the palm with the finger indicates the sexual act. 'Giving the finger' is represented by two gestures: pointing the middle finger upwards the American way; and pulling up the right forearm while intersecting the left hand in the crook of the elbow (European style). Winking, considered innocuous in many societies, is a come-on sign if performed by a man to a woman.

Personal Space

Even though the population is made up of so many Asians, no part of the body is really taboo, except those considered 'private', of course. It is perfectly all right to touch somebody on the shoulder or arm. Patting the head, unless it is a child, is considered condescending and might be taken as an offence. Men tend to slap each other's backs when they are in high spirits and to show friendship. Putting an arm around the shoulder is another sign of cordiality. Holding hands, however, is reserved for lovers and children. Two men holding hands, especially, is sure to attract some dirty looks.

Kissing on the cheeks is very common and you should not read anything into it. Women kiss both men and women, children kiss adults, but men do not kiss each other. A handshake will do. Kisses usually come in pairs (on both cheeks) and sometimes in three's (alternating the cheeks). Most kisses are usually just a fleeting touching of the cheeks, so there is no need to be apprehensive if you are not used to such close contact. Hugs are less common unless the person is a long lost friend or relative. Some children are taught to hug adults ('squeeze the neck' in Creole) as well as kiss. Muslim men and women do not shake hands with each other, but a Muslim businesswoman would readily offer her hand for shaking if the man is non-Muslim. Indians might greet each other with a *namaste*, two hands brought together in a praying gesture but with non-Indians, they usually shake hands.

Mauritians stand at a comfortable distance when talking to people, close enough to be clearly audible but not so close as to be embarrassing. The space between a woman and a man should be slightly wider than between two women or two men.

THE MEDIA

The Mauritian government prides itself on being very liberal and democratic about the dissemination of information. The prime minister is also the minister of information and the only television and radio network in the country is a parastatal body controlled by civil servants and pro-government officials. So much for freedom of speech.

The radio broadcasts on two channels: one for French, English and Creole programmes and the other in Indian and Chinese languages. Air time for the second channel is limited and it helps to know the programming times before tuning in (newspapers publish the list of programmes). Very little air time is devoted to English-language programmes, although there are news programmes in English in the morning and in the evening. English programmes tend to be educational and are relegated to the less popular time slots, like late at night (BBC news or VOA). You can also listen to a few private radio stations, but most of them broadcast in French and they tend to focus on light entertainment.

There are three television channels, broadcasting in English, French, Chinese, Hindi and Indian and Chinese dialects. English-language programmes are scarce and the daily news bulletin is limited. Very little Creole is heard and the Creole news summary at the end of the main bulletin is almost a joke with no effort made at translating the headlines into simple and clear Creole. Movies and drama serials are almost totally in French, with English-language shows dubbed in French.

If you want to hear English language on television, you should subscribe to the cable channel, Sky News. However, this only broadcasts news, as its name implies, and British news at that. The rest of the world is relegated to barely one hour of coverage. There is a variety of other satellite channels showing movies, cartoons, sports and documentaries and variety shows.

Newspapers

The island's first newspaper was published in 1773, and since then there has been a steady stream of publications in a variety of languages and catering to different segments of the population. Local newspapers pride themselves on being independent and they are fairly successful at keeping government intervention at bay. There are seven dailies on the newsstands, with the morning *L'Express* and evening *Le Mauricien* enjoying the highest circulation. (They are also the freest of the lot.) Out of the seven, two are in Chinese and the rest in French. The only newspaper that is written mostly in English is the weekly *Mauritius Times*.

Now and then a newspaper will print an English article, usually an opinion piece contributed by an academic or someone else outside the journalistic world (journalists rarely, if ever, write in English). Although the style and manner of expression are not of the same standard as that of an English-language publication, it makes a refreshing change to read something other than in French. If you do not read French and would like to have a look at these occasional English articles, ask a Mauritian friend to keep a look out for these on your behalf. At other times, papers publish news from international news agencies in the original English language. Sometimes, though, the editing is fairly spotty and the news items may not even make sense.

Foreign Publications

Foreign newspapers are scarce and even when available, they would be a few days old. Magazines are more plentiful and current. The most popular English-language publications are *Time* and *Newsweek*. Sports publications are also very popular with Mauritian youth. *The Economist* is available, but not widely read. Lifestyle magazines in English are also available but transportation costs and the unfavourable foreign exchange rate often make foreign publications expensive.

DOING BUSINESS WITH MAURITIANS

CHAPTER 9

'The reason that worry kills more people than work is
because there are more people who worry than work.'
—Robert Frost

From a mainly agricultural economy at the time of independence in 1968, Mauritius has evolved into a diversified economy with the manufacturing sector leading in terms of revenue. No longer do Mauritians have to put up with the talk of deficits and currency devaluation that was current in the 1970s. The late 1980s saw high growth of 6–8 per cent that was likened to an economic miracle by those in power. The economy has now slowed down, but there are still wondrous opportunities for making money in Mauritius.

OPPORTUNITES
Although it is small, Mauritius aspires to be a high-tech society. As the country develops, more and more opportunities will arise for the keen-eyed entrepreneur. The government has identified a list of priority industries and offers attractive packages of incentives to those interested in the industries. The aim is to move away from the dependence on sugar towards a broader based economy that features manufacturing, finance and construction.

The EPZ
The Export Processing Zone (EPZ) was set up to give impetus to the manufacturing sector in Mauritius. Industries in the EPZ manufacture goods for re-export and benefit from tax breaks and preferential rates. The

Textiles and garment industries play a major role in the Mauritian economy.

powerhouse driving the Mauritian economy, it is no longer contained within a single location but covers the whole island.

For a long time, the EPZ was dominated by textile factories, mainly for woollen garments (Mauritius is one of the largest exporters of woollen knitwear in the world). The expertise of the local knitwear industry can be seen in the high quality of the garments produced by the factories. Textile was an obvious choice because it is labour intensive and requires very low skills. It brought in the cash and now, the Mauritian government wants to move towards a more high-tech economy.

Today, the government is actively promoting the development of the following industries:

- Electronics (production of parts like printed circuit boards, PABX systems, etc.)
- Printing and publishing (including desktop publishing, colour separation, as well as the production of books and magazines)
- Information techonolgy (software development, computer aided publications)
- Engineering (together with its support industries)
- Jewellery

Anyone interested in starting one of the above industries will still have to go through the usual channels, but the chances of approval are much higher. To set up a factory in the EPZ, you need an Export Enterprise Certificate delivered by the Ministry of Industry. A detailed feasibility study of the project as well as a bank status report are essential before you even file your application. Next you go to the Prime Minister's Office to seek authorisation to invest in the country. With these two approvals in hand, the next step is to apply to the Bank of Mauritius for Approved Status for Foreign Investment. It is only after all this that you can start operating in the country. In between, you need to apply for a manufacturing licence, building permits, electricity motor permit, police approval for vehicle parking facilities, fire brigade clearance, sanitation and hygiene authorisation and a host of other permits. The amount of red tape involved is mind-boggling. However, the machinery is well oiled and you will be directed from one office to another with competence and rapid efficiency.

Moreover, the government has set up the Mauritius Export Development and Investment authority (MEDIA) to help coordinate all EPZ investment projects. Its aim is to cut through the red tape so that you can start to contribute to the Mauritian economy as soon as possible. Made up of both public and private sector officials, it assists in factory start-up as well as identification of overseas markets. MEDIA operates offices in the following countries: England, South Africa, USA, France, Germany and India. For the respective addresses, go to the Mauritian embassy in the country. In addition, there are a number of private consultancy firms offering support services as well as legal and financial advice.

Operating a Factory and its Advantages

To operate a factory in the EPZ, you do not need phenomenal amounts of money. As long as your project lies within the targeted industries and it is sound, you can start with a couple of machines, a handful of workers and lots of hard work. The advantages are manifold: flat corporate tax of 15 per cent throughout, dividends tax-free for 20 years, complete exemption from customs duties on machinery and raw materials, free repatriation of profits. In addition, you get to enjoy a quality of life that is the envy of both developing and developed countries.

The Financial Sector

The government is also actively promoting the development of the financial sector in order to achieve a more sophisticated economy. The Stock Exchange of Mauritius is actively supported by the government and is seen as a means of mobilising funds on behalf of listed companies. You can trade in both local and foreign shares and, in spite of its small size, the exchange has been thriving.

Ultimately, Mauritius aims to become an important offshore centre for international businesses. To engage in offshore activities, you should first set up a company, either in Mauritius or in your home country, and then apply for an Offshore Certificate from the Mauritian government. If you are not a resident, then all business is conducted in currencies other than the rupee and you are not allowed to deal in property. If you already own a company in your country and want to establish an office in Mauritius, you must lodge a certificate of incorporation together with your company's memorandum and articles with the Registrar of Companies. If your documents are not in English, you should provide a translation. You must also register your office in Mauritius.

Benefits

Offshore companies enjoy a host of benefits: very low income tax, free repatriation of profits, no capital gains tax, no exchange control, double taxation avoidance. The Offshore Authority closely supervises all offshore activities so that the country does not become an avenue for money laundering by foreign drug lords and other dishonest characters.

The Mauritius Freeport

Another sector that is actively being promoted by the Mauritius government is the freeport, a duty-free logistics, distribution and marketing hub for the region. Mauritius is an ideal location for such a facility since the country provides access to the whole eastern and southern African region, a huge market comprising 425 million consumers. In addition, several trade agreements ensure preferential access for goods of Mauritian origin to the European Union and the United States.

The two key areas for freeport business are textiles and seafood. Mauritius is now the logistics hub for the storage and supply of raw textile materials to the EPZ companies of countries fronting the Indian Ocean, such as Zimbabwe, Madagascar, Namibia and Botswana. These companies also market their finished products through the Mauritius Freeport. As for the seafood hub, it provides storage and processing facilities for all seafood catch coming from the southern Indian Ocean. With the Indian Ocean holding one of the largest stocks of tuna in the world, Mauritius is poised to become a major centre for tuna processing and transhipment.

Setting up a company in the freeport is extremely simple. Through an electronic licensing system, applications are processed within 24 hours. With a Freeport certificate issued by the Freeport Unit and a Freeport Operator licence issued by the Customs and Excise Department at a cost of Rs 10,000 per annum, your company is ready to operate in the Mauritius Freeport, without any limitation on the range of products to be commercialised. Furthermore, foreign companies only need to register their company locally before starting operations.

Benefits

The benefits of operating in the freeport are manifold, with very attractive corporate tax incentives, free repatriation of profits without exchange controls, exemption from customs duties, reduced port handling charges as well as access to offshore banking facilities. As of 2005, more than 350 companies have taken advantage of the freeport facilities.

Construction

Mauritius is experiencing a veritable property boom as a result of its relentless development. Old ramshackle buildings in the town centres are making way for spanking new high-rises while more and more agricultural land is being cleared for residential development. Property development definitely offers immense opportunities for making money. You can either buy up a row of shops, raze everything to the ground and put up a skyscraper combining shops, office space and residential apartments; or buy a plot of land and build houses for sale. The latter option is not as profitable since Mauritians are still in the habit of buying their own land and building their houses according to their specification. However, condominiums in the popular coastal villages are a real money-spinner. Or you can build service apartments by the beach. Whatever option you decide upon, though, remember that non-residents are not allowed to buy land, so you will need a local partner.

Dabbling in property requires considerable capital. But, if you do not have unlimited means, you can still join the fray by starting out small, then using your profits to go into bigger ventures. Local banks and other institutions are willing to finance your business to a large extent, especially if you or your partner personally know the manager. Finally, remember that with the unfavourable rate of the rupee against major currencies, your small capital might go a long way in Mauritius.

Related skills are in high demand, such as architects, engineers and decorators. Judging by some of the ugly monsters that dot the landscape, an architect who understands the climate and the heritage of the country should do good business.

The Creative Industries

If you are good with a pen, pencil or paintbrush, there is a lot of scope for striking it rich. The creative industries (advertising, publishing, or design) are still in their infancy and look set to grow at a good pace. Image is taking on more importance and advertisements as well as office decor tend to become more sophisticated. An office is not just a collection of desks, chairs and filing cabinets any more, although you will find that most offices are just that. Managers now want their offices to feel and look comfortable so as to offer a pleasing view to visitors as well as staff. Individuals also seek

A thriving industry is the manufacturing of model ships. Mauritian artisans are highly skilled and learn quickly.

out interior designers to decorate their multimillion-rupee houses. However, artistic talent alone will not take you very far. To be successful, you should read up on the heritage of the people and mix around for a while in order to get a feel of the tastes of the various segments of the population. Mauritian society is divided by race and education level, as well as income.

Mauritians are innately artistic, but lack technical knowledge. They can come up with the best colour combination for a room, but will not always be able to maximise the use of space. However, they are sharp and learn quickly—a few pointers from you and they are ready to tackle the next job. So you will have no problem recruiting staff and training them on the job if you wish to venture into design or advertising. When you are dealing with words,

Pifalls

Watch out for certain pitfalls:
- Bureaucracy is slow and tortuous. Give yourself ample time to secure all the relevant permits before starting operations. It will not do to take orders and then find out that you will not get clearance from the fire brigade or town council until a few months later.

though, remember that the average Mauritian is much more fluent in French than in English.

> **Be Warned**
>
> If you decide to venture into any of the creative industries, be warned that it will take a while to turn in a profit. Although good designers and copywriters are scarce, you will still have to convince people that they do need your services.

Employment

What if you have no inclination for big money? Or do not have enough capital and are unwilling to put in the effort to open a factory in the country? Perhaps you only want to earn enough money to make a decent living in Mauritius. You can

- Mauritian workers are skilled and learn fast. However, they have not been exposed to certain types of industries, such as high-tech manufacturing. So, do a proper survey of the labour force. Otherwise, you might have difficulty recruiting qualified staff.
- Despite the government's assurances, infrastructure is sometimes not adequate. Electricity, for example, might not be powerful enough to operate your machines.
- Mauritian workers like to take short-cuts to do less work or show that they are smarter. (In fact, taking short-cuts is almost a national pastime.) Make sure that their short-cuts, such as disposal of wastes, do not land you in trouble.
- The Mauritian legal and financial systems are a hybrid of French and English systems. Do not assume that you are familiar with the whole system if you notice that parts are similar to what you already know.

always apply for employment in the country. This means that you come here as a tourist and then look for a company that is willing to take you in. Then you apply for a work permit from the Minister for Employment. Processing usually takes about two months. Approval is more likely to be granted if you have a skill that is in short supply in the country or have found a job at director level in a foreign company. You also need a work permit if you are going to be doing business in the country for more than three months.

Alternatively you could try your hand at a small business venture that does not require much capital outlay. The retail sector still offers scope for novelty or gift shops. Or you can offer consultancy services from home, anything from etiquette to language lessons. With some resourcefulness, the possibilities are boundless.

SETTING UP

As they say, setting up is always the toughest part. Once you have started working in Mauritius, then everything will be that much easier. And you will learn the ropes as you go along. Before you start, it is good to have an idea of the type of environment you will be working in and of the resources available to help you.

Partnerships

You want to do business in Mauritius but are unsure of whether you can go it alone? Then the obvious answer is to get a local partner. Your contacts in Mauritius may be able to suggest someone who will be interested in setting up a company with you. Or there are a number of establishments, one of which is the MEDIA, that will help identify a reliable partner for you. Do not advertise for one in the press. Any bona fide entrepreneur looking for a partner is already registered with the MEDIA or local consultancy firms. The next step is to incorporate your company, which can be limited by shares or by guarantee. After this, you apply for all the relevant permits and can start operations.

It pays to be cautious when dealing with a would-be partner, especially one who has come through informal channels. Try to check up on their background. This is going to be difficult, but a look at the registry of companies, for example, might give you an idea of whether the person was involved in criminal breach of trust with a previous partner. There have been instances where trusting foreigners have been duped of their money by 'hit-and-run' partners, not quite con artists but dishonest enough to slowly siphon the funds into other ventures. Also make sure that the collateral put up by your partner is equal to their share. Obviously you will not be able to do the background check by yourself. The best person to help you would be a reputable legal or accountancy firm.

You should also not be offended if your would-be partner seems to be suspicious of you. In front of you, they will seem eager to set up business with you, but they are not naïve. Enough Mauritians have been conned by foreigners to make them wary. They will run checks on you and question your sources of income because they do not want to be part of a money laundering operation.

BUSINESS MEETINGS

Mauritians are an informal people and they conduct business in a leisurely fashion. They do not like to be rushed into approving a plan or placing orders. The American-style fast talker is irritating because they want decisions on the spot. In the face of such forceful attitudes, the Mauritian business person is more likely to clam up. They will not listen to a glib sales pitch because they do not want to be taken for a ride. On the other hand, meetings must produce a result. Decisions are taken, albeit after much discussion. Everyone is allowed their say and all suggestions are studied seriously, which is why meetings tend to drag. If you come from a culture where everyone comes armed with statistics and a meeting moves like a military drill, then you will be frustrated by what you perceive to be the lack of preparation of your colleagues and the way some people seem to make comments just for the sake of talking. Sometimes you might be taken aback that your business contact is still asking questions when you thought that the meeting was called to seal a deal. And be prepared for changes of mind; they might go back and think that they have been too easily convinced by you and would like to reconsider.

Meetings are non-confrontational and if you cannot agree on a price or a course of action, you go back and think about it. If you have other suggestions, you can call for another meeting. But, if you cannot offer anything constructive, then the rest of the business is carried on over the phone. Your Mauritian partner is always polite and will make compromises if need be. This is why their occasional frankness can be really disconcerting. They think nothing of asking you, "Are you sure you are not taking me for a ride?" right in the middle of your conversation. This will be said with a rather sheepish smile and in a jesting tone, but they are dead serious. Do not treat it as a joke. You should do your utmost to convince your contact that you are genuine and serious about doing business with them.

If your meeting takes place in an informal setting, like a hotel coffee house, then the custom is to have a drink (either tea or coffee) while discussing business. If the meeting is in an office, however, it is unlikely anything will be offered to you. Mauritian business people make sure that they schedule meetings at 'safe' times, that is, well away from meal times. But, if you are thirsty, go ahead and ask for something to drink. It might just be a glass of water, but it will be welcome relief for a parched tongue. Never expect anything to eat, not even a light pastry.

Punctuality

It is of utmost importance that you make it on time, especially if this is your first meeting. If you are still staying in a hotel, your Mauritian partner will come and meet you there. If your meeting is elsewhere, then you could use the excuse of not being familiar with the place for any tardiness. However, this will create a bad first impression. Punctuality is a virtue and indicates your eagerness to do business. If you are always late for your meetings, maybe you will not be able to deliver the goods on time.

At work, you can be late for a meeting, provided you arrive before the boss. Take your cue from the boss. If they are in the habit of delaying the start of a meeting, then you can give yourself a few minutes' grace. But if they are always punctual then you had better be there on time. Actually some bosses expect everybody to be waiting for them; it is a sign of respect. Ask your colleagues about the boss's habits.

Dress

Like the tone of the meeting, attire is also informal, but not to the point of being casual. Suits are not required, since most Mauritian men possess only one or two, which they wear for special occasions. However, men should wear well cut trousers, not jeans, with a long-sleeved shirt and a tie. Sleeves can be rolled up, but never wear a tie with a short-sleeved shirt, even if you find the weather much too hot. A tie over a short-sleeved shirt is the hallmark of a country bumpkin, and such attire might lead your business contact to treat you less seriously. As for the colour of your clothes, there is no restriction, although white or pale blue is preferred for shirts

and dark colours for trousers. However, if you prefer dark shirts or a trendy colour, do not let the local preference for pastel cramp your style. Always wear dark shoes.

Women have a wider choice, but again informality dictates the dress. A suit complete with jacket and classic blouse is much too formal and would put the others ill at ease. The usual attire is a plain dark skirt (red is OK) and a pastel-coloured blouse. Printed dresses are also appropriate, but choose one with a simple classic cut. Trousers are not frowned upon, but it is safest not to wear them for a first meeting. Traditional dresses, like the Indian *sari* or African robe, will also do. The Chinese *cheongsam*, however, has a kinky image not in keeping with a serious businesswoman. Shoes should have at least a one-inch heel. Flat pumps and loafers, however comfortable, are too casual. But sandals (with heels) can look quite elegant, especially with a *sari*.

It is all right for both men and women to wear jewellery, but never anything flashy and gaudy. Usually men should wear no more than a watch, a wedding or signet ring and perhaps a crucifix on a small chain. Women are allowed slightly more, such as earrings and bracelets. Costume jewellery can be worn, but good quality costume that does not look too fake. Do not wear anything that clinks or makes noise when you are explaining yourself.

Briefcases are not necessary, but if you do have one, it will impress the people you meet. It is perfectly all right to attend a meeting with a wad of loose papers, perhaps in a folder or a soft cardboard file, and a pen in your pocket. Some Mauritians may even carry just a diary.

Name Cards

Exchanging business cards is slowly making its way into the Mauritian business culture. So, in order to avoid any embarrassment, do not whip out your name card upon being introduced. Wait for others to offer theirs first—if they have one, they will do so immediately because it is a 'document' they are proud of possessing. There is no specific etiquette governing the giving and receiving of cards since they do not form part of the local business culture. However, holding the card with both hands and bowing slightly denotes respect for the other person. On receiving a card, glance at it and make some comment. It shows you have been impressed. If the person you are meeting does not have a name card, you can still give yours, at the end of the meeting, just before the parting handshake. Say, "This is just to remind you of my contact number" or something to the same effect. Do not make it look as if you are establishing your superiority.

Printing Your Own Name Cards

In Mauritian firms, junior executives and even middle managers are not given name cards by their companies. If you are used to carrying one and feel that it befits your status to have one, then you have to print your own. Ask for permission to include your office address and phone number. Otherwise, you should only put your residential address on the card.

Greetings

Mauritians are still conservative and using first names is not considered dignified enough. Even if you have been dealing with the same person for years, but your relationship has not moved beyond business, you still call each other Mr, Mrs or Miss. Do not ask them to use your first name; they will be put in an awkward position. Even among colleagues, the older ones expect the title—sometimes with the first name, but the honorific is important.

All business encounters start and end with a handshake. Women might offer their cheek to be kissed, but only after they have become familiar with you and you have established a cordial relationship. At work, you do not have to shake hands with colleagues. A cheerful 'Good morning' and 'Goodbye' are enough. If you are greeting an older person, it is good to call them by their name.

The Bill Fight

When you are having a business lunch or dinner, it is understood that you do not have to pay since you are the visitor. You do not have to fight to pay the bill. If you want to pay, just say so and your guest will not put up any objection unless it is blatantly a case of bribery. Splitting the bill is not done.

If you are eating out with colleagues, however, going Dutch is the norm. You pay for your share of the meal and, if you are the only person to have ordered a beer, you do not expect your friends to foot the bill for that. Sometimes the bill is split evenly among the diners, but if you have ordered individual portions, then the norm is for each person to pay for what they have ordered. However, if you go out on a regular basis with a group of colleagues, then you might decide to take turns to call for the bill. When this happens, make sure you do not order more expensive stuff than the others when it is not your turn to pay.

WOMEN IN BUSINESS

The business world is still dominated by men, although there are a few very successful women in the field. Mauritian businesswomen still like to be treated as women and expect the men they meet to show them little courtesies, like opening the door for them. Paying them a compliment on their appearance will not be construed as making a pass or sexual harassment. Mauritian businesswomen are feminine and might pour your tea for you, but make no mistake about their competence. They can be as sharp and incisive as any man, even though they appear soft-spoken and gentle. However, you do not have to limit your conversation to business matters only. After you have closed your discussion, you can ask about their family and they will be very happy to talk about their children and other domestic matters.

Businesswomen have no hang-ups about male chauvinism. Even though they are operating in what is basically a man's world, they do not want to be treated as men and have no need to assert themselves.

If you are a woman coming to Mauritius to do business, try not to be too forceful. Even though the attitude of the male businessperson may be labelled condescending if applied in your country, do not take offence. They mean no harm and do not consider you their inferior. Many a time you will probably be mistaken for a secretary. If you come with a male partner, you might even be taken for his mistress! No need to raise your hackles. After your identity has been established, your Mauritian counterpart will treat you with due respect. Here, you can be relaxed and as feminine as you want to be. But never flirt with the men you meet (they might try to, but you should not respond). However efficient you are, you will lose all credibility.

BUSINESS ETHICS

Although morality dictates that everything must be above board and open to scrutiny, underhand methods and backdoor procedures are still very much part and parcel of doing business. There is much hypocrisy in the business world in the sense that everybody is aware that some firms use not-quite-transparent methods, but no one will criticise them for it.

Accounting

Many Mauritians still view taxes as robbing them of what is rightfully theirs. They have worked hard for their money and are reluctant to part with even one cent. Which is why many small businesses, especially shops, have been operating at

a loss for decades—on paper. One of the main tasks of the accountant is to ensure that the company pays as little tax as possible. Tax avoidance is the name of the game, and tax evasion is also sometimes played.

Most large companies, especially public ones that are accountable to their shareholders, keep their books in proper order. If there are loopholes in the law, they will certainly exploit them. But they will not create 'loopholes' so as to evade taxation and cheat shareholders.

It is those smaller companies managed by the owner which might display spotty bookkeeping. The accounts are purposefully complicated so that it is not easy to ascertain the state of the finances. In cases where partners are involved, the dormant ones may not receive a dividend for several years, or the funds may be diverted by the active partners into their private individual concerns. Many companies do not balance their accounts until the end of the year. By then, it might not be possible to detect irregularities.

Kickbacks and Corruption

The general perception is that corruption is not as rife as it used to be. Corruption of public officers is perhaps unavoidable in a society where everyone is scrambling to better themselves financially. Sometimes you will find that there is no other course of action but to grease the palm of somebody in authority in order to move your project forward. In fact, some officials will sit on your files until you offer them some incentive.

The private sector also witnesses its fair share of kickbacks. The purchaser in your company might go to a particular supplier because the latter offers them personal advantages, like a commission on the orders they place. If you come across cases of corruption and have no means to right them, then it is better to just keep quiet. Making the whole thing public might attract antagonism and life could become difficult for you. If you are the object of unwanted gifts, tell the bearer off in a diplomatic way. Do not be censorious and act offended. Just make it clear that you are not used to such practices and do not condone them.

THE WORK ETHIC

If you come from a culture that venerates hard work, you might be shocked by local work attitudes. Work is only a means of making a living; very few people take undue pride in their work. They are satisfied that they have completed their task, but do not derive much satisfaction from doing the job. Few are those who will put in weekends just to complete a job; if they cannot make it by the deadline, they cannot make it—it is no big deal. They are not going to lose any sleep over the matter. They will complete it when they can.

You might find your colleagues lazy because they come in and leave on the dot, and work the strict minimum number of hours required. They, on the other hand, probably think that you are a fool for slaving away longer than necessary at your desk. It is just a different philosophy. Life is made for having fun; work is a necessary evil because it gives you the means to have fun. So, as long as you have put in a decent number of hours each day, you have earned your salary and deserve to have fun. In a country which is so conducive to having fun, who can blame them? You might find yourself adopting the same attitude as you ease yourself into the relaxed way of life.

Nepotism

One of your colleagues comes up to you one day and tells you that a cousin or nephew/niece has applied for the vacant clerical post in your department. Can you help? You might find that such a request smacks of nepotism, but it is perfectly normal in Mauritius. It is one's duty to help one's family, and your colleague might think they are doing the company a favour since they know the character of the job applicant. What should you do in the face of such a request? Do not reject it outright. If the relative is qualified for the job and would not be depriving a much more deserving applicant, then it costs you nothing to employ them. On the other hand, you win the gratitude of a respected colleague. Who knows, you might need their help some day. However, make it very clear to your colleague that, had the relative not been qualified for the job, you would not have given them a second chance, not even for their sake. Otherwise you will end up having to entertain other similar requests, sometimes unreasonable ones as well.

Favours

Colleagues are always asking favours from each other, such as standing in for them at a meeting or helping them complete an urgent task. These are standard requests and it is not very nice to refuse, unless you are caught up in something else. Remember that if you do not help your colleagues, no one will come to your help when you are in need. However, there are certain requests that could compromise your integrity. If a colleague asks you to tell the boss they are busy in the storeroom when, in fact, they have left the office early, you can draw the line here and say that it is against your principles. Say that you will not tell the boss that your colleague has left, but that you cannot lie. There will be some resentment, especially if the person is caught. You will also not gain the admiration of everyone for your integrity—solidarity among workers is an overriding principle—but you will not attract such requests again.

Sick Leave

Every worker is entitled to a certain number of days of annual leave—'local' leave in Mauritian parlance. The amount varies according to the category of the worker. You can take a 'local' any time you want, but have to give three days' notice. Unless the office will go bust without you, the application is usually granted. If you are the boss and absolutely need the presence of an employee on a day they have applied for leave, try to work out a compromise, such as giving them half a day off. In Mauritius, personal matters come before the needs of the company. Appealing to the sense of loyalty does not work because workers feel that their leave is their due and they can take it whenever they want to.

In addition to the fixed 'local' leave, a worker can take sick leave for up to three days at a stretch without having

to provide a medical certificate. You just call up your boss and say that you will not be turning up today because you are sick. No questions are asked, and you can do the same thing the next day. If you will not be working on a fourth day, then you go to see a doctor on the third day and ask for a medical certificate. You send in the document on the fourth day, not when you resume work. The number of sick days is also fixed, but this little scenario can repeat itself a few times in a year. Basically, you can take all your sick leave without ever having to see a doctor. If you have consumed all your sick leave, you can still fall sick, but this time you need to furnish a medical certificate. The employer has the discretion to pay your full salary, half-pay or no pay.

Of course, such generous legislation leads to abuse. Absenteeism and malingering are serious problems, especially among the lowly-skilled. Fridays and Mondays are the favourite days for falling sick, and you might hear a colleague wishing you a good weekend and telling

'Bridges'

When a public holiday falls on a Thursday or Tuesday, many workers take the Friday or Monday off so as to get a long weekend. This is called a 'bridge' because they are using the 'local' leave to connect two off days. It's a really good idea and sometimes the whole office closes for the day because too many workers are 'bridging' to make it viable to open.

you not to expect them on Monday because they are going to be on sick leave!

Office Politics

Like elsewhere in the world, you cannot escape office politics. There are always a few individuals jostling for advancement, currying favour from the boss or generally bootlicking those in authority. The key is to be able to recognise such people for what they are and not to be taken in by their wiles. Of course, you should never get drawn into office politics. However, as an outsider (since you are a foreigner), you might find yourself being used as a pawn by the various factions. Make it clear to all sides that you want to remain above their petty politicking. You can be good friends, but in the office you will treat everyone with equal fairness.

Office politics in Mauritius is complicated by the spirit of communalism. However fair you are, some venomous tongue could accuse you of favouring people of your own race or of one community in particular. There is nothing much you can do about this, except maintain a high standard of fairness at all times.

One of the most insidious ways office politics is conducted is through gossip and rumour-mongering. Certain rumours can be very damaging to a person's career or personal life. Never lend your ear to such gossip and never help to propagate it. Above all, never allow rumours to cloud your judgment of your colleagues.

Office Supplies

It is generally assumed that once you work in an office, you can make some office property yours. In fact, little things like stationery items are not even considered office property. Your workers have no qualms helping themselves to pens, staplers and paper for their own personal use. In addition to wasting quite a bit of stationery in the office, they think nothing of taking some back home.

If the situation is under control, do not make a big fuss about it. Your secretary will really be taken aback if you scold her for taking a few pens home. If you want to cut down wastage in the office, you will face an uphill battle. Recycling is still alien to most Mauritian workers and they see no reason to save on supplies because these do not belong to anybody in particular. They are just the property of this nebulous entity called the office.

Lead by example. If you consistently ask your secretary to photocopy both sides of the sheet of paper, and point it out to her when she forgets, it will become a habit after a while. She will then tell the other employees that this is your habit and they will follow suit.

The physical set-up of an office is no different from elsewhere in the world. The open-office concept, however, has not gained much ground yet. Managers are each given a cubicle while the clerks are grouped according to their department. For example, you will find all accounts clerks huddled in one room near the accountant's office. Secretaries and typists or general administration clerks are lumped together in the typing pool, which is an open space outside the managers' rooms. Filing cabinets are also stored here. Personal secretaries take dictation in the boss's office, but do their typing and filing outside.

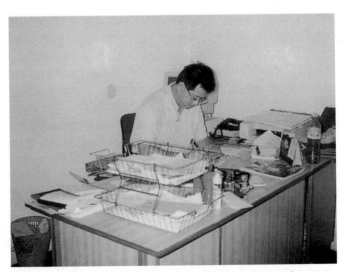

The Mauritian office set-up is basic: a desk with an in-out tray and a computer for the lucky ones.

The size of the office is proportional to the person's importance in the company. The accountant, who is considered more important than the personnel manager, is housed in more comfortable surroundings than the latter. When an office is part of a factory, the administrative area is generally one floor above the production department. Which is why Mauritian workers always say, "Go up to see the boss."

Hierarchy

Office hierarchy is generally fixed and there is not much interaction between one level and another. Clerical and junior staff rarely address the management by their first names. On the other hand, bosses always call their subordinates by their first names, unless the person is quite elderly. Some managers do stop by the typing pool for some light-hearted banter, but that is as far as it goes. Higher level staff do not discuss serious matters with the juniors.

Certain departments are considered more important than others. The finance people always receive more respect because they are dealing with the money side of the business (and also because the employees receive their pay packets from them). The marketing department is usually composed of people with lower qualifications who have made their way up from the sales contingent. So, even if their contribution is greater, they are treated with less awe.

As far as promotion is concerned, most Mauritian companies still value seniority over youthful dynamism. New staff have to earn their grade, even when they are more productive than the old guard. A young person is promoted above an older one only if the former has more paper qualifications. A new employee who is promoted rapidly always arouses the suspicions of colleagues and speculation about their relationship with the boss is bound to go round the office.

Many a time, academic qualifications are the sole criterion for employment and promotion. There is a general perception that people with degrees in the sciences are more intelligent than those in the humanities. So two persons doing the same job might be paid differently because of their different academic background.

'Boys'

Every office has one or two 'boys', (middle-aged or elderly) men with only primary education who are employed to shuffle the files from one department to another and to run errands for the company, such as taking the mail to the post office every day. Some offices prefer to call them messengers, although they do not really relay messages. Another important duty of the 'boy' is to attend to the needs of the administrative staff, especially making tea and coffee. You will be pleasantly surprised to find that most offices provide these beverages free to their staff. Of course, you are not supposed to order the 'boy' to make tea for you any time you feel like it. He prepares the beverages in mid-morning and serves every manager in their own office. The clerical staff usually help themselves at the little tea corner.

One of the unofficial perks of working in an office with a 'boy' is that he will also run personal errands for you. Do not make it a habit, though. But, if you have forgotten to pay your electricity bill and this is the last day, you can ask him to do you a favour and make a trip down to the CEB office. You will notice that some colleagues use the office 'boy' on a regular basis, even asking him to go to the market for them. Do not gripe about abuse of company resources. This is considered a private arrangement between the colleague and the 'boy', even though the errands take place during office hours.

Office Functions

Most companies have an annual party, usually on Christmas or New Year's Eve. Some have separate functions for management and junior staff, but in general this is the only occasion in the year for a token gesture of integration. Most executive staff put in a brief appearance and then perhaps move off to a separate, more elaborate lunch or dinner. The usual party is just a gathering of all the employees in a large room in the office, with drinks and snacks provided. You eat, drink and chat with your colleagues. This is probably the only informal occasion you will have to get to know some of them better. Emboldened by the liquor and the informal atmosphere, some junior staff might say certain truths to you about your management style that you do not want to hear. If you are afraid of being faced with such embarrassing moments, then by all means leave early. If, however, you feel that your credibility and authority will not be impaired, then go ahead and enjoy yourself with your workers. You might end up winning more loyalty than you expected.

Some factories organise an annual picnic for the factory operators. They hire a few buses and provide a packed lunch of fried noodles or *briani* and some drinks, including rum and beer. The workers never find the provisions adequate, so they come with their own supply of liquor. Again here, you can decide to board the bus with all the workers and spend the whole day with them, or take your car to the chosen beach and have lunch and maybe a game of football with them. In this case, it is advisable not to be too familiar with the workers, especially if you are a man and most of the operators are women. You never know what kind of accusation can be levelled at you the next day, especially if some of them get drunk.

LABOUR UNIONS

All workers in Mauritius have a constitutional right to join a labour group, called a trade union here to differentiate it from other types of union. (The French word is *syndicat*, but it does not have the shadowy overtones of its English equivalent.) The various unions are in turn grouped into federations, some affiliated to certain political parties. The trade unions have lost much of the power they wielded in the 1970s and early 1980s. Today's style is more consultative than confrontational, and labour disputes are fewer and are resolved through discussion.

If you are entitled to join a union, you should do so. Monthly subscription is minimal and you will have the full strength of the union behind you if ever you have a dispute with your employer. Joining the union also gives you a sense of solidarity with your colleagues.

Discipline

Mauritian workers are generally cooperative, but there is always the odd one who will try to create trouble. When faced with such indiscipline, the usual course of action is to warn the troublemaker and inform the company's union representative. Any disciplinary action you would like to take has to be discussed with the other managers. Never lay a hand on an employee, however provoked you are, and remember that whatever you say in the heat of the moment can be used against you. You might think nothing of scolding an employee for what you believe to be a flagrant mistake, but you will be in hot soup when the union files charges of intimidation against you.

Strikes

The incidence of strikes has greatly diminished. In the 1970s, crippling strikes by the port workers damaged the economy and led to them being made redundant when the government decided to build the bulk sugar terminal. Since then, unions have realised that strikes can backfire and have used them only as a last resort. However, threats of strike are still common.

When a strike ends, both parties go back to work, picking up from where they left. You should behave as if nothing has happened. Never show your resentment at the workers' attitude or blame them. When they went on strike, they were only exercising their constitutional right. Accusations may have flown during the dispute, and you should look at them objectively and see whether there is any truth to them.

FAST FACTS

CHAPTER 10

FOR MY NEXT TRICK
I'LL DISAPPEAR
IN A FLASH

'I've known, in scented lands that suns caress,
Under a canopy of reddened trees,
Where palms deluge the eyes with laziness,
A Creole lady's charms that no one sees.'
—Charles Baudelaire in his poem, 'To a Creole Lady'

Official Name
Republic of Mauritius

Capital
Port-Louis

Flag
Four equal horizontal stripes in a red, blue, yellow and green sequence from the top.

National Anthem
Motherland

Time
Greenwich Mean Time plus 4 hours (GMT + 0400)

Telephone Country Code
230

Land
Island in the Indian Ocean, off the east coast of Madagascar

Area
total: 2,040 sq km (787.6 sq miles), including the islands of Rodrigues, Saint Brandon and Cargodos Agalega

Highest Point
Piton de la Rivière Noire (828 m / 2,716.5 ft)

Climate
Tropical weather with trade winds from the south-east.

Natural Resources
Arable land and fish

Population
1,230,602 (July 2005 est)

Ethnic Groups
Indo-Mauritian (68 per cent), Creole (27 per cent), Sino-Mauritian (3 per cent), Franco-Mauritian (2 per cent)

Religion
2000 census: Hindu (48 per cent), Roman Catholic (23.6 per cent), other Christian denominations (8.6 per cent), Muslim (16.6 per cent), other (2.5 per cent), unspecificied (0.3 per cent), none (0.4 per cent)

Official Languages
English and French

Government Structure
Parliamentary democracy

Adminstrative Divisions
9 districts: Black River, Flacq, Grand Port, Moka, Pamplemousses, Plaines Wilhems, Port-Louis, Rivière du Rempart, Savanne
3 dependencies: Cargados Agalega Islands, Saint Brandon Island, Rodrigues Island

Currency
Mauritian rupee (Rs or MUR)

Gross Domestic Product (GDP)
US$ 15.8 billion (2004 est.)

Agricultural Products
Bananas, corn, potatoes, pulses, sugar cane and tea

Other Products
Cattle, fish and goats

Industries
Chemicals, clothing, food processing, metal products, non-electrical machinery, sugar milling, textiles, tourism and transport equipment

Exports
Clothing, cut flowers, molasses, sugar and textiles

Imports
Capital equipment, chemicals, foodstuffs, manufactured goods and petroleum products

Airports
The only international airport is Sir Seewoosagur Ramgoolam International Airport at Plaisance.

WRITING NUMBERS
Dates are written as day-month-year (dd-mm-yy). Commas indicate thousands and millions, and full stops are used for decimals, e.g. 5,250,789.34.

FAMOUS PEOPLE
Sir Seewoosagur Ramgoolam (1900–1985)
First local prime minister. Led the struggle for Independence and is still remembered, especially among the Labour Party, as the 'father of the nation'.

Sir Gaetan Duval (1930–1996)
Creole leader of the PMSD, the social-democratic party that opposed Independence. Served as cabinet minister in several

governments. Remembered for his political astuteness as well as his flamboyant lifestyle. Known as the 'king of the Creoles'.

Ti Frère (1900–1992)
Stage name of Jean Alphonse Ravaton, an extremely talented *séga* singer who could improvise a song on the spot. His broken voice was his trademark.

ACRONYMS

BoM	Bank of Mauritius
CEB	Central Electricity Board
CPE	Certificate of Primary Education
CWA	Central Water Authority
DBM	Development Bank of Mauritius
DWC	Development Works Corporation
EPZ	Export Processing Zone
GM	Government of Mauritius
MBC	Mauritius Broadcasting Corporation
MCB	Mauritius Commercial Bank
MEDIA	Mauritius Export Development and Investment Authority
MEF	Mauritius Employers Federation
MEPZA	Mauritius Export Processing Zone Association
MLA	Member of the Legislative Assembly
MMM	Mouvement Militant Mauricien, a powerful political party
MTC	Mauritius Turf Club
NHDC	National Housing Development Corporation
NPF	National Pension Fund
NTA	National Transport Authority
OTS	Overseas Telecommunication Services
PS	Permanent Secretary
SBM	State Bank of Mauritius
WC	Water Closet

HELPFUL HINTS FROM A TO Z
- Appliances can be bought locally, but they tend to be more expensive and with a limited range.

- Beaches ring the whole island. They are some of the best in the world and will feature regularly in your life in Mauritius.
- Creole is a language you will definitely learn. It is almost like the cement of Mauritian society.
- Dodo is the flightless bird exterminated by the Dutch as soon as colonisation began. Mauritius' only claim to international fame.
- Entrepreneurs fare very well in Mauritius. In addition, the local population has great admiration for anyone who earns big money.
- French is the language most Mauritians speak. It is very useful to know at least a smattering.
- Gambling rules the life of many Mauritians. There is certainly nothing wrong with wagering a few hundred rupees on a horse or at the casino, but do not allow addicted friends to lead you astray.
- Hotels are expensive but really pamper their guests.
- Invitations to dinner need not be reciprocated, but do your best to turn up at your friend's dinner party because Mauritians are usually very eager to get better acquainted with foreigners.
- Kissing on the cheeks is just a greeting, nothing more. Women kiss each other on both cheeks, and men as well. Kissing between two men is not accepted.
- Laid-back is what living in Mauritius is all about. You might think your colleagues are lazy, but their relaxed lifestyle makes for a happier population.
- Marriage is an entrenched institution in the country. If you and your partner are not married, there is no need to tell your Mauritian friends about it. They assume that you are.
- Neighbours are friendly, but the relationship rarely develops into first-name basis.
- Patience is a trait you will need a lot of when dealing with public officers.
- Quality of life is what you will enjoy in Mauritius: great weather, beautiful beaches, friendly people.

- Racism does not exist in Mauritius. Here it is known as 'communalism'.
- *Séga* is the song and dance of the slaves. It is easy to learn and no party is complete without it.
- Tea houses open very long hours and they are the best place to grab a bite when you get hungry in the middle of the night.
- Unions are worth joining if you are entitled to. Subscription is nominal and you get the full force of the union behind you in case of dispute with your employer.
- Visiting is an important part of the social fabric. Few people drop in unannounced, but it does happen when your friend has some business in your area.
- Whisky is the liquor of choice. No entertaining is complete without it.

CULTURE QUIZ

By now you should have a good grounding in what it takes to handle life in Mauritius. Although the island is known for its laid-back lifestyle it is not always a simple matter to become a part of that culture; from housing to doing business, you are sure to find things that are foreign and strange to you. Each situation you encounter while you are there will, of course, be unique but certain aspects of any culture remain constant. Test your skills with the following questions to see how ready you are to cope with life in Mauritius.

SITUATION 1

This is your first invitation to a Mauritian wedding. You are quite excited to experience this event as you have been told that weddings are a big thing among the local society. You certainly want to mark the occasion with an appropriate gift. You:

A Ask the groom-to-be what he would like to receive and tell him that your budget is around Rs 400.

ⓑ Go out and buy a beautiful painting which would look really nice in your own living room.

ⓒ Make a trip to an upmarket store and select a set of crystal glasses that cost about Rs 600.

ⓓ Put Rs 500 in an envelope and hand it to the couple on the wedding day.

Comments

If the couple is Chinese, then money is definitely an acceptable gift. However, you should try to find a *foong pao* (red envelope) and slot the Rs 500 note in. A safer bet is **ⓒ**. Glassware always makes a beautiful gift and your friends will be happy to see that you have made the effort to select a gift personally. They will be impressed by the fact that you bought it from an upmarket store; it shows you hold them in high esteem. You should certainly never tell a wedding couple what your budget is: it might be embarrassing if you find out that it is too low by local standards. Giving a painting is also not such a good idea because there is no guarantee that your friends will like it, even if you are absolutely in love with it. Few Mauritians display paintings on their walls.

SITUATION 2

Your teenage children need to attend a secondary school. Of course you want the best school for them, one that combines good teaching with a Christian education. You:

ⓐ Write to the Minister of Education and request that your child be admitted into a religious school.

ⓑ Pay a visit to the principal of the nearest 'confessional' school and enquire about vacancies.

ⓒ Call up the best school recommended by Mauritian friends and ask them to send you admission forms.

ⓓ Ask your church pastor to get your child into the school affiliated to your Church.

Comments

If you want your child to receive some form of Christian education, you have to go to a 'confessional' school.

Government schools managed by the Ministry of Education do not offer structured religious instruction. And it is no use asking for admission forms because these do not exist. Asking your pastor to help you may work, but the easiest course of action is ❸, that is, apply directly at the 'confessional' school of your choice.

SITUATION 3

There is a cyclone and a Class III warning has been issued. This is going to be your first experience of this tropical phenomenon. You want to be prepared for it. You:

ⓐ Rush home and make sure that all windows and doors are well secured.
ⓑ Make a trip to the nearest supermarket to stock up on emergency supplies.
ⓒ Carry on working because the cyclone has not hit the island yet.
ⓓ Call your friends to come over for a game of cards.

Comments

When a cyclone has reached Class III, the weather is already very bad and going out is very dangerous. It is no use trying to stock up on essentials now because all shops are closed. Calling your friends over is also putting their lives at risk. The only solution is to rush home and make sure that your house is well protected. You can certainly weather the cyclone out in the office, but there will be no electricity and you will not be comfortable at all.

SITUATION 4

You have been invited to have dinner at a new friend's house. The invitation includes your children as well. As this is your first time, you:

ⓐ Check the Yellow Pages to find a babysitter for the night.
ⓑ Bring your children along with you.

❸ Leave the kids at home by themselves and call up regularly to check on them.

❹ Decline the invitation because you do not know what to do with your children.

Comments

It is no use looking around for a babysitter because the custom of leaving young children with a stranger while the parents are out in the evening does not exist in Mauritius. And leaving the children alone at home would shock your Mauritian friends, in addition to being dangerous for the children themselves. The obvious solution is **❸** because your friends sincerely want to meet your children as well. Mauritian families always go out with children in tow. Declining the invitation would only deprive all of you of a good night out.

SITUATION 5

This is your first visit to your friend's house. It is a beautiful house and you are really impressed by the design. All of you are in the living room chatting and having a drink. However, you are really curious about the rest of the house. Dying to see more, you:

❹ Wait for your hosts to take you on a tour of the house.

❸ Say that this is the most beautiful house you have ever seen and ask for a tour.

❸ Ask about the size of the house and who built it.

❹ Request to use the toilet and cast a discreet glance on the way there.

Comments

Most Mauritian owners have their houses designed especially for them. But this is such a common practice that they never think that guests are interested in their house. So they rarely offer to take guests on a tour. Asking for one, however, is not polite. But you can certainly ask questions about the house and show your interest, but even then, they might not get the hint. The best is solution **❹**; as you walk towards the toilet, your host will point out the different rooms to you and you can find an opportunity to voice your admiration.

SITUATION 6

It is your colleague's birthday and they have invited your family for a dinner party. But you are not that close and do not know the person too well. In addition, you are feeling rather tired by the end of the week, and it has just been one invitation after another since your arrival. You have not had much time for your family. You decide to:

Ⓐ Give the party a miss but make sure to give your colleague a small present the next day at work.

Ⓑ Call up just before the party and say you are feeling unwell.

Ⓒ Turn up for the party and leave soon after dinner is over.

Ⓓ Tell your colleague to reschedule the party because you are feeling tired.

Comments

Even if it is your colleague's birthday, the party is also thrown in your honour, as a kind of welcome. They have invited friends to come and meet you and are looking forward to this opportunity to get to know you better. So, in order not to disappoint them, you should attend the party. You never know, it might turn out to be more enjoyable than you expected. So the correct answer is **Ⓒ**. Calling up just before the party to tell your colleague that you are not coming will cause great disappointment and make them lose face. And, of course, not letting them know is even worse.

SITUATION 7

It is the end of the week and your colleagues suggest going to a restaurant for a good lunch. You all select different dishes from the à la carte menu. Feeling relaxed, you order a beer to go with your meal. None of your colleagues does. When the bill comes, you:

Ⓐ Take out money for your share of the meal, plus the beer and a small tip for the waiter.

Ⓑ Tell your colleagues to split the bill evenly; it makes things easier.

Ⓒ Offer to pay for everyone since your meal is the most expensive of the lot.

Ⓓ Wait for someone to pick up the bill.

Comments

Colleagues do not expect a treat from anyone, unless it is a special occasion. Just because you ordered more food than the rest does not mean you have to pay for them. And just because you are a foreigner does not mean that you do not have to pay. Splitting the bill evenly does make things easier, but it is done only if the same group goes out together on a regular basis. Ⓐ is the usual scenario: everyone pays for their share, and if you have some loose change, you can leave it as a tip.

SITUATION 8

A colleague tells you that his niece has applied for the clerical post in your department and asks for your help. She has all the necessary qualifications, but there is another applicant who can type slightly faster. You:

Ⓐ Scold your colleague for offending your integrity.

Ⓑ Offer the job to the better qualified person and tell your colleague that the niece does not deserve the job.

Ⓒ Drop the girl from consideration because you cannot condone nepotism.

Ⓓ Give the job to the niece, but tell your colleague that it is only because she is qualified for the job.

Comments

In Mauritius, helping one's family is not considered nepotism. In fact, it is this family spirit that is at the root of many enterprises' success. Your colleague is helping both their niece and the office since they can vouch for her character.

❶ is your best course of action; you are recruiting a qualified person and helping a colleague at the same time.

SITUATION 9

Some friends suggest that you join them over the weekend for a game of gin rummy. You know that they play with money, but you yourself have never gambled before. Actually, you have always been apprehensive about venturing your money in a card game, but do know the rules of the game. You:

Ⓐ Decline politely, giving the excuse that you are not free over that weekend.

Ⓑ Tell your friends that gambling is a sin and that they should give up these evil habits.

Ⓒ Say 'yes' in a vague manner, never intending to take up their invitation.

Ⓓ Agree to have a game as long as the stakes are low and your friends refresh your memory about the rules.

Comments

If you really believe that gambling is evil, then you should just decline your friends' invitation, saying that you do not gamble. Saying 'yes' or telling them that you are not free will only make them invite you another time. Lecturing your friends on the evils of gambling is not going to help; it will only make you lose friends. So why not follow **Ⓓ** and join them in a game? As long as the stakes are low, it is great fun and cements your friendship.

DO'S AND DON'TS

DO'S

- Greet your neighbours and colleagues every morning.
- Shop at the market for fresh meat, fruits and vegetables.
- Try the foods sold by vendors on the streets.
- Boil tap water before consumption.
- Provide a meal for your maid.
- Bring your children along when visiting Mauritian friends.
- Leave a reasonable tip if you are satisfied with the service in a restaurant.
- Give a New Year tip to the rubbish collector, newspaper delivery person, etc.
- Make full use of the lovely beaches.
- Accept the small New Year gifts presented by your staff.
- Visit Rodrigues and the other islands around Mauritius.
- Dress modestly when visiting places of worship.
- Celebrate your holidays and festivals by offering some of your delicacies to neighbours and friends.
- Stand in for a colleague once in a while. The favour will always be returned.
- Ensure you keep a set of emergency supplies during the cyclone season.

DON'TS

- Don't sunbathe topless on public beaches.
- Don't allow your dog to foul the pavement in front of your neighbour's house.
- Don't confront a colleague for taking some office supplies home.
- Don't use the terms *malbar* and *lascar*.
- Don't be drawn into office politics, especially those along racial lines.
- Don't refuse to consider a colleague's relative for a job in the office.
- Don't accept valuable gifts from suppliers or colleagues.
- Don't be late for meetings and appointments.

- Don't leave your rubbish on beaches and in forested areas. Pick up after yourself.
- Don't ask for cutlery at an Indian wedding dinner. You are supposed to use your hands.
- Don't hold noisy parties beyond midnight.
- Don't think a cyclone is over when there is a lull and everything is still. It's the eye of the cyclone and it will rage with even greater intensity when the tail comes in.

GLOSSARY

Many words used in Mauritius are derived from the French language. English terms, on the other hand, take on entirely different meanings. Here is a selection of common terms that one is likely to come across.

achard	pickled vegetable
affranchi	freed slave
Ahir	a sub-caste of the Vaisya caste
ami	intimate friend
Baboujee	Hindu of the Kesatria caste
banian	a middleman between the fisherman and the fishmonger
bazar	market selling fresh foods
Bazar Central	the main market in Port-Louis; the largest in the country
bouillon	soup
boy	office boy whose function is to run errands
boutique	grocery
briani	dish of rice, meat and spices usually served at Muslim weddings
brioche	bun given out for a Catholic child's First Communion
cabinet	medical or dental surgery
camarade	friend
Casernes	the police headquarters in Port-Louis
catless	spicy deep-fried meat patty
clinic	private hospital
coca	fizzy soft drink
Code Noir	the legislation governing the trade and treatment of slaves in colonial times

colon	the French coloniser
confessional schools	schools run by the religious authorities
corsair	an 18th-19th century French seafarer with written permission from the king to attack and plunder enemy ships
Creole Lascar	descendants of the early Muslim settlers
deg	big pot to cook briani
dhoti	traditional garment worn by Indian men
double cut	system by which an employer is allowed to retain two days' wages from a coolie for every day off work
dragée	small sweet given out at a christening
Eid Mubarak	'the blessings of Eid be with you'
fleur-de-lis	lily flower; emblem of the French kings
foire	the weekly open-air market held in villages and some towns
foong pao	red envelope used by the Chinese to present money to others
frigidaire	refrigerator
gajack	snack eaten with alcoholic beverages
gamat	Indian wedding party
Ganga Talao	Grand Bassin
gâteau la cire	sweet sticky pudding eaten at Chinese New Year
gâteau piment	fried snack of ground dholl
goyave de Chine	small tart guava
Grand Nation	Hindu belonging to the Brahmin and Kesatria castes

Gros Creole	very dark Creole with African features
guérisseur	faith healer
hill coolie	labourer who came from India to work in the sugarcane fields
horni	light-weight long scarf
Indian	a Hindu
Jamaat	Muslim welfare association
kameez	straight-cut trousers worn by Indian women
kanwar	structure made of bamboo carried by Hindu devotees to celebrate Maha Shivaratri
kavadee	wooden structure carried by Tamil devotees during the Thai Poosam procession
kovil	Tamil temple
Koyri	a sub-caste of the Vaisya caste
Kurmi	a sub-caste of the Vaisya caste
kurta	Indian shirt for men
langouti	traditional garment worn by Indian men
lascar	pejorative term for a Muslim
local	annual leave (as opposed to medical leave)
lunghi	traditional garment worn by Indian men
Lycée	French school
Madras	a Tamil
Madras *baptisé*	a Christian of Tamil origin
madrassa	religious school for Muslim children
magasin	sundry shop
maison	round loaf of bread

majeur	when a young person reaches the age of 18
malbar	pejorative term for a Hindu
Mamzelle	Miss (title)
manioc	cassava
maravane	rattler
Maraze	a high-caste Hindu; a Brahmin
marron	runaway slave
masala	any kind of curry
Mazambic	Creole with pronounced African features
meuble	furniture
Milat	light-skinned Creole
moule	rectangular loaf of bread
nan	unleavened bread consumed by the Muslims
Nas	a Creole
nénenne	maid
paille en queue	an unusual seagull with a long black tail; the mascot of the local airline
pain fourré	loaf of bread stuffed with meat
plat au pain	dish eaten with bread
pomme d'amour	tomato
puja	Hindu prayer service
puri	deep-fried pancake
rakhi	colourful wristlet given by Indian women and girls to their brothers
ravane	thin, wide drum used to set the rhythm in *séga*
Rosenbergi	large freshwater prawn
roti	Indian pancake
rougaille	dish of tomatoes, onions, garlic and chillies, with or without meat

roulement	a form of credit system used by shopkeepers in villages
salwar	knee-length Indian tunic
samoussa	fried triangular packets with a potato curry filling
satini	sauce of crushed tomatoes, onions, chillies and coriander (also called *chatini* in restaurant menus)
séga	the traditional song of Mauritius
séga typique	séga using only traditional instruments; the most authentic form
seggae	mixture of *séga* and reggae
seine	fishing nets
soup	rice porridge
syndicat	labour union
tantine	auntie
taxi-train	taxi with a fixed route operating between the town centre and the suburbs
teahouse	café serving tea and Muslim snacks
tea money	small amount of cash drivers slip to the traffic policeman for minor traffic offences
thali	yellow cord with a pendant that signifies a Hindu woman's married status
ti bazar	mini market
Ti Nation	Hindu belonging to the Sudra caste, the lowest caste
tip-top	mini- or full-size bus servicing the suburbs of the large towns
ton	uncle
toque	fez, the traditional headwear for Muslim men

tuyau	tip in horse-racing
Vaish	a Hindu of the Vaisya caste; the largest caste in the country
van lak	a form of blackjack
waqf	property willed by a Muslim to the community
zakaat	a 2.5 per cent annual levy on income for Muslims to be used for the benefit of the whole community
zed mo	riddle
Zulu	an African

RESOURCE GUIDE

EMERGENCY TELEPHONE NUMBERS

- Airlines departures/arrivals — 603-3030
- Alcoholics Anonymous — 302-6093
- Ambulance (SAMU) — 114
- Anti Drugs and Smuggling Unit (ADSU) — 208-8398
- Central Electricity Board (CEB) — 601-1100
- Central Water Authority (CWA) — 170
- Child Abuse Unit — 240-3900
- Child Development Unit — 113
- Domestic Violence — 213-0001
- Emergency — 999
- Fire Services — 995, 115
- International Directory Assistance — 10-090
- National Directory Assistance — 150
- Police — 112
- Red Cross — 676-3064
- SOS Women — 433-3391, 676-5770
- Telephone fault — 92

TELEPHONES
Fixed Lines
- Mauritius Telecom
  Telecom Tower, Edith Cavell Street, Port-Louis
  Tel: (230) 203-7000; fax: (230) 208-1070
  E-mail: ceo@mauritiustelecom.com
  Website: http://www.mauritiustelecom.com

Cellular Phones
- Cellplus (a subsidiary of Mauritius Telecom)
  9th Floor, Telecom Tower, Edith Cavell Street, Port-Louis
  Tel: (230) 203-7500; fax: (230) 211-6996
  Email: cellplus@cellplus.mu
  Website: http://www.cellplus.mu

- Emtel Ltd
  1 Boundary Street, Rose Hill
  Tel: (230) 454-5400; fax: (230) 454-1010
  Email: emtel@emtelnet.com
  Website: http://www.emtel-ltd.com

AIRLINES

- Air France
  c/o Rogers Aviation and Travel Services, 5 President John
  Kennedy Street, Port-Louis
  Tel: (230) 202-6747; fax: (230) 212-0218
  Website: http://www.airfrance.com/mu
- Air Mauritius Ltd
  Air Mauritius Centre, President John Kennedy Street,
  Port-Louis
  Tel: (230) 202-7070; Fax: (230) 208-8331
  E-mail: contact@airmauritius.com
  Website: http://www.airmauritius.com
- British Airways
  Ireland Blyth Ltd, IBL House Ground Floor, Caudan
  Waterfront, Port-Louis
  Tel: (230) 202-8000; fax: (230) 208-8080
  Website: http://www.ba.com
- Emirates Airlines
  Ground Floor, Harbour Front Building, Place D'Armes,
  Port-Louis. Tel: (230) 213-9100; fax: (230) 213-0550
  Website: http://www.emirates.com
- Singapore Airlines
  Currimjee Jeewanjee & Co (GSA), 3 President John Kennedy
  Street, Port-Louis
  Tel: (230) 208-7695/96/97, 210-5100. Fax: (230) 210-1722
  E-mail: sia@currimjee.intnet.mu /
        mu_feedback@singaporeair.com.sg

AIRPORT

The SSR International Airport, Plaisance, is the only
international airport of Mauritius. For flight arrival and
departure information, call tel: (230) 603-3030.

TOURIST OFFICES
Mauritius Tourism Promotion Authority
Website: http://www.mauritius.net

- Head Office. 11th Floor, Air Mauritius Centre, 5 President John Kennedy Street, Port-Louis
  Tel: (230) 210-1545; fax: (230) 212-5142
- SSR International Airport
  Arrival Lounge, Plaisance
  Tel: (230) 637-3635
- Port-Louis Waterfront
  Tourism Office
  Tel: (230) 208-6397

PUBLIC TRANSPORT
Taxi

There is no taxi company operating in Mauritius. All taxis are privately owned and have to display their operation base on the side of the front doors. There are taxis operating from major hotels and taxi stands in all towns and most large villages. Taxis have white number plates with black letterings.

- Doomun Preetum Taxi Plus Service
  Place d'Armes, Port-Louis
  Tel: (230) 508-1682
- Taxi Stand
  Royal Road, Beau Bassin
  Tel: (230) 454-2818
- Taxi Stand
  Place Margéot, Rose-Hill
  Tel: (230) 464-4112
- Taxi Stand
  La Louise, Quatre Bornes
  Tel: (230) 425-5669
- Taxi Stand
  Curepipe
  Tel: (230) 676-2714

Car Rental

- ABC Car Rental Ltd
  Albion Docks Building, Trou Fanfaron, Port-Louis
  Tel: (230) 242-8957, 216-3805
  Fax: (230) 242-8958
  Email: abccar@intnet.mu
  Website: http://www.abc-carrental.com
- Avis Rent A Car
  Al Madina Road, Cassis
  Tel: (230) 208-1624, 208-6031, fax: (230) 211-1420
  Email: avis@avismauritius.com
  Website: http://www.avismauritius.com
- Europcar
  Avenue Michael Leal, Les Pailles
  Tel: (230) 286 0143
  Fax: (230) 286-4705
  Website: http://www.europcar.com
- Hertz Rent A Car
  Gustave Colin Street, Forest Side, Curepipe
  Tel: (230) 674-3695/96; fax: (230) 674-3720
  Website: http://www.hertz.com/rentacar

BANKING
Accountants

- De Chazal Du Mée
  10 Frère Félix de Valois Street, Champ de Mars, Port-Louis
  Tel: (230) 202-3000, 202-9500; fax: (230) 208-0086
  Email: dcdm@dcdm.intnet.mu
  Website: http://www.dcdm.biz
- Price Waterhouse Coopers
  6th Floor, Cerné House, Chaussée, Port-Louis
  Tel: (230) 207-5011; fax: (230) 207-8037
  Website: http://www.pwcglobal.com/ (select 'Mauritius' from the drop-down menu)

Bank Accounts

It is quite easy to open a bank account in Mauritius. Most banks request a minimum deposit of some Rs 1,000 (approximately US$ 30) for a savings account. Proof of identity, such as ID card, passport or birth certificate may be required.

Major banks in Mauritius are the Mauritius Commercial Bank, State Bank of Mauritius, Hong Kong and Shanghai Bank, and Barclays Bank.

Credit Cards
The most commonly accepted cards are MasterCard, Visa, American Express and Diners Club.

Income Tax
For individuals, income tax is charged in incremental steps up to a maximum rate of 30 per cent of chargeable income.
- Commissioner of Income Tax
  8th Floor, Emmanuel Anquetil Building, 15 Jules Koenig Street (corner of SSR and Jules Koenig Street), Port-Louis
  Tel: (230) 201-1830; fax: (230) 212-9246
  Email: incometax@mail.gov.mu
  Website: http://www.gov.mu/portal/site/incometax

Value Added Tax
A 15 per cent Value Added Tax (VAT) is charged on most goods and services.
- Value-Added Tax Department
  Rabadia Building, 38 Mère Barthelemy Street, Port-Louis
  Tel: (230) 208-1261/65; fax: (230) 212-9454
  Email: vat@mail.gov.mu
  Website: http://www.gov.mu/portal/site/vat

GAS COMPANIES
Cooking gas is on sale at petrol stations throughout the island. It may also be home delivered, but this normally applies for large quantities and is at an additional cost.

- ELF Gaz (Maurice) Ltd
  Marine Road, Quay D, Port-Louis
  Tel: (230) 240-8047

- Yip Tong Group
  Yip Tong House, Royal Road, Cassis, Port-Louis
  Tel: (230) 212-3326

DOCTORS
Cardiologists
- Professor Soorianarain Baligadoo
  De Chazal Lane, St Paul Avenue, Vacoas
  Tel: (230) 686-0228
- Dr Mamode Aniff Khan Yearoo
  24 Raoul Rivet Street, Port-Louis
  Tel: (230) 212-3132

Dermatologists
- Dr Yusuf Mahomed Jeetoo
  5 Rennards Street, Beau Bassin
  Tel: (230) 454-0558
- Dr Philippe Li Loong
  George Town Complex, St Jean Rd, Quatre Bornes
  Tel: (230) 424-9757

ENT Surgeon
- Dr Kwet Kian Ng Kee Kwong
  4B Dr Edwin Ythier Street, Rose Hill
  Tel: (230) 464-1906

Gastroenterologist
- Dr Denis Li Ting Fong Li Kam Wa
  25 Jummah Mosque Street, Port-Louis
  Tel: (230) 240-3137

Gynaecologists
- Dr Guy Gerard Jacques Gnany
  Les Camphriers, 3 Brown Sequard Avenue, Quatre Bornes
  Tel: (230) 425-9347
- Dr Ah Fat Wong Ten Yuen
  Labourdonnais Court, St Georges Street, Port-Louis
  Tel: (230) 211-1401

Neurosurgeon
- Dr Rabindranath Ji (Ramesh) Modun
  Chapman Hill, Royal Road, Beau Bassin
  Tel: (230) 454-1608

Ophthalmologists
- Dr Jean José Isabelle
  Impasse Esnouf, Curepipe
  Tel: (230) 675-2272
- Dr Indurdeo Gaya
  9 Alfred Brown Avenue, Quatre Bornes
  Tel: (230) 425-1257

Orthopaedic Surgeon
- Dr Maheswarnuth Hurryparsad Gunesee
  45 Bernardin de St Pierre Avenue, Quatre Bornes
  Tel: (230) 424-7944

Paediatrician
- Dr Mohamed Gafoor Bholah
  Desforges Medical Centre, Sir S Ramgoolam Street,
  Port-Louis
  Tel: (230) 212 3260

Psychiatrist
- Dr Maryam Bibi Mahmad Timol
  50 Route du Jardin, Curepipe
  Tel: (230) 676-5026

Plastic Surgeon
- Pierre Louis De Larue
  Coastal Road, Cap Malheureux
  Tel: (230) 262-7795

Chest Disease
- Dr Louis Pierre Roland Donat
  Lallah Street, Floréal
  Tel: (230) 686-4909

HOSPITALS

There are several hospitals over the island, and health service is free. In addition, Area Health Centres (AHC) and Community Health Centres (CHC) are available in populated areas to dispense health services on an outpatient basis. Apart from the more general services available in the main hospitals of Port-Louis (Dr Jeetoo Hospital), Pamplemousses (SSRNH) and Rose-Belle (J Nehru Hospital), there are specialised hospitals for specific ailments. Eye problems are treated at the Moka Eye Hospital while ENT problems will receive specialised treatment at the ENT Hospital of Vacoas.

- Dr Jeetoo Hospital
  Volcy Pougnet Street, Port-Louis
  Tel: (230) 212-3201; fax: (230) 212-8958
- Princess Margaret Orthopaedic Hospital
  Candos
  Tel: (230) 425-3031; fax: (230) 425-8958
- Sir Seewoosagur Ramgoolam National Hospital (SSRNH)
  Royal Road, Pamplemousses
  Tel: (230) 243-3661; fax: (230) 243-3740
- Moka Eye Hospital
  Royal Road, Moka
  Tel: (230) 433-4015
- ENT Hospital
  Vacoas
  Tel: (230) 686-2061–64
- J Nehru Hospital
  Emmanuel Anquetil Building, Rose Belle
  Tel: (230) 603-7000

HEALTH SERVICES
Private Hospitals

There are several private hospitals (called 'clinic') dispensing good quality health care at a relatively high cost. Most are located in the upper Plaines Wilhems region. Rates and other fees are normally advertised in the patients' room.

- Nouvelle Clinique Du Bon Pasteur Ltée
  Mgr J Mamet Street, Rose Hill
  Tel: (230) 464-2640, 464-7238; fax: (230) 454-0632
- City Clinic
  102-106 Sir Edgar Laurent Street, Plaine Verte, Port-Louis
  Tel: (230) 242-0486
- Clinique Darné
  Georges Guibert Street, Floréal
  Tel: (230) 601-2300; fax: (230) 696-3612
  Email: clinique.darne@intnet.mu
- Clinique Mauricienne
  Le Réduit
  Tel: (230) 454-3061–63; fax: (230) 464-8813
- Clinique Ferrière
  College Lane, Curepipe
  Tel: (230) 676-3332; fax: (230) 670-2300
- Clinique de Lorette
  Higginson Street, Curepipe
  Tel: (230) 675-2911; fax: (230) 276-2695
- Clinique du Nord
  Royal Road, Baie du Tombeau
  Tel: (230) 247-2532; fax: (230) 247-1254
  Email: cdnord@intnet.mu

Ambulance Services

Some private hospitals operate their own ambulance service. However, most ambulances are operated by the public service. In cases of emergency, the SAMU ambulance will be best equipped to deal with urgent cases. Ambulances are available at the main hospitals and also from certain police stations.

- Candos:
  Princess Margaret Orthopaedic Hospital.
  Tel: (230) 425-3031
- Curepipe Police Station (Night)
  Tel: (230) 675-3031
- Port-Louis:
  Dr Jeetoo Hospital (day & night). Tel: 212 3201

- Pamplemousses:
  Sir Seewoosagur Ramgoolam National Hospital
  Tel: (230) 243-3661
- Rose Hill Police Station (Night)
  Tel: (230) 454-2022

Medical Assistance

- Medic Assistance International (Mtius) Ltd
  Newry Complex, 85 St Jean Road, Quatre Bornes
  Tel: (230) 464-2019

INTERNET SERVICE PROVIDERS

- http://www.servihoo.com

Cybercafés

- Borneo Ltd
  41 St Georges Street, Port-Louis
  Tel: (230) 211-5564
- Central Interactiv' Agency
  Office 216, TMC Building, Freeport, Zone 6, Mer Rouge,
  Port-Louis
  Tel: (230) 206-2630
- Click & Go
  Astrolab Building, Port-Louis Waterfront, Port-Louis
  Tel: (230) 208-2213/14
  Email: clickngo@intnet.mu
- Cyber 2000
  Centre Commercial Phoenix, Sivananda Street, Phoenix
  Tel: (230) 698-5473; fax: (230) 698-5096
  Email: cyber2000@intnet.mu
- Cyber Lanarena
  Kadel Building, Royal Road, Beau Bassin
  Tel: (230) 467-8326
- Cybersurf
  Labourdonnais Street, Mahebourg
  Tel: (230) 631-2350

- Cyberyder Ltd
  Ground Floor, Telecom Tower, Edith Cavell Street, Port-Louis
  Tel: (230) 203-7277
- Dils Internet Cafe
  Above Dil's Snack, Commercial Centre (Arcades Sunnassee), Rose-Hill
  Tel: (230) 467-1133
  Email: dislinternet@intnet.mu
  Website: http://www.ziaaddils.uklinux.net/dilsinternetcafe/
- FRCI E-Services Ltd
  Sibotie House, L'Anse Courtois, Pailles
  Tel: (230) 286-9636
- Globe Trotter Cyber Cafe Ltd
  286A Royal Road, Rose-Hill
  Tel: (230) 465-8800
- Homesite Internet Club
  St Jean Road, Quatre Bornes
  Tel: (230) 424-1155
- Le Cyber Campus Pub
  1st Floor, Palladium Complex, Trianon
  Tel: (230) 467-5277
- Mediatool Ltd
  9th Floor, Stratton Court, La Poudrière Street, Port-Louis
  Tel: (230) 210-0877
- Oxygen Surfgrafx Ltd
  Ramdenee Building, Forest Side
  Tel: (230) 670-7170
- Sunbow Technology Ltd
  Newry Complex, 85 Route St Jean, Quatre Bornes
  Tel: (230) 467-7200
- Telecom Plus Ltd
  Level 6, Telecom Tower, Edith Cavell Street, Port-Louis
  Tel: (230) 203-7575
- V-Street.com
  Baden Powell Building, Lord Baden Powell Street, Port-Louis
  Tel: (230) 211-9118

POST OFFICES

Headquarters
    Quay Street, Port-Louis
    Tel: (230) 208-2851
    Website: http://www.mauritiuspost.mu/
Opening hours
    Mondays to Fridays   8:15 am to 4:00 pm
    Saturdays   8:15 am to 11:45 am

EMBASSIES

Most foreign embassies and consulate offices are either in
Port-Louis or in Floréal. With respect to formalities for the
Schengen visa to visit several European countries, please
contact the French Embassy.

- Australian High Commission
  2nd Floor, Rogers House, 5 President John Kennedy Street,
  Port-Louis
  Tel: (230) 202-0160; fax: (230) 208-8878
  Website: http://www.mauritius.embassy.gov.au/
- Consulate of Austria
  5 John Kennedy Street, Port-Louis
  Tel: (230) 208-6801
- Consulate of the People's Republic of Bangladesh
  AG Joonas Industrial Estate, 1 Military Road, Port-Louis
  Tel: (230) 242-6333
- British High Commission
  7th Floor, Les Cascades Building, Edith Cavell Street,
  Port-Louis
  Tel: (230) 202-9400; fax: (230) 202-9408
  Email: bhc@bow.intnet.mu
- Consulate of Brazil
  18 Edith Cavell Street, Port-Louis
  Tel: (230) 207-3000
- Consulate of Canada
  c/o Blanche Birger Co Ltd, 18 Jules Koenig Street, PO Box
  209, Port-Louis
  Tel: (230) 212-5500

- Consulate of Chile
  18 Edith Cavell Street, Port-Louis
  Tel: (230) 207-3000
- Embassy of the People's Republic of China
  Royal Road, Belle Rose, Rose-Hill
  Tel: (230) 454 9111, 464-5556; fax: (230) 464-6012
- Embassy of Egypt
  Forest Lane, Floréal
  Tel: (230) 696-5012; fax: (230) 686-5775
- Delegation of the European Commission to the Republic
  of Mauritius
  8th Floor, St James Court, St Denis Street, Port-Louis
  Tel: (230) 207-1515; fax: (230) 211-6624
- Consulate of Finland
  c/o Rogers & Co Ltd, 5 John Kennedy Street, Port-Louis
  Tel: (230) 208-6801
- French Embassy
  14 St Georges Street, Port-Louis
  Tel:(230) 208-3755, 202 0100; fax: (230) 202-0140
  Website: http://www.ambafrance-mu.org/
- Honorary Consul General Federal Republic of Germany
  32 Bis St Georges Street, Port-Louis
  Tel: (230) 212-4100; fax: (230) 211-4111
- Consulate of the Republic of Ghana
  Ghana House, 13 Queen Mary Avenue, Floréal
  Tel: (230) 696-7002; fax: (230) 696-1879
  Email: ghanahouse@intnet.mu
- Consulate of The Republic of Indonesia
  AG Joonas Industrial Estate, 1 Military Road, Port-Louis
  Tel: (230) 242-6333; fax: (230) 242-1471
  Email: novaind@intnet.mu
- Japanese Consulate
  4th Floor, Wing b, Ken Lee Building, Edith Cavell Street,
  Port-Louis
  Tel: (230) 211-1749; fax: (230) 211-1789
- Consulate of the Republic of Korea
  Scott & Co Ltd, 4 Edith Cavell Street, PO Box 51, Port-Louis
  Tel: (230) 210-7255, 250-1309; fax: (230) 212-3333
  Email: nchong@intnet.mu

- Consulate of Madagascar
  Guiot Pasceau Street, Floréal
  Tel: (230) 686-5015; fax: (230) 686-7040
- Consulate of Portugal
  18 Edith Cavell Street, Port-Louis
  Tel: (230) 207-3000
- Russian Embassy
  Queen Mary Avenue, Floréal
  Tel: (230) 696-1545, 696-5533; fax (230) 696-5027
- Consulate of the Republic of Seychelles
  Suite 616, St James Court, St Denis Street, Port-Louis
  Tel: (230) 211-1688; fax: (230) 211-1688
  Email: gfok@intnet.mu
- South African High Commission
  4th Floor, British American Insurance (BAI) Building, 25
  Pope Hennessy Street, PO Box 908, Port-Louis
  Tel: (230) 212-6925–30; fax: (230) 212-5704, 213-1171
  Email: sahc@intnet.mu
- Consulate of Sweden
  c/o Taylor Smith & Co Ltd, Aqualia Building, Old Quay D
  Road, Port-Louis
  Tel: (230) 206-3203; fax: (230) 240-2884
  Email: colin.taylor@rogers.mu
- Embassy of Switzerland
  2 Jules Koenig Street, Port-Louis
  Tel: (230) 208-8763
- Consulate of Thailand
  5 Duke of Edinburgh Avenue, Port-Louis
  Tel: (230) 208-0877
- Consulate of Ukraine
  St Julien Village, Union Flacq
  Tel: (230) 412-8710
- Embassy of The United States of America
  4th Floor, Rogers House, 5 President John Kennedy Street.
  Port-Louis
  Tel: (230) 202-4400
  Email: usembassy@intnet.mu
  Website: http://mauritius.usembassy.gov/

BUSINESS CONTACTS

- Board of Investment Mauritius
  Level 10, One Cathedral Square Building, 16 Jules Koeing Street, Port-Louis
  Tel: (230) 203-3800; fax: (230) 208-2924
  Email: contact@investmauritius.com
  Website: http://www.boimauritius.com
- Mauritius Chamber of Agriculture
  Plantation House (PO Box 312), Duke of Edinburgh Avenue, Port-Louis
  Tel: (230) 208-0812, 208-2747; fax: (230) 208-1269
  Email: mca312@intnet.mu
  Website: http://www.mchagric.org/
- Mauritius Chamber of Commerce & Industry
  3 Royal Road, Port-Louis
  Tel: (230) 208-3301; fax: (230) 208-0076
  Email: mcci@intnet.mu
  Website: http://www.mcci.org/
- Financial Services Promotion Agency (FSPA)
  5th Floor, Barkly Wharf, Le Caudan Waterfront, Old Pavilion Street, Port-Louis
  Tel: (230) 211-8383; fax: (230) 210-8560
  Email: info@fspamauritius.com
  Website: http://www.mauritius-finance.com/
- Mauritius Export Processing Zone Association (MEPZA)
  6th Floor, Unicorn House, 5 Royal Road, Port-Louis
  Tel: (230) 208-5216; fax: (230) 212-1853
  Website: http://www.mepza.org/
- Mauritius Freeport Authority
  1st Floor, Trade and Marketing Centre (TMC), Freeport Zone No. 6, Mer Rouge, Port-Louis
  Tel: (230) 206-2500; fax: (230) 206-2600
  Email: mfa@freeport.gov.mu
  Website: http://www.efreeport.com
- Mauritius Industrial Development Authority
  PO Box 1184, 2nd Floor, BAI Building, 25 Pope Henessy Street, Port-Louis
  Tel: (230) 208-7750; fax: (230) 208-5965
  Email: mida@media.intnet.mu

LAWYERS

- Banymandhub Boolell Chambers
  Temple Court, 2 Labourdonnais Street, Port-Louis
  Tel: (230) 212-9810; fax: (230) 212-9868
- Bhayat A Kader, Senior Counsel
  PCL Building, Sir Virgil Naz Street, Port-Louis
  Tel: (230) 208-2767; fax: (230) 208-5258
- Collendavelloo Chambers
  10 Frere Felix de Valois Street, Champs de Mars, Port- Louis
  Tel: (230) 208-5164; fax (230) 212-6234
- Mohamed Chambers
  Suite 503-505, 5th Floor, Sterling House, Lislet Geoffroy
  Street, Port-Louis
  Tel: (230) 212-1155; fax: (230) 210-5193
  Email: smohamed@intnet.mu

MECHANICS

- ABC Body & Paint
  Allées des Mangues, Les Pailles
  Tel: (230) 212-8283
  Email: abcpaint@intnet.mu
- Garage Bala & Sons Ltd
  Royal Road, Grand River North West
  Tel: (230) 212-5382

REAL ESTATE BROKERS

- Coprim Ltée
  13 Rue Dauphine, Port-Louis
  Tel: (230) 212-3666; fax: (230) 208-3974
  Email: coprim@intnet.mu
- Pam Golding Properties
  7 Wilson Lane, Vacoas
  Tel: (230) 686-6006; fax: 9230) 686-3842
  Website: http://www.pamgolding.co.za/areas/mauritius/
    mauritius.asp
- Soproges Ltée (Soc. Professionnelle de Gestion Ltée)
  1st Floor, George Town Building, St Jean Road, Quatre Bornes
  Tel: (230) 454-3046; fax: (230) 454-6726
  Email: soproges@intnet.mu

SCHOOLS

Education is free in Mauritius at both primary and secondary levels. However, there are several private schools, most of them using French as teaching medium, for example the Lycée Labourdonnais and the École Du Centre. The English medium private schools are:

- Clavis Primary School
  Montagne Ory, Moka
  Tel: (230) 433-4439
- Le Bocage International School
  Montagne Ory, Moka
  Tel: (230) 433-1159, 433-0941; fax: (230) 433-4914
  Email: lbis@intnet.mu
- Saint Nicholas Grammar School
  Corner Palmerston Road and Golf Course Road, Phoenix
  Tel: (230) 526-9010; fax: (230) 251-0967
- Northfields International High School
  Labourdonnais Village, Mapou
  Tel: (230) 266-9448; fax (230)266-9447
  Email: Northfields@intnet.mu

RELIGIOUS AND SOCIAL WORK

The Hindus constitute the main religious group, with a large Roman Catholic congregation as the next religious group. Islam is also an important religion.

- Evêché de Port-Louis
  13 Mgr Gonin Street, Port-Louis
  Tel: (230) 208-3068; fax: (230) 230-6607
  Email: eveche@intnet.mu
- Anglican Diocese of Mauritius
  Bishop's House, Nalletamby Road, Phoenix
  Tel: (230) 686-5158; fax: (230) 697-1096
- Caritas/Abri de Nuit
  Roman Catholic Diocese of Port-Louis, Abattoir Street, Port-Louis
  Tel: (230) 242-9030

- NATRESA (National Agency for the Treatment and Rehabilitation of Substance Abusers)
  Maxcity Building, 16 Poudrière Street, Port-Louis
  Tel: (230) 210-8017/18, 210-6775; fax: (230) 210-8015
  Email: na251996@intnet.mu
- Mauritius Council of Social Services (MACOSS)
  Astor Court, 34 Lislet Geoffroy Street, Port-Louis
  Tel: (230) 212-0242, 208-4425; fax: (230) 208-6370
  Email: macoss@intnet.mu
  Website: http://www.macoss.org

CYCLONE INFORMATION

Cyclones and tropical depressions occur in the summer months. Officially, the cyclone season starts in December and ends in May. However, cyclones are most likely to hit the island between January and March. Wind speeds exceeding 200 kmph have been recorded with the most intense cyclones.

- Weather information services (only during cyclonic periods)
  Tel: 96, 170
- Mauritius Met Office for weather forecast
  Tel: (230) 302-6071/686-1031

FURTHER READING

BOOKS

- *A New History of Mauritius*. John Addison and Kissoonsingh Hazareesingh. Mauritius: Editions de l'Océan Indien, 1993.
- *Slaves, Freedmen and Indentured Labourers in Colonial Mauritius*. Richard B Allen. Cambridge: Cambridge University Press, 2000.
- *Convicts in the Indian Ocean: Transportation from South Asia to Mauritius, 1815-53*. Clare Anderson. London: Palgrave Macmillan, 2000.
- *The Best of Mauritian Cooking. Barry* Andrews and Paul Jones. Singapore: Times Editions, 2000.
- *Flora of Mauritius and the Seychelles*. J G Baker. Delhi: Asian Educational Services, 1999.
- *Servants, Sirdars and Settlers: Indians in Mauritius, 1834–1874*. Ed. Marina Carter. India: Oxford University Press, 1995
- *Creolization of Language and Culture*. Robert Chaudenson. Oxford: Routledge, 2001.
- *The Rape of Sita*. Lindsey Collen. London: Bloomsbury, 2001; New York, NY: The Feminist Press at CUNY, 2004.
- *Return of the Crazy Bird: the Sad, Strange Tale of the Dodo*. Clara Pinto Correia. New York, NY: Copernicus Books, 2003.
- *The Mauritian Economy: A Reader*. Ed. Rajen Dabee and David Greenaway. London: Palgrave Macmillan, 2001.
- *Journey to Mauritius*. (*Lost and Found: Classic Travel Writing* series). Bernadin de Saint Pierre. Trans. Jason Wilson. Northampton, MA: Interlink Publishers, 2002.
- *Mauritius in the Making: Across the Censuses, 1846-2000*. Monique Dinan. Mauritius: Nelson Mandela Centre for African Culture, 2003.
- *Lonely Planet Mauritius, Reunion & Seychelles*. Jan Dodd and Madeleine Philippe. Victoria: Lonely Planet, 2004.
- *Golden Bats and Pink Pigeons*. Gerald Durrell. London: House of Stratus, 2002.

- *Mauritius: Light and Space*. Dan Callikan and Christian Bossu-Picat. Mauritius: Editions de l'Ocean Indien, 2002.
- *Mauritian Creole in Seven Easy Lessons*. Mark Frew. Mauritius: Ledikasyon Pu Travayer, 2003.
- *Dodo: From Extinction to Icon*. Errol Fuller. New York, NY: Universe, 2003.
- *Dodo: The Bird Behind the Legend*. Alan Grihault. Mauritius: Imprimerie & Papeterie Commerciale Ltd, 2005.
- *History of Indians in Mauritius*. Kissoonsingh Hazareesingh. London: Macmillan, 1977.
- *History of Muslims in Mauritius*. Moomtaz Imrith. Mauritius: Editions Le Printemps Ltée, 1994.
- *War and Empire in Mauritius and the Indian Ocean (Studies in Military and Strategic History)*. Ashley Jackson. London: Palgrave Macmillan, 2001.
- *The Dodo and Mauritius Island: Imaginary Encounters*. Harri Kallio. London: Dewi Lewis Publishing, 2004.
- *Rights of Women in Mauritius*. Marie Lourdes Lam Hung. Mauritius: S.N., 2003.
- *Mauritius: Its Creole Language (The Ultimate Creole Phrase Book: English-Creole Dictionary)*. Jacques K Lee. London: Nautilus Pub. Co, 2004.
- *Séga: The Mauritian Folk Dance*. Jacques K Lee. London: Nautilus, 1990.
- *A Concise History of Dutch Mauritius, 1598–1711*. P J Moree. London: Kegan Paul, 2001.
- *The Dive Sites of Mauritius: Comprehensive Coverage of Diving and Snorkelling*. Alan Mountain. New York, NY: McGraw-Hill/Contemporary Books, 1997.
- *The Mauritian Shekel: The Story of Jewish Detainees in Mauritius, 1940-1945*. Genevieve Pitot. Portland, OR: Rowman & Littlefield Publishing, 2000.
- *This is Mauritius*. Alain Proust, with text by Alan Mountain. Cape Town: Struik Publishers, 2003.
- *Beyond Inequalities: Women in Mauritius*. Bhagiawatty Gunganah, Satinder Ragobar and Oomandra Nath Varma. Harare: Southern African Research and Documentation Centre, 1998.

- *Festivals of Mauritius*. Ramesh Ramdoyal. Mauritius: Editions de l'Ocean Indien, 1994.
- *Mauritius: A Geomorphological Analysis*. Prem Saddul and David W Mphande. Mauritius: Mahatma Gandhi Institute, 2002.
- *Comprehensive History of Mauritius*. Sydney Selvon. Mauritius: Mauritius Printing Specialist, 2001.
- *English-Creole Dictionary*. K Goswami Sewtohul. Mauritius: K Goswami Sewtohul, 1997.
- *Field Guide to Coastal Fishes of Mauritius*. Hiroaki Terashima. Mauritius: Albion Fisheries Research Centre, 2001.
- *Mauritius Style: Life on the Verandah*. Christian Vaisse, with text by Christian Saglio, Isabelle Desvaux de Marigny and Henriette Valentin Lagesse. Singapore: Editions Didier Millet, 2003.

WEBSITES

- General information about Mauritius
  Website: http://www.ile-maurice.com
  Website: http://www.mauritius-info.com
- Mauritius Island Online
  Website: http://www.maurinet.com
- Official website of the Government of Mauritius
  Website: http://www.gov.mu/
- Mauritius Tourism Promotion Authority
  Website: http://www.mauritius.net
- Republic of Mauritius, Central Statistics office
  Website: http://www.gov.mu/portal/sites/ncb/cso/index.htm
- Mauritius Freeport Authority (Board of Investment, Freeport Unit)
  Website: http://www.efreeport.com
- The Stock Exchange of Mauritius
  Website: http://www.semdex.com
- Mauritius Chamber of Commerce and Industry
  Website: http://www.mcci.org
- Bank of Mauritius
  Website: http://bom.intnet.mu/
- Mauritius Commercial Bank
  Website: http://www.mcb.co.mu

- Mauritius Yellow Pages
  Website: http://www.themauritiusyellowpage.com/
- Air Mauritius (official website of the national airline)
  Website: http://www.airmauritius.com
- Institute of Environmental and Legal Studies
  Website: http://www.intnet.mu/iels
- University of Mauritius
  Website: http://www.uom.ac.mu
- Le Mauricien (online version of the daily newspaper)
  Website: http://www.lemauricien.com
- L'express (online version of the newspaper in French)
  Website: http://www.lexpress.mu
- Mauritius News (newspaper for overseas Mauritians)
  Website: http://www.mauritius-news.co.uk
- Maritius Scout Association
  Website: http://www.angelfire.com/nj/mauscout
- Recipes from Mauritius
  Website: http://ile-maurice.tripod.com/
- Classic Stamps of Mauritius
  Website: http://www.stampsmauritius.com

ABOUT THE AUTHOR

Born in Mauritius, Roseline NgCheong-Lum spent the first 20 years of her life on the island, making friends with and learning from all the various ethnic groups that make up the country. These formative years have instilled in her a deep interest in peoples and their cultures.

After graduating from Oxford University, she worked as a teacher in a large Mauritian secondary school, sharing her love for literature with her pupils. In 1988, she moved to Singapore where she became an editor, continuing her association with books.

Roseline has lived in England, the United States and Thailand, and has travelled to almost every region in the world. She now lives in Singapore with her husband and two daughters. She spends at least one month every year in Mauritius, taking in the sights, sounds and smells of her beloved country. Despite her hectic schedule, Roseline has managed to author several books in the *Cultures of the World* and the *Countries of the World* series and *Journey Through Bangkok*. Her book *Not Just a Good Food Guide: Bangkok* won the 2005 Gourmand International Award for Best Culinary Travel Guide.

INDEX

A

accommodation 108–113
  furnishing 114–116
  pets 118
  rubbish 118–119
  living quarters 110–113
  utilities 116–117
arts and culture 193–197

B

beach activities 179–186
beaches 178–179, 270
business and employment
  237–262, 270
  bill fight 251–252
  business ethics 253–254
  dress 249–250
  employment 245–246
  greetings 251
  industries 240–245
  labour unions 262–264, 271
  Mauritius Freeport 241–242
  meetings 247–248
  name cards 250–251
  partnerships 246–247
  pifalls 244–245
  punctuality 248–249

C

clubs 200
cohabiting 100
conversation 87–88
cyclones 139–143

D

districts 8–26
  Black River 19–20, 267
  Flacq 14–15, 267
  Grand Port 16–17, 267
  Moka 23–24, 267
  Pamplemousses 12–13, 267
  Plaines Wilhems 20–23, 267
  Port-Louis 8–12, 267
  Rivière du Rempart 13–14, 267
  Savanne 18–19, 267
divorce 99–100

E

eating out 162–170
education 130–134
entertaining 172–176
EPZ *See* Export Processing Zone
etiquette 79–87, 270
  being a house guest 85–86
  dress 80–81
  forms of address 79–80
  greetings 84–85
  introductions 80
  neighbours 86–87, 270
  table manners 170–171
  visiting 82–83, 271
Export Processing Zone
  (EPZ) 11, 77, 237–240, 241, 269

F

family 67–71
  children 70–71, 81–82
  typical household 67–68
festivals 201–216
  Chinese New
    Year 72, 199, 202, 205–207
  Christmas 202, 211, 215–216, 262
  Divali 202, 214
  Easter 202, 209–211
  Eid-ul-Fitr 72, 208–209
  Feast of the Holy Virgin
    202, 211–212
  Ganga Asnan 202, 214–215
  Holi 202, 207–208
  Maha Shivaratri 18, 207
  New Year 197, 202–203, 262
  Père Laval 124, 202, 212–214
  Rakhi 202, 211
  Thai Poosam Kavadee 50, 202,
    204, 204–205
finances 134–136
food and drink 145–156
  drinks 153–156, 271
  ethnic cuisines 145–151
  fast foods 151–153
  taboos 156–157
foreigners 76–78
formalities 106–107
  citizenship 107
  permanent residence 107
  vaccinations 106
  visa regulations 106–107

G
gambling 197–200, 270
geography 8

H
history 26–37
household help 119–120

L
language 218–233
 body language 231–233
 Creole 225–229, 270
 English 218–221
 French 221–225, 270
 mother tongues 229–230
 status symbol 230–231

M
making friends 88–90
media 233–235
medical care 136–139

O
outdoor activities 188–193
outer islands 187

P
population
 'general' population 60–61
 communalism 65–67, 271
 ethnic groupsCreole 48–65

R
religion 71–74
resorts 5, 110, 192, 198
rites of passage 100–104
Rodrigues Island 30,
 37–46, 191, 192, 266, 267

S
security 120–121
séga 20, 39, 63–65, 96, 98, 195,
 196, 211, 269, 271
shopping 126–129
 bazars 158–161
 best buys 127–128
 food shopping 157–161
 markets 126
 service 129
 shops 126–127
 supermarkets 161–162
 trading hours 128–129

T
telecommunications
towns
 Beau Bassin 21, 22, 62
 Curepipe 11, 21, 23, 110, 111, 112,
  115, 116, 117, 123, 126, 128, 134,
  138, 163, 190, 195, 198, 199
 Floréal 111, 112, 128
 Grand Baie 13, 14, 110, 112, 113,
  163, 166, 179, 184, 194, 201
 Mahebourg 17, 30, 115, 194, 212
 Péreybère 14, 26, 110, 113, 179
 Phoenix 22, 55, 56, 133, 154, 161
 Port-Louis 8, 9, 10, 11, 12, 13, 20,
  21, 28, 29, 31, 37, 47, 55, 58,
  72, 107, 110, 111, 113, 117, 122,
  123, 128, 129, 137, 138, 151, 154,
  159, 160, 163, 166, 167, 169, 189,
  194, 197, 200, 205, 266
 Quatre Bornes 22, 62, 110, 111, 112,
  115, 123, 163, 167
 Rose-Hill 11, 21, 22, 62, 101, 123,
  126, 138, 189, 194, 195, 197, 205
 Vacoas 22, 50, 137, 189, 191,
  200, 214
transport 121–123
 'tip-tops' 124–125
 buses 123–124
 driving 122–123
 roads 121–122
 taxi-train 125
 taxis 124

W
weddings 91–99
 Chinese 97–98
 Creole 95–96
 gifts 98–99
 Indian 92–94
 Muslim 94–95
women 68–69, 252–253
work ethic 255–256
 'boys' 261–262
 favours 256
 hierarchy 260
 nepotism 255–256
 office functions 262
 office politics 258
 office supplies 258–260
 sick leave 256–258

Titles in the CULTURESHOCK! series:

Argentina	Hawaii	Pakistan
Australia	Hong Kong	Paris
Austria	Hungary	Philippines
Bahrain	India	Portugal
Barcelona	Indonesia	San Francisco
Beijing	Iran	Saudi Arabia
Belgium	Ireland	Scotland
Bolivia	Israel	Sri Lanka
Borneo	Italy	Shanghai
Brazil	Jakarta	Singapore
Britain	Japan	South Africa
Cambodia	Korea	Spain
Canada	Laos	Sweden
Chicago	London	Switzerland
Chile	Malaysia	Syria
China	Mauritius	Taiwan
Costa Rica	Mexico	Thailand
Cuba	Morocco	Tokyo
Czech Republic	Moscow	Turkey
Denmark	Munich	Ukraine
Ecuador	Myanmar	United Arab
Egypt	Nepal	Emirates
Finland	Netherlands	USA
France	New York	Vancouver
Germany	New Zealand	Venezuela
Greece	Norway	Vietnam

For more information about any of these titles, please contact any of our Marshall Cavendish offices around the world (listed on page ii) or visit our website at:

www.marshallcavendish.com/genref